Ferdinand and Isabella

PROFILES IN POWER

General Editor: Keith Robbins

CAVOUR
Harry Hearder

DISRAELI
Ian Machin

CASTRO (2nd edn)
Sebastian Balfour

MUSSOLINI
Martin Clark

LENIN
Beryl Williams

WILLIAM PENN
Mary Geiter

THE YOUNGER PITT
Michael Duffy

EISENHOWER
Peter G. Boyle

MARTIN LUTHER KING
John Kirk

FERDINAND AND
ISABELLA
John Edwards

Ferdinand and Isabella

John Edwards

Harlow, England • London • New York • Boston • San Francisco • Toronto
Sydney • Tokyo • Singapore • Hong Kong • Seoul • Taipei • New Delhi
Cape Town • Madrid • Mexico City • Amsterdam • Munich • Paris • Milan

PEARSON EDUCATION LIMITED

Edinburgh Gate
Harlow CM20 2JE
United Kingdom
Tel: +44 (0)1279 623623
Fax: +44 (0)1279 431059
Website: www.pearsoned.co.uk

First edition published in Great Britain in 2005

ISBN 0 582 21816 0

British Library Cataloguing in Publication Data
A CIP catalogue record for this book can be obtained from the British Library

Library of Congress Cataloging in Publication Data
Edwards, John, 1949–
    Ferdinand and Isabella / John Edwards.
        p. cm. — (Profiles in power)
    Includes bibliographical references and index.
    ISBN 0–582–21816–0 (pbk.)
    1. Spain—History—Ferdinand and Isabella, 1479–1516.   2. Ferdinand V, King of Spain,
1452–1516.   3. Isabella I, Queen of Spain, 1451–1504.   I. Title.   II. Profiles in power
(London, England)

DP164.E37 2004
946′.03′0922—dc22

                                                                                        2004052941

10   9   8   7   6   5   4   3   2   1
08   07   06   05   04

Set by 35 in 9.5/12pt Celeste
Printed in Malaysia

The Publishers' policy is to use paper manufactured from sustainable forests.

Contents

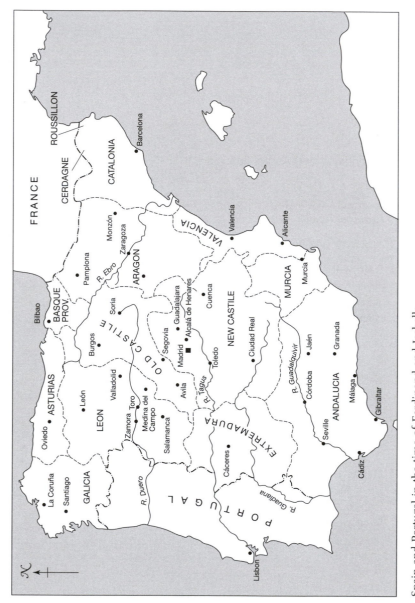

Spain and Portugal in the time of Ferdinand and Isabella

Source: Based on John Edwards, *The Monarchies of Ferdinand and Isabella* (Historical Association pamphlet), p. 4

Introduction

The political figures included in the 'Profiles in Power' series, ranging from the sixteenth century to the twentieth, have generally achieved dominance as individuals: they have also generally been male. Ferdinand and Isabella of Spain are unusual in two ways. They are chronologically the earliest in the series and, crucially, they ruled as a couple and generally in harmony. Although the first few months of Isabella's reign in Castile, in 1474–5, saw some stormy times, while the shape of her husband's role in the kingdom was hammered out, they eventually gained the reputation, not always justified as will be seen, of possessing virtually indistinguishable ideas and policies. At least until recently, in both popular and official circles in Spain, Ferdinand's personal motto, '*Tanto monta*' ('It amounts to the same'), was familiar, in the expanded form: '*Tanto monta, monta tanto, Isabel y Fernando*'. This implied a unity of personality and purpose between the two monarchs, but it is as false as most medieval etymologies, since Ferdinand's motto refers, in fact, to the equal difficulty, or impossibility, of using any one of its threads to undo the Gordian knot of Greek mythology.[1] Generally respected in Spain, both in their own time and subsequently, Isabella and Ferdinand became political and cultural role models during the dictatorship of General Francisco Franco (himself included in this series), between his victory in the Spanish Civil War, in 1939, and his death in 1975. For Franco and his ideologues, the 'Catholic monarchs', as they were entitled by Pope Alexander VI in 1496, represented all that was virtuous. They were, indeed, devout Catholic Christians, whose religion was claimed to give the lie to the secularist creeds of socialism, communism and anarchism, against which Franco's war was supposedly fought. They 'unified' Spain – Castile, Aragon, Navarre – under one government, thus, like Franco, attempting to suppress the culture and national identity of minority peoples, notably the Basques and Catalans, and securing the political, linguistic and cultural dominance of Castile. By means of war in Granada, they ended Muslim rule in Spain and they also affirmed the country's Catholic Christian identity by expelling from their domain those Jews who would not become Christians and enforced religious orthodoxy by means of a new Inquisition. Finally, in the third major event of 1492, after the conquest of Granada and the expulsion of the Jews, they sent Christopher Columbus to discover, albeit unwittingly, a 'New World'.

One of Franco's main academic and cultural achievements was to bring together, in 1940, many Spanish research centres, under the aegis of the Consejo Superior de Investigaciones Científicas (Higher Council for Scientific Investigations). The combination of this institutional co-ordination and the 'cult' of Ferdinand and Isabella was to foment, especially after 1960, a large quantity of excellent archival and historical work by Spanish scholars on the monarchs and their reigns. The debt owed to the scholars concerned is readily acknowledged here and will be evident in these pages. Perhaps inevitably, the developments that followed Franco's death – the 'transition' to democracy and constitutional monarchy, the division of Spain into partly or largely autonomous regions in which minority languages could flourish, the growth of religious freedom, secularism and cultural diversity, some of it wild and anarchic – seemed to bring about a decline in interest in two rulers who apparently represented the values of a largely discredited 'Old Regime'.[2] More recently, however, the balance has shifted once more. Royal biographies are in fashion and often concentrate on anniversaries, such as the 400th anniversary of Philip II's death in 1998, the 500th anniversary of Charles V's birth in 2000 and the 500th anniversary of the death of Isabella herself in 2004.

This change in taste also represents a change in historical methodology. Franco's Spain was never totally immune from the spectacular historiographical developments that took place in mid twentieth-century France, especially in association with the so-called Annales School. Those influenced by these trends, which also led to the foundation of the journal *Past and Present* in England in 1952, frequently, though by no means universally, represented Marxist and/or socialist ideas and approaches and, in this context, kings and their personal histories were distinctly unfashionable. Instead, the focus was on the 'material' base of money and taxation, of military manpower and supplies and the organization of agricultural and industrial production. On the surface, it appears surprising that such 'left-wing' interests and techniques should have had an influence even on non-Marxist Spanish historians in the 1950s–1970s, in a political climate that, on the surface at least, could hardly have been more uncongenial to such approaches. Apart from French, and to a lesser extent Italian, influence, however, there were two important developments in Spain that encouraged such academic approaches even before the 'transition' of the 1970s. One of these was a spectacular improvement in archival work, especially in municipal and notarial archives, which greatly expanded the possibility of serious academic research, the improvement being particularly noticeable in the former Crown of Castile, since Aragonese and Catalan records had traditionally been superior in both quantity and availability. The second development was the expansion of higher education in the Spain of the 1960s and 1970s, which provided a much enhanced institutional base for young researchers. These trends have, of course, continued, as new researchers, including undergraduates, invade local archives in search of primary material, much of which is still relevant to the concerns of the most rigorous adherent to the values of *Annales* and *Past and Present*. Perhaps, though, it is fair to say that, as the twenty-first century begins, some kind of equilibrium has been reached, in which it is once again acceptable to consider the lives of 'great men' – and of course 'great women'.

This work unashamedly views the history of Spain, in the late fifteenth and early sixteenth centuries, from the perspective of the rulers and their government. A survey of the period is offered in an earlier study by this author, *The Spain of the Catholic Monarchs, 1474–1520* (Blackwell, 2000), which treats more briefly such matters as the ideological and cultural characteristics of Isabella and Ferdinand's monarchy. Here, however, the court and its culture take centre stage, along with an exploration of what is known about the personalities of the rulers, their strong and weak points, their hopes and fears. Familiar events are discussed, including Isabella's seizure of power in 1474–5, the establishment of the new Inquisition in 1478 and the achievements, as the monarchs themselves saw them, of 1492. The main focus, though, will be on the personal role of the king and queen in these developments, with the purpose of discerning the degree to which personal royal initiative could bring about change in these European monarchies.

It is customary, at this stage as this, to mention helpers and funders who have supported the author in bringing the project concerned to fruition. It would be possible to name many individuals who have encouraged and assisted this writer in his work on Ferdinand and Isabella for over 30 years and they are collectively acknowledged here. I am also deeply grateful to Heather McCallum for her patience and support over a number of years and for Helen Marsden's help in the later stages, as well as Keith Robbins' editorial labours. As this book was nearing completion, the death of my father-in-law, Bill Baggs, occurred. His skill, integrity and devotion, in quite another field of human endeavour, really have made continuous work on this much delayed project a possibility and the result, whatever the faults of its author, is dedicated to his memory.

Notes

1 Macpherson, I. (1998) 'Solomon's knot' in Macpherson, I. and MacKay, A. (eds) *Love, Religion and Politics in Fifteenth-century Spain*, Brill, p. 219.

2 Calderón, José Manuel (2001) *Felipe el Hermoso*, Espasa Calpe, p. 11.

Chapter 1

Inheritance and Apprenticeship

On the night of Saturday to Sunday 11–12 December 1474, Henry IV of Castile lay dying in the castle (*alcázar*) of Madrid. Already in poor physical and mental health, the king had for several weeks been seeking well-being by hunting in the nearby royal forest of El Pardo. He died in the early hours of the 12th, his death apparently being sudden and its direct cause uncertain.[1] What happened next can best be described as a partially constitutional coup, in which Henry's half-sister Isabella immediately claimed the Castilian throne, thus precipitating four years of civil and international conflict. First thing on Sunday morning, one of Henry's courtiers, Rodrigo Ulloa, travelled north to Segovia, where Isabella was awaiting events with her little court, having used the city, in which royal archives and treasure were stored, as her base since the beginning of 1474. Although, on the instructions of the committee of nobles that had been appointed to run the kingdom during his illness, Ulloa asked her to do nothing concerning the throne and to await a judicial determination between her and Henry's officially recognized daughter, Joanna, the action she took was very different. The rest of that Sunday was spent in preparations for her proclamation as queen. She rehearsed the ceremony, but rumblings from those among her entourage who were subjects of John II of Aragon meant that much of the day was spent on legal niceties. Her husband Ferdinand was absent during the whole proceeding. The next day (13 December), being the feast of St Lucy, a simple ceremony took place in the main square of Segovia, in which Isabella swore to obey the commandments of the Church and respect its prelates, to seek the common good of the Castilian people and the expansion of its Crown's domains, which she swore never to divide or give away. She promised to respect all the privileges, liberties and exemptions of the nobility and of the towns and villages. After this, she was accepted by the assembly as queen of Castile and this was confirmed by the conventional cry, led by the royal heralds, of 'Castile, Castile, Castile, for the queen and our lady,

1

Queen Doña Isabella and for the king Don Ferdinand, *as her legitimate husband!'* The only other thing known for certain about the ceremony in Segovia on 13 December 1474 is that no first- or second-rank nobles were present and at most one prelate, the local diocesan bishop, Juan Arias Dávila. With this limited amount of open backing, she had not only to secure the allegiance of Castile but also to obtain the support of her husband, who was then over 200 miles away, in the Aragonese capital, Zaragoza.

The subordinate regions, known as 'kingdoms', of the Crown of Castile, which Isabella had effectively seized by means of a coup, covered about three-quarters of the Spanish landmass and contained a similar proportion of its natural and human resources. The Iberian territories of the Crown of Aragon, which her husband Ferdinand would inherit in 1479, amounted to no more than one-quarter of those of Castile, although the Aragonese king also ruled various Mediterranean islands, including the Balearics, Sardinia and Sicily, this last giving Ferdinand his current royal title. The independent kingdom of Portugal, which adjoined Castile, had less than one-sixth of the latter's population, although it, too, was beginning to acquire an overseas empire in the Atlantic and interests on the African mainland (see Chapter 5). The Pyrenean kingdom of Navarre would retain its independence until 1512 and the Muslim emirate of Granada until 1492, but there was no doubt that Isabella's decisiveness in Segovia, in December 1474, brought her the potential to achieve hegemony over the entire Iberian peninsula.

As every serious historian of her life and times has noted, Isabella's path to the throne had not been straightforward, let alone inevitable.[2] Until the death of her brother Alfonso, on 5 July 1468, the princess had had no prospect at all of becoming queen of Castile and, even after that, the obvious successor was Henry IV's daughter, Joanna, offspring of his marriage to his second wife, Joanna of Portugal, who had been born in February 1462. Much ink has been spilt in the attempt to assess the truth of the claims made by numerous chroniclers and propagandists, after Isabella's accession, that Princess Joanna was in fact the result of an illicit alliance between Henry's queen and one of his favourites, Beltrán de la Cueva, count of Ledesma – hence the nickname given to her by her enemies, 'La Beltraneja'. Insofar as it is possible to determine the question, however, it seems right to accept Tarsicio Azcona's contention, in a recent study, that the unfortunate Joanna was 'misnamed' (*mal llamada*) the 'Beltraneja' and was, in fact, the legitimate heir to the Castilian throne.[3] What is undeniable, however, is that the existence of a rival candidate was to blight particularly the earlier years of Isabella's reign and test the mettle of her husband as a military commander as well as a political leader. Henry IV had not helped the situation, first, by allowing both women to be sworn in as heirs by the Castilian parliament (*cortes*) – Joanna in May 1462 and Isabella in September 1468 – and, second, by leaving no clear will when he died in 1474.

There is some debate about the order of events in the communication of the news from Segovia to Ferdinand, but it seems certain that the first person from whom he heard of the new regime was not his wife. The chronicler Alfonso de Palencia, who was on a diplomatic mission in Zaragoza at the time, reports that the news leaked through from various sources, the first being the archbishop of Toledo, Alfonso Carrillo, who was followed by a servant of the archbishop of Seville, Cardinal Pedro González de Mendoza. On 16 December, as Isabella was issuing a letter from Segovia to the cities and authorities of Castile, which announced her accession and asked them, in the terms of the ceremony that had been held three days earlier, to recognize her as their 'Queen and natural Lady and sister', and Ferdinand 'as my legitimate husband', Gaspar de Espés arrived in Zaragoza with a short letter from his wife, which did no more than announce her half-brother's death. Not surprisingly, Ferdinand was sufficiently alarmed to leave for Castile on 19 December and it was at Calatayud, on the 21st, that he finally received an account of the events in Segovia from his wife and from her faithful henchman Gutierre de Cárdenas, who had scandalized some by carrying the unsheathed sword of state before her on the 13th. Thus it was revealed to Ferdinand that Isabella, in her proclamation, had relegated him to the role of 'king consort', one that he was evidently unwilling to accept. On Christmas Eve, one of the king of Sicily's legal advisers, Alfonso de la Cavallería, wrote on his behalf to John II, asking him to help reconcile the couple who, he indicated, had seriously fallen out over the manner of the Castilian proclamation.

The Aragonese court had evidently expected Ferdinand to have executive power in the neighbouring kingdom, where his father and other relatives had been so influential for many decades. He hurried to Segovia, only pausing at Almazán to celebrate Christmas, but received what looked like a further snub, when he was effectively refused entry to Segovia and made to cool his heels in the neighbouring village of Turégano, supposedly while preparations were made to receive him in state. Isabella's few noble supporters, the Enríquez and the Manrique, came out of the city to kiss hands and finally on 2 January 1475, he made his formal entry. He swore at the San Martín gate to observe the city's privileges and moved on to the cathedral to swear another oath to uphold the laws of the kingdom as a whole. He then went to meet his wife in the Alcázar where, after a banquet, the couple seem immediately to have begun a 'debate' about how royal powers in Castile were to be divided between them. By then, Isabella's initial stance had received the backing of the archbishops of Toledo and Seville and several leading Castilian nobles, who had signed an agreement to that effect on 27 December 1474. The result of the January negotiations in the castle at Segovia was a concordat (*concordia*) between the spouses, who had been lobbied beforehand by three main groups. The first consisted of those Castilians who fully committed themselves to Isabella's service and saw Ferdinand as no more than a king consort. The second group, consisting of Ferdinand's Aragonese entourage, naturally wished him to have executive powers alongside the 'proprietary queen' of Castile, but Azcona has argued that the most militant pro-Aragonese stance was adopted by those Castilians who had supported the Trastamaran 'Aragonese princes' (*infantes de Aragón*), including Ferdinand's father, during the reigns of the previous two Castilian kings, John II and Henry IV.[4] Inevitably, a major bone of contention would be the matter of female succession, which was said not to be permitted in the Crown of Aragon, but the princess's early upbringing had given her knowledge and experience of women with political power.

During the first few years of her life, Isabella lived with her mother, Isabella of Portugal, who is commonly portrayed as being devastated in 1454, when her daughter was only three years old, by the death of her husband, John II of Castile, 'sinking gradually into despair and madness', although the opinions of recent biographers vary on this point.[5] Another important influence on Princess Isabella in her earlier years was her grandmother, Isabella of Barcelos, who arrived in Castile from the neighbouring and wholly independent kingdom of Portugal as a widow and was regarded as being of such political substance that she was invited by her son-in-law, John II, to attend meetings of the Royal Council (*consejo real*). After the king's death, she accompanied her daughter to Arévalo, although she appears to have retained some political influence at the court of Henry IV, seeing that she was one of the negotiators of his marriage with Juana of Portugal. She died in 1465, just as civil war was breaking out in Castile. Also not to be forgotten is a third strong political woman, who had influence on the young princess of Castile. This is her aunt, Mary of Castile, who married Alfonso V of Aragon and Naples, and from 1434 until her death, in 1458, governed the diverse and difficult territories of the Crown of Aragon on his behalf. Noted for the contrast between the weakness of her body and the vigour of her political judgement and activity, Mary spent three years in Arévalo, between 1454, when she came to renegotiate Aragonese–Castilian relations after the death of her brother, and 1457.[6] During her daughter's subsequent reign, Iñigo López de Mendoza, first marquis of Santillana, hailed Isabella of Portugal, on that basis, as the 'fourth liberator of mankind', after Judith and Esther in the Old Testament and the Virgin Mary in the New. Clearly, Isabella of Portugal did once possess political acumen and strength, whatever her later psychological problems. It is also worth stressing, at this stage, the considerable Plantagenet and Lancastrian influence in Isabella of Castile's dynastic background, which came through both her Castilian and her Portuguese descent. Not only was Catherine of Lancaster, regent of Castile early in the fifteenth century, her paternal grandmother, but her maternal grandmother, Isabella of Barcelos, was both the granddaughter of João I of Portugal and the daughter-in-law of Catherine's half-sister, Philippa of Lancaster, who was herself the daughter of Blanche of Lancaster, the first wife of Edward III's brother, John of Gaunt.[7] These connections would be of renewed interest when Isabella and Ferdinand's daughter Catherine married into the Tudor dynasty (see Chapter 7).

As early as July 1468, after her brother Alfonso had died and even though she refused to accept the title of 'queen' while her half-brother Henry still lived, Isabella began to receive personal advice on government. Martín de Córdoba, an Augustinian friar, dedicated to her his treatise entitled 'Garden of noble ladies' (*Jardín de nobles donzellas*), which he wrote in order to refute the arguments of those who opposed government by women:

Some men, Lady, of lesser understanding, and perhaps lacking knowledge of natural and moral causes, and not having turned the pages of chronicles of past times, thought it a bad thing when any kingdom or other polity comes under the rule of women, but I, as I shall state below, am of the contrary opinion.[8]

Fray Martín follows the example of his predecessor Juan García de Castrojeriz, who, in 1344, published a 'Rule of princes' (*Regimiento de príncipes*) and whose work was still influential in the late fifteenth century. Thus he stresses the need for a ruler to have a thorough education, in order to govern himself or herself, the royal household and the kingdom as a whole. He cites cases of powerful women in ancient times, including goddesses and sibyls, but notes the absence of examples of successful female rulers in his own day. In particular, contemporary candidates lacked letters, 'because now, in our century, women do not give themselves to the study of liberal arts or of other sciences, rather it seems as though they are forbidden'.[9] To Fray Martín, Isabella's noble birth made her eligible to rule and he was fond of comparing her with the Virgin Mary, whom he also regarded as the daughter of kings. He noted, in the conventional manner of the period, that Mary, by her obedience to God in giving birth to His son, Jesus, redeemed the sin of Eve, in eating the forbidden fruit in the Garden of Eden (Genesis 3). If God created paradise for Eve, Mary was paradise in herself, an idea that was to be developed further by writers after 1474. In this context, Martín identified three degrees of female chastity – virginal purity, honourable widowhood and marital fidelity. Citing the example of numerous female saints, he vainly urged Isabella, just a year before her marriage to Ferdinand, permanently to preserve her virginity.[10]

In the Castilian context, the absolutist theory of monarchy had been fully developed in the second section of the seven-part law code of Alfonso X, the *Siete Partidas*, which had not received full legal force in the kingdom until 1348. According to this text, which provided the basis for monarchical government in Castile in the fifteenth century, the king governed by grace (*gobierno de gracia*). Chancery documents, both before and during Isabella and Ferdinand's reign, habitually talked of the ruler's 'absolute royal power' (*poderío real absoluto*), which he exercised by means of his 'certain knowledge and by his own will' (*cierta ciencia y moto propio*). This 'absolute' power was exercised through the granting to subjects by the king, as 'natural lord' (*señor natural*) of the kingdom, of lands and other Crown resources, in the form of royal graces or grants (*mercedes reales*). Thus the king was the sole repository of legal power and also exempt from subjection to his own laws, which he might annul or suspend, simply by exercising his 'absolute power' and 'certain knowledge' and will. During the reigns of John II and Henry IV, Alfonso X's concept and project of monarchy had been further developed, so as to give much greater emphasis to the divine authority and attributes of monarchy. Thus, like the Jewish monarchs of the Old Testament, as well as the Christian emperors of Rome and Byzantium, Castilian rulers in the fifteenth century saw themselves as 'anointed kings' (*reyes ungidos*). As a result of the efforts of John II's constable (*condestable*) of Castile and favourite (*privado*), Álvaro de Luna, after 1430, this 'theological' concept of monarchy was further developed, receiving its fullest expression at the Cortes of Olmedo, in 1445.[11] The conflicts of the later years of John II's reign, as well as much of Henry IV's, failed to dilute this Christianized form of monarchical absolutism, so that its continuation was effectively the only policy in Isabella's mind, when she seized power in December 1474. The events of the previous decades had pointed up, however, the consequences of a ruler's failing to live up to this exalted form of monarchism. Absolutism could never function without the co-operation of oligarchic groups, such as the nobility, the Church and municipal councils, so that Isabella and her husband's aim was simply to restore an equilibrium that had tilted too far against the Crown. As for the other contemporary models of monarchy, 'baronial' or knightly monarchy, in which the nobility had a legally recognized place in the government of the kingdom, was still favoured by some political theorists. Nevertheless, fifteenth-century notions of 'knightly monarchy' were clearly based on the king as the *creator* of nobles, so that the noble and knightly classes derived their very status not merely from prowess in warfare or other personal and 'aristocratic' virtues but also from the divinely sanctioned authority of the monarch himself. This subordination seems to have been recognized even by those nobles who had rebelled against Henry IV in 1465–8. The two remaining models for monarchy, the 'popular' and the 'Aristotelian', had little influence in the last three decades of the fifteenth century. It is true that, in the wake of the Alfonsine rebellion, the Cortes of Ocaña (1469) demanded greater participation by the major towns, which remained under royal jurisdiction, in the government of the kingdom, but it was only in the first years of the sixteenth century that 'communal' political ideas once again became a force to be reckoned with.[12] Meanwhile, Aristotelian notions of 'citizen rule' were largely confined to the lecture halls of the universities.[13]

An unprecedentedly large number of writers during Isabella and Ferdinand's reign stressed the divine aspect of monarchy. They included not only poets, such as Fray Iñigo de Mendoza and Juan del Encina, but chroniclers and historians such as Fernando del Pulgar and Andrés Bernáldez, and the Italian humanists Lucio Marineo Siculo and Piero Martire d'Anghiera (Pedro Mártir de Anglería). It was inevitable that such an apparently unprecedented exaltation of the divine character of monarchy should have an effect on literary portrayals of the characters of the king and queen themselves. One consequence of this increasing stress on the religious aspect of monarchy was to encourage the judgement of individual rulers, such as Isabella and her husband, for their deeds, not by their relationship to the law, for example in the form of their accession oaths to uphold the laws of the kingdom, but in terms of their personal characteristics as Christians. Thus Isabella was ever more frequently seen as a good queen, not because she upheld the law, but because she was, in Fernando del Pulgar's phrase, 'Catholic and devout' (*católica e devota*).[14] This process of 'moralization of the royal image', to use Nieto Soria's phrase, fomented the growth of the 'crusading' ideal in Castile, particularly after the Cortes of Toledo in 1480, in a manner that encouraged the development of messianic and even millenarian ideas, at the highest political level.[15] With this stress on monarchy as a matter of personal faith rather than law, in other words, rule that was to be judged by a divine rather than a secular standard, came a desire to justify the actions of the Castilian monarchy by historical precedent. Thus the work of historians and chroniclers was increasingly devoted to interpreting the monarchs' actions teleologically, as part of the long-term divine plan, for Castile and the world. Victory in the war of 1475–9 against Portugal (see later) saw a downplaying of earlier notions of the voice of the people as being the voice of God (*vox populi, vox Dei*) and their replacement by references to the just judgement of God (*juicio recto de Dios*). St John the Evangelist and sometimes St John the Baptist were adopted as icons of the religious authentication of the now victorious Castilian regime.[16]

When Isabella and Ferdinand acceded to their respective thrones, they inherited a strong historiographical tradition, in both Castile and Aragon, and quickly turned it to their own advantage. The dynastic, if not legal, unification of the two Crowns, was thus seen in terms of the restoration of the unitary Visigothic Christian monarchy that had existed in Spain from the fall of the western Roman Empire until the Muslim invasion of 711. In this way, Ferdinand and Isabella came to be regarded as the direct inheritors of the mantle of the Visigothic kings and the later medieval ideology of 'Reconquest' was thereby reaffirmed. Similarly, the new rulers' victory over Afonso V of Portugal, and his wife Joanna, was regarded by official propagandists in Castile as divine vengeance for the Portuguese defeat of John I at Aljubarrota (Batalha) in 1385. In addition, efforts were made to play up the historic role of Castile in the formation of Spanish identity. It seems to have been but a short step from such historical claims to a religious belief in the monarchs' destiny as both Spanish and world rulers. In order to pursue this perceived destiny, however, Isabella and Ferdinand would find it necessary to accentuate Spanish identity and autonomy in a manner that would later be described as 'nationalistic'. This development was particularly noticeable in relations between Spain and the Papacy in this period and was based on the professed identification of late fifteenth-century Spain with the pre-711 Visigothic monarchy. Finally, a further consequence of the king and queen's sense of 'manifest destiny' was the desire to reform the customs and morals of Aragonese and Castilian subjects, as well as the institutions that governed their lives. In the administration of justice, as in other manifestations of royal power, the medium was indeed the message. Although the legal system continued to function behind the scenes, and indeed received vigorous support and reform from the king and queen, such public ceremonies were clearly intended to encourage literary and political propagandists to praise them as the sole dispensers of punishment and reward. Like other European rulers of the period, Isabella and Ferdinand used the rhetoric of written texts to promote their ideals and political programme.

Such techniques had been perfected by Fernando del Pulgar, in his collection of pen portraits entitled 'Famous men of Castile' (*Claros varones de Castilla*), which was dedicated to Isabella.[17] Sometimes it was desirable to pay lip service to other notions of monarchy. Thus, despite their 'absolutist' basis, royal ceremonies of entry to cities often presented a public appearance of *pactismo*, or government by consent between Crown and city authorities. Councillors might be allowed to speak up before the ruler(s) and such formal acts often began with a royal oath to uphold traditional local privileges. At least in appearance, Isabella and her husband respected the political and legal diversity of the territories they had inherited. Among the many facets of the language of propaganda, which was developed in Isabella and Ferdinand's reigns, there was a historical component, which claimed and emphasized a sharp contrast between the disorder of the recent past and the peace and order of the present. According to this analysis, the 'tyranny' of Henry's reign (meaning, in this case, weak and bad government rather than excessive authoritarianism) had been replaced by the good government of his successors and genealogy was created in order to emphasize the supposedly direct link between the current rulers and their Visigothic predecessors. In Nieto Soria's phrase, the aim was evidently to 'restore dreamed-of lost paradises'.[18] Writers worked to build up the reputation (*fama*) of the king and queen as the personification of justice and the custodians, both of the honour of their kingdoms and of the common good. In this discourse, the monarchs were portrayed as more or less omnipotent, under God, while their warfare, most notably in the conquest of Granada, but before that in the defence of Isabella's throne against Afonso and Joanna, was seen as not only just but also necessary.

In Segovia in January 1475, when the earliest attempt was made to lay down a basis for putting such exalted ideas into practice, pragmatic considerations inevitably imposed themselves as well. In addition, not all contemporary writing took such an exalted and complimentary view of the queen. The most acerbic critic was the humanist historian Alfonso de Palencia (1424–92), who was dismissed as royal chronicler in 1480, but nonetheless wrote, in Latin, a history of the reign of Henry IV, as well as that of Isabella and Ferdinand up to the conquest of Granada. It was entitled 'Hispanic deeds' (*Gesta Hispaniensia*), but is commonly known as the 'Decades' (*Décadas* in Spanish).[19] Throughout his work Palencia stressed the importance of sex in government and politics. In the case of Henry IV, he made the supposed impotence of the king a fundamental cause of his failure as a ruler, but he seems to have found a female ruler, in the form of Isabella, particularly hard to accept. In some cases, as Brian Tate has pointed out, Palencia attacked the queen through her female supporters and advisers, just as Isabella's grandmother, Catherine of Lancaster, had been criticized for her involvement with Leonor López de Córdoba and Inés de Torres. In the period 1430–80, several prominent Castilian women came under the historian's critical scrutiny. They included Henry IV's own mother, María de Aragón, María de Silva, daughter of the count of Cifuentes and wife of the count of Fuensalida, Leonor Pimentel, countess of Plasencia, Beatriz Pacheco, countess of Medellín, and Beatriz Fernández de Bobadilla, marchioness of Moya. Beatriz de Bobadilla led the trail directly to Isabella herself, whom Palencia startlingly described as the 'mistress of dissimulations and deceits' (*magistra dissimulationum simulationumque*).[20] Her father, Pedro de Bobadilla, was governor (*alcaide*) of the castle at Segovia and she became one of Princess Isabella's ladies-in-waiting. During the 1460s, she married Andrés Cabrera, who was a royal page (*doncel*) and the king's chief steward (*mayordomo mayor*). Cabrera, in turn, became governor of Segovia's *alcázar* and, on 30 June 1463, received from Henry IV the grant of the frontier castle of Moya (Cuenca).[21] Cabrera had difficulty in establishing control in Moya, probably for the same reason as had caused him problems in Segovia. There, many leading citizens apparently felt that a fortification of such importance should not have been placed in the hands of a *converso* who was, in Tate's words, 'an upstart, the plaything of the wishes of his wife [Beatriz]'.[22] The Segovians removed Cabrera, but Isabella restored him in 1480, upgrading the small town of Moya to a marquisate, as a reward for the couple's support during the war against Joanna and the Portuguese. Palencia reports continuing resistance in Segovia to the new marquis and marchioness, referring to the 'domination' and 'insolence' of Beatriz.[23] By attacking Beatriz's behaviour in Segovia, the chronicler was also inevitably criticizing her royal mistress. He had already done so in his account of Isabella's self-proclamation as queen, in Segovia, and especially of the carrying in front of her of the sword of state, on the grounds that many observers thought it wrong for a woman to show 'that ostentation of the attributes of the husband [Ferdinand]'.[24]

After this incident, Palencia begins to compose a portrait of Isabella that would lead to his demotion five years later. His approach to a female ruler, in an overwhelmingly patriarchal society, is complex and interesting.

Having criticized her brother Henry for effeminacy and impotence, the latter both sexual and political, the historian now saw the queen as a usurper of the masculine role, who nevertheless still retained her feminine wiles. To him, this made her doubly dangerous and the relevant passages of his chronicle read more like a private memorandum than an official history. According to his own account, early in the reign, Palencia told Ferdinand, during a private conversation, that he was aware that his criticism of Isabella was known to her and was placing him under unjust suspicion in other matters.[25] In subsequent pages of his chronicle, Palencia referred to the 'womanly mind of the queen' and 'the queen, after all a woman'. This writer frequently combined political criticism of Isabella in government with aspersions on her female gender. In general, he referred scathingly to:

The arrogance and massive power of Lady Isabella, in no way disposed to accept the rules of government which, since the most remote centuries, have favoured the male.

To test the accuracy of this perception, it is important to examine closely the Segovia agreement of 1475, and the war that followed it.

The text of this *concordia*, which appears to have been drafted by Archbishops Carrillo and Mendoza, with the legal advice of Rodrigo Maldonado de Talavera for Castile and Alfonso de la Cavallería for Aragon, was signed at Segovia on 15 January 1475 and confirmed by those dignitaries then present in the city. The formal involvement of these individuals indicates that this was a public rather than a private agreement that was to be ratified by the Castilian Cortes at Madrigal in 1476. The drafters seem to have worked, not from general Castilian precedent, but on the basis of the original marriage agreement between Isabella and Ferdinand, which had been signed at Cervera in October 1469, when the throne had seemed a distant and improbable prospect. None of those mainly involved was a professionally trained lawyer, since Isabella still, in these early and uncertain days, had no access to the relevant government department, the chancellery in Valladolid. Nevertheless, the main heads of the 'Agreement for the governance of the kingdom', as it was entitled, were clear enough and directly tackled the question of Ferdinand's juridical status in Castile.

First, all chancellery documents were to open in a common form, with Ferdinand's name coming before Isabella's. Second, allegiance (*pleitohomenaje*) by governors of royal fortresses should be made to the queen alone, while, third, royal revenues were to be for the indiscriminate use of both rulers, this last provision applying to Aragon and Sicily, as well as Castile. The catch was that Isabella would appoint all Castilian treasury officials and Ferdinand would have to take what his wife gave him, in terms of the estates and revenues of the Crown. All grants of cash and rents made to subjects, and appointments to all offices, were also to remain in the queen's hands. She also retained absolute ultimate control over appointments to masterships of military orders and to senior offices in the Church, such as bishoprics, abbacies and other ecclesiastical benefices, although these might be asked for through Ferdinand. The implications of this for papal authority in Castile are not specified in the Segovia accord. In the case of the administration of justice, however, both spouses were to have full powers, including decisions on cases, whether they acted together or separately. Local royal governors (*corregidores*) in the major towns (see Chapter 2), contrariwise, were to be appointed by the queen alone. These terms appear to be based on the 1469 Cervera agreement, but circumstances had changed in the intervening years. Government in the most powerful Spanish kingdom was no longer hypothetical for Isabella and Ferdinand and the latter had, in the meantime, become ruler of Sicily in his own right, by the grant of his father, John II of Aragon. It was hard to be a sovereign in one place, yet a semi-cypher in another, especially given the high Trastamaran doctrine of monarchy that both spouses inherited. In any case, the war with Portugal was soon to change things radically, so that, on 28 April 1475, Isabella felt constrained to concede to her husband complete powers, even in her absence, to 'provide, command, do and ordain everything necessary (*visto*)'. Ferdinand could now appoint royal officials, make grants from royal revenues, in fact exercise all his wife's powers as 'heiress and legitimate successor' in Castile.[26]

Given the circumstances of Isabella's accession, it was inevitable that she and her husband would have difficulties to face in establishing themselves in Castile. The king's will had remained uncertain unto death, the Cortes was yet to meet and the views of numerous nobles and major towns were at best neutral and at worst hostile. Things were equally unstable internationally and Isabella took the wise precaution of quickly renewing the traditional Castilian alliance with France by despatching to Paris, on 7 February, her secretary Fernando del Pulgar, who would later chronicle her reign, and another secretary, surnamed Christián, to represent Ferdinand. Louis XI, characteristically, hedged his bets and thus the couple failed to neutralize the main threat facing them, which came from Isabella's slighted rival, Joanna, and her new husband, Afonso V of Portugal. In addition, they sent troops to help Ferdinand's father defend his northern frontier against French attack. What was worse, at this time, in the first half of 1475, it would have been inaccurate to equate 'Castile' with Isabella and her husband's regime and everyone, including the rulers themselves, knew it. Indeed, before Pulgar and Christián even set off for Paris, Louis had written to Afonso, suggesting that, on the assumption that Afonso became king of Castile as well as Portugal, they might partition John II's Crown of Aragon between them. In February 1475, it looked as though such a scheme might well be put into effect.

When Henry IV died, in the previous December, Afonso already had an ambassador at the Castilian court, Pedro de Sousa. Isabella took the precaution of summoning him immediately afterwards to Segovia, sending him back to Lisbon with protestations of friendship towards Afonso. Her precaution was wise, since, on 27 December 1474, Afonso wrote to magnates, including the marquis of Cádiz, Rodrigo Ponce de León, and to towns, urging them to acknowledge his new wife, Joanna, as heir to the Castilian throne. The Portuguese king then held a council, at Estremoz, at which a plan was agreed for defence and re-armament, this to be ratified by the Cortes on 15 January 1475. Military action eventually began in May of that year and between the 10th and the 30th of that month, Portuguese forces crossed the frontier at various points. The king's own force entered Castile at La Codosera, near Alburquerque, but the action was neither co-ordinated nor decisive and by the 12th Afonso had re-crossed the border to sign, at Arronche, a document that set out the succession to the Portuguese throne. His son John would succeed him and his grandson Afonso in case of the former's death, this specification evidently being intended to avoid precisely the kind of succession dispute that he was about to foment in Castile. The invading Portuguese forces seem to have totalled about 5000 light cavalry (*jinetes*) and 10–15,000 infantry and this not inconsiderable army was expected to be reinforced by Joanna's Castilian supporters. Meanwhile, the princess herself awaited her husband in the Zúñiga town of Plasencia, where he arrived on 29 May. The uncle and his 13-year-old niece were married that same day. On the 30th, Joanna issued what was, in effect, a manifesto, justifying her claim to the Castilian throne, in precedence over Isabella.

Ferdinand and Isabella's feeling of insecurity had been plain during the previous two months. On 4 March, well before the May events at Plasencia, Isabella's court established itself at Medina del Campo, in the castle of La Mota, where she would eventually die. There, the marquis of Santillana and the constable of Castile did homage to her, but the threat from the west caused a move to Valladolid, where the king and queen based themselves in houses belonging to the count of Benavente.

On 3 April, to raise morale, not least within themselves, they organized a series of public festivities in Valladolid, in which the young queen might display her charm, while the chancellery worked to retain the support of major cities, such as Burgos and Toledo, by confirming their privileges. In addition, energetic, but ultimately unsuccessful, diplomatic efforts were made to persuade Afonso to abandon his ambitions. It did not help that Isabella had quarrelled with Archbishop Carrillo of Toledo, who played such a large part in her attainment of the throne. In these straitened circumstances, she was forced to display a public modesty and humility that would not be characteristic of her reign in later years. She not only appealed for the support of her nobles, knights and towns, but also issued general pardons to those guilty of crimes in earlier years, so that they would help her to crush rebel Castilian nobles and resist the Portuguese. At the end of April, she also made a visit to Alcalá de Henares, in a vain attempt to effect a reconciliation with Archbishop Carrillo.

Yet still, despite all warnings and precautions, Afonso managed to surprise his opponents while they were separated, with Isabella in Toledo and Ferdinand in Medina del Campo. On 19 May, Ferdinand wrote to the *adelantado* of Murcia, Pedro Fajardo, empowering him to attack the nearby marquisate of Villena, the stronghold of Juan Pacheco, who was one of Joanna's main supporters. Isabella followed this letter with her own, to the same effect, on 23 May, and the next day she issued a general letter to her realm, ordering her subjects to withdraw allegiance and financial support from the rebels, transferring revenues to the royal fisc. The comings and goings of the next few days, during which the spouses were often uncertain of each other's locations, culminated in a personal disaster for Isabella. On 31 May she arrived in Cebreros and there had a miscarriage, requiring the whole of June to recover, in Ávila. It is unlikely that she knew, at this stage, of Joanna's manifesto. Meanwhile, Afonso had attempted to set up a base in Arévalo, a place much associated with Isabella, in order to provide a link with the garrison of Burgos, which had declared for him. But Ferdinand had gathered forces to prevent this salient into the heart of Castile and Afonso's scheme failed. Instead, he received the bonus of an offer of allegiance from the Leonese town of Toro, which led him to concentrate his effort in the Zamora region and the lower Castilian reaches of the Duero (Douro). In response, the queen, now recovered, joined her husband at Tordesillas on 12 July and within two days they had at their disposal a significant force of 2000 heavy cavalry (*hombres de armas*), 6000 light cavalry (*jinetes*) and 20,000 infantry, to send to Toro. In the traditional manner, which was not to be followed for much longer in Castile, this army consisted mainly of seigniorial contingents, flying the banners of their lords, and the militias of the major royal towns. In these circumstances, the royal couple rightly felt that they were in great danger, threatened by external attack, from France as well as Portugal, and by known or potential dissent within Castile. Already, on 12 May, Ferdinand had made a will, which was drawn up by the queen's confessor, the Jeronymite friar Hernando de Talavera, of whom much more will be heard. In it he declared that he would defend Castile 'to the shedding of blood, if necessary' and that he wished to be buried with his wife, wherever that might be. In view of the personal and political disputes between the couple, which were sometimes gleefully recorded by court chroniclers, it is interesting to note that he entrusted to Isabella, after his death, the care not only of his illegitimate children, Aldonza Ruig (or Ruiz) and the future archbishop of Zaragoza, Alfonso de Aragón, but also of their mothers. Crucially, he made her the heiress both to the kingdom of Sicily and, after his father's death, to the Crown of Aragon.

The war began badly and quickly led to marital strife. While Isabella remained in Tordesillas, Ferdinand led his army towards Toro, arriving in its neighbourhood on 20 July 1476. News then came that the larger nearby town of Zamora had declared for Afonso and Joanna and, in order to preserve his forces for an attack on this more significant target at a future date, the king abandoned plans to besiege Toro and discharged the urban militias among his forces. The first to object to this move were Ferdinand's Basque and Cantabrian troops, who saw it as weakness and perhaps treachery, protesting outside the royal tent. Worse was to come, however, when the news reached Isabella's camp. In one of the better known incidents of public dispute between them, according to the 'Incomplete chronicle' (*Crónica incompleta*), the queen and her entourage prepared a rough reception, when Ferdinand returned to Tordesillas on 24 July, without having fought a battle:

When the queen heard of his coming, she became very agitated, and could not bear not to ride out herself, together with some horsemen, and she ordered them to stick their lances in those [of Ferdinand's] cavalry who were coming along in front, and she tried to have them captured, using the strong words of a man, rather than those of a timorous woman.[27]

Isabella had evidently not calmed down by the time of the meeting of the Royal Council held the next day, which, as everyone knew, was ironically the feast of Spain's patron saint, James the Greater, the traditional heavenly sponsor of military victories. The chronicle records a public diatribe by the queen against her husband and also his calming reply using the royal plural, which appears to give a good indication of the character of the disputes that arose at times between them:

Madam, give the anxieties of your heart a rest, because time and days will bring you such victories that, though they may have thwarted us in this, you will forgive them a thousand times. Let me gain your pardon for this offence, even though that's what it was. I thought that, arriving back frustrated, I would have from your tongue words of consolation and encouragement, and with us coming back safe and with honour, you complain? We're going to have a lot of trouble with you from now on! But women always, even though men may be well-disposed, vigorous, dynamic and gracious, are so dissatisfied – especially you, madam, since the person who could satisfy you is yet to be born![28]

This passage, with its colloquial not to say blunt language, is an exceptional illustration both of the tensions caused by the Portuguese threat and of the sometimes fiery nature of Ferdinand and Isabella's relationship.

The king had, of course, been defeated mainly by treachery rather than military force, but the retreat from Toro required a major strategic rethink. The main danger was that, from bases there and in Zamora, Afonso would be able to link up both with his supporters in Burgos castle and with French troops, which threatened to attack through the Basque country and perhaps Navarre. A series of councils of war were held, in Tordesillas and Medina del Campo, and three decisions were made as a result. First, it was decided that, given their continuing lack of access to most of the theoretical revenues of the Crown, further military action should be funded by tapping the wealth of the Church, in the form of liturgical plate (see Chapter 4). Second, it was agreed that Ferdinand should immediately march east to Burgos, with the aim of recapturing its castle for his cause and, finally, he should ask his father, John II, to send him his illegitimate son Alfonso of Aragon, who was reckoned to be the best general in the Peninsula at the time. In addition, during late July and early August, further appeals for support were made to the Castilian towns and regions.

In the second half of 1475 the king and queen both pursued war measures with vigour. Ferdinand concentrated on the rebels in Burgos, while Isabella stayed in Valladolid, to organize forces that aimed to prevent Portuguese troops in Toro and Zamora from reinforcing Burgos castle. Archbishop Carrillo of Toledo sent troops to help Afonso and, in September, his men managed to capture Baltanás and take the count of Benavente prisoner, but Isabella managed to block the Portuguese advance at Palencia. During the next few weeks, Afonso tried to use the count as a bargaining token, offering to release him in return for the raising of the siege of Burgos castle, but, by November 1475, the military stalemate in Old Castile had encouraged Isabella and Ferdinand to view their situation in a more optimistic light. From the 5th to the 10th of that month, they held a further council of war at Dueñas, where the agenda included the likely contribution to be made by Alfonso of Aragon, secret negotiations with supporters which had been taking place in Zamora, aimed at the surrender of the city, the possibility of Aragonese military help, on land and sea, and the idea of buying off Louis XI of France, thus further isolating the Portuguese king. Husband and wife continued to pursue their own parallel and co-ordinated schemes but, on 3 December, the Zamora plot was discovered and the prospect of capturing Afonso and Joanna disappeared. Nonetheless, Ferdinand sent an army along the Duero, in the direction of Zamora, and within an hour of its arrival the city had fallen. The castle, however, remained in Portuguese hands, its garrison being under orders to hold out until Prince John brought reinforcements from Portugal. Thus Christmas 1475 was a bleak time for Isabella and Ferdinand, who were physically separated and realistically fearing a renewal of the war. The king regarded the siege of Zamora castle as such a high priority that it required his personal presence, so that he had to entrust to his wife the task of receiving the surrender of the Burgos garrison, at the end of January 1476.

This strategic act began a revival in Ferdinand and Isabella's prospects. The troops that had been engaged in Burgos could now be directed westwards, to Toro and Zamora, and, at the beginning of February, Ferdinand wrote optimistically to the city councillors of Barcelona. But the roller-coaster of events continued into 1476, as he failed both to enter Toro secretly and to prevent the town being reinforced by Prince John, on 9 February. At last, however, a military climax seemed likely and both husband and wife engaged in active preparations. From Tordesillas, Isabella organized an army of reserves, under the command of Alfonso of Aragon and including the newly released count of Benavente. Ferdinand's image, in his wife's eyes, as a warrior king was soon to be redeemed, but John II of Aragon still seems to have doubted his son's ability in open warfare (*guerra guerreada*), preferring him to concentrate on winning over his neutral or rebel subjects by diplomacy. Realities on the ground made battle inevitable, especially after Prince John of Portugal and his army marched out of Toro on 13 February, to attack the assembling Castilian forces. They failed to make contact, however, and returned to base, but the prince and his father then made an unwise decision to divide their forces by attempting to regain Zamora. If he were hoping thereby to obtain better surrender terms – for example the retention after the war of Toro and Zamora, perhaps even of Galicia to the north – Afonso's plan failed. Zamora remained loyal to Isabella and Alfonso of Aragon's army continued to march westwards, managing to harry the Portuguese forces as they returned to Toro. At dawn on 1 March 1476, on a field appropriately called Peleagonzalo ('Gonzalo's fight'), Afonso and Ferdinand's armies finally met in pitched battle. The Portuguese king's forces had been chased there and Ferdinand first attacked them with the central units of his front, consisting of urban militias. In defiance of the then current prejudice of upper-class military men against such 'armies of shopkeepers', the king's troops defeated Afonso's crack Portuguese division, while the seignorial contingents of Cardinal Pedro González de Mendoza, the duke of Alba, and other leading nobles, were equally successful on the right flank. On the left, Prince John's Portuguese did much better, but could not influence the overall outcome.

Thus, this old-fashioned 'feudal' field battle (*batalla campal*) ended with Ferdinand's triumphal return to Zamora, which he entered at one in the afternoon, in time for lunch. On 19 March, the castle there surrendered to him and a procession of nobles began to transfer allegiance from Joanna to Isabella. Hearing the news, Louis XI abandoned his plans to send troops to the peninsula. What may have meant most of all to Ferdinand, however, was the likely reaction of his wife. Isabella was not on the battlefield, but awaited the news in Tordesillas. The next day, as soon as she heard the result, she summoned her secretary, Fernando Álvarez, and they drafted a brief triumphal message, which was to be despatched to the main cities of the kingdom. After this, she rushed to her husband's side, being reunited with him in Zamora on 5 March. The official celebration of the victory was held in the town square there on 22 March and other festivities were organized throughout the kingdom, on Isabella's orders. The queen also ordered, an 'action of grace' to God, this being the building of a Franciscan church in Toledo, to be dedicated to the couple's patron, St John the Evangelist, and named San Juan de los Reyes ('St John of the Kings').

Hopes that the victory at Peleagonzalo would end the Castilian rulers' troubles proved to be unfounded. For one thing, there were still problems in Galicia, which Afonso had invaded at the beginning of the war, and which he hoped to keep when a peace treaty with Castile was eventually made. The Portuguese occupied a triangle of territory in southern Galicia, between Tuy, Ourense and Pontevedra, being greatly helped by the treachery of Isabella's chief representative in Galicia, the 'scout' (*adelantado*) Fernando de Pareja, who had his lands and rents in Castile confiscated as a result. When the bishop of Tuy, Diego de Muros, tried to

regain his see, he was captured and Galicia remained a focus of dissidence for some years. Also still in operation, at least potentially, after
Peleagonzalo, was the Guipuzcoan front in the Basque country further
east, where the threat came from France. Up to 1477 Isabella and her
husband benefited, and Afonso of Portugal suffered, from Louis XI's
preoccupation with the destruction of his relative Charles the Bold,
duke of Burgundy. Thus, although Alain d'Albret was appointed, on 21
December 1475, to command the French invading force, the only actual
fighting took place around Hendaye, in March 1476, and the invasion
was abandoned two months later, on Louis's orders. This did not, however, prevent Afonso V's extraordinary travels in France, beginning in
1476, in a vain search for support. Disillusioned by his failure, the Portuguese king wrote a letter, at Harfleur on 23 September 1477, in which he
announced his intention to abdicate in favour of his son John and enter
a monastery. Meanwhile, Isabella hastened to sign agreements with her
rebellious nobles and, on 18 September 1476, her troops finally attacked
Toro itself and its castle eventually surrendered on 22 October. With the
western front largely under control, she and her husband were able to
turn their attention to other pressing problems, including not only Galicia
but also other focuses of rebellion, such as the marquisate of Villena in
the east and, in central Spain, the lands of the archbishop of Toledo and
of the masters of the military orders of Santiago and Calatrava. Although
Archbishop Carrillo came reluctantly to heel, finally making an agreement with Isabella and Ferdinand on 4 March 1477, a full-scale war had
to be fought, with the help of Murcian forces, to subdue the marquis of
Villena's vassals, as well as the rebel castles of the orders of Santiago and
Calatrava. After extensive negotiations, in Spain and in Rome, Pope Sixtus
finally agreed to allow Ferdinand to act as administrator of the powerful
order of Santiago, following the death of its master, Rodrigo Manrique,
count of Paredes, on 11 November 1476. Finally, in April or May 1477,
the two rulers felt able to begin a campaign to subdue, and achieve full
allegiance from, regions which had been either hostile or neutral during
the recent war, beginning with Extremadura and continuing in Andalusia
(see Chapters 2 and 4).

The Portuguese threat had not gone away, however, since Afonso did
not fulfil his plan of becoming a monk, instead returning to his kingdom,
in November 1477. The new year saw plans being made for a second
invasion of Castile and a Cortes, held at Santarem, voted money for such
an expedition. But Afonso seems to have lacked support from Castilian
magnates for a second attempt, although Isabella and Ferdinand took the
precaution of closely monitoring likely supporters. Indeed, during the

first half of 1478, the true venom of the couple, particularly the queen, towards their Portuguese relatives became ever more obvious. While in Seville that summer, Isabella made efforts to assemble forces for a final assault on the Portuguese, this time in their own country. The commander was to be the new master of Santiago, Alonso de Cárdenas, whose election had followed the administration of the order in Ferdinand's name, and the expedition was to be supported at sea by an Aragonese naval squadron. Meanwhile, the king temporarily put to one side his own kingdoms' traditional hostility towards France, renewing, on 10 January 1479, Castile's alliance with Louis XI and thereby removing Afonso's only possible ally. Nevertheless, it was undeniable that, despite bellicose noises made by both sides during 1478, both Castile and Portugal were exhausting their resources in the pursuit of the conflict.

As early as August 1477, Isabella had authorized the count of Feria to sign a peace treaty with Portugal, which was to apply to the frontier zones between Alburquerque and Seville, and this seems to have held for about a year. Now, however, in 1479, serious negotiations began, aimed at ending the war altogether. Attempts by Pope Sixtus IV to mediate were unsuccessful but, in February 1479, a most intriguing episode took place, in which two women attempted personally to negotiate an international peace treaty. The protagonists were Isabella and her aunt, Princess Beatrice of Portugal, who was also sister-in-law to Afonso V. The initiative came from Beatrice and the talks took place face to face, at Alcántara in Extremadura, from 18 to 22 March 1479. The Portuguese proposals, quickly rejected by Isabella, were that a double marriage should take place, between Joanna and the infant Prince John of Castile (born on 30 June 1478) and also between Princess Isabella of Castile and the eldest son of the Portuguese heir, Prince John. In addition, Castile was to pay all the costs of the war to date and a general pardon was to be issued to all Castilian subjects who had supported Afonso and Joanna. Clearly, though, family ties were no substitute for hard-headed diplomacy and the negotiations failed. Thus it was left to professionals to reach a settlement, in the Portuguese town of Alcáçovas, in September 1479, Isabella's plenipotentiary being Rodrigo Maldonado de Talavera. Two treaties were concluded, one of them ending the war and the other dealing with the human consequences of the conflict at the royal level and, in particular, the fate of Joanna of Castile.

The peace treaty purported to renew its predecessor, which had been made at Almeirim on 27 January 1432, and proclaimed 'perpetual peace' between the neighbouring kingdoms. The frontier was to be that which existed at the death of Henry IV of Castile, the Portuguese were to release their Castilian prisoners and all Castilian rebels, who had declared for Joanna and her husband, were to be fully pardoned. Afonso agreed not to invade Castile again and not to support any Castilian subjects in rebellion against their rulers. In return, Castile abandoned all financial claim on Portugal for the cost of the war and both sides agreed to demolish any provocative border fortifications and avoid any kind of incitement to future conflict. In addition, and significantly for future Iberian adventures in Africa and the Atlantic (see Chapter 5), Castile formally abandoned all claim to territories in which Portugal had an interest and over which there had previously been military conflict between the two powers – Guinea, Mina de Oro, Madeira, Cape Verde and the Azores. The Canaries were allocated to Castile, but Portugal was to be given a free hand in the kingdom of Fez. Isabella confirmed her assent to the treaty, at Trujillo in Extremadura, on 27 September 1479 and Ferdinand, who was then in his hereditary Aragonese domains, gave his formal assent in a separate document.

The second treaty of Alcaçovas, which had been drawn up earlier in Moura, concerned hostages (*tercerías*) for the general settlement. This complex and long-winded document evidently had the primary purpose of settling the fate of Isabella's defeated rival Joanna. It provided that the latter should enter the state of *tercería*, in the charge of Princess Beatrice, on 26 October 1479. This meant that, at the age of 18, she would be permanently deprived of her liberty unless, having lost her much older husband Afonso, she chose one of two unappetizing marriages, with man, in the form of Ferdinand and Isabella's son John, or with God, by means of entry to a convent. Both would have the effect of extinguishing for ever her claim to the Castilian throne. It is impossible not to see these demands by Isabella as vindictive, as well as self-interested. The prospect of her son's marrying Joanna seems only to have been included as a sop to her aunt Beatrice, while her real intention was that her rival, and almost certainly her niece, should go into a convent and never emerge from it, as indeed eventually occurred. Isabella seems to have expressed the wish, when the negotiations with her aunt first began at Alcántara, that Joanna should enter a Castilian convent, so that, once again, it was a gesture to Portugal, of which she had briefly been queen, that she should after all be allowed to reside in a Portuguese house. Isabella's relations with Portugal, and to a lesser extent her husband's, would remain a constant preoccupation for many years to come (see Chapter 7), but the fact that Joanna died as late as 1530, without any kind of reconciliation with her 'Spanish' relations, should always be borne in mind.

Some no doubt said, at the time, that a peculiarly female vindictiveness was involved in the relationship between Isabella and Joanna, using it to bolster their prejudice against the exercise of sovereign power by women. Certainly, the chronicler Alfonso de Palencia states that, during the Portuguese invasion of 1475, many 'also criticised the queen for trying, with feminine determination, to exclude the leading Andalusians [such as the duke of Medina Sidonia in Seville and Don Alonso de Aguilar in Córdoba] from the government of cities and towns'.[29] The chronicler attributes Isabella's politics not to reason of state but to her female nature. Noting that this weak point in her character was exploited by many Castilian magnates, 'with the aim that she should not be subordinated to her husband and that, because of discord between the spouses, the cement of the throne should be unpicked'.[30] The obvious implication of this comment is that the enemies of Isabella and Ferdinand's regime saw the possibility of exploiting the couple's distinction of gender, as well as the duality of their rule in Castile.

As a part of this process which, given Palencia's close involvement with politically active members of the nobility, is likely to have been at least to some extent real rather than imaginary, the reputation of Ferdinand appears to have suffered as well. According to the humanist historian, after 1475, 'driven by insane love of his wife', the king quickly became hesitant and weak willed in both domestic and public affairs.[31] In 1479, a year before he was replaced by Hernando del Pulgar as chief royal chronicler, Palencia summarized the situation as follows:

The queen had been preparing for a long time – since just after she was married – something that in the judgement of any prudent man was not fitting for the future succession in these kingdoms: reducing the influence of her husband, in case, as a result of her death, any contingency presented itself in the regular course of the inheritance, if she was survived by her husband.[32]

Palencia seems to have been referring here to Isabella's determination to see that her first child and namesake, born in October 1470, should succeed her on the Castilian throne. Ferdinand and his supporters, of course, believed that he should be her heir, yet such an arrangement was still excluded when she eventually made her will and its codicil, in the autumn of 1504.[33] In any event, it seems to have been as a consequence of his criticism of the queen and his defence of his own professional integrity at Toledo in 1480 that Alfonso de Palencia described Isabella as the 'mistress of dissimulations and deceits'. What is interesting is that the chronicler was firmly of the opinion that sexuality, and in particular female sexuality, had a material effect on the politics of the period. Not only did Palencia employ sexual innuendo as a means of discrediting Henry IV and his regime, but he went on to highlight the personal relationship between Isabella and Ferdinand as a vital factor in their conduct of government. There were two novelties in the regime of the future 'Catholic Monarchs', these being the accession of a woman as 'proprietary queen' of Castile and her exercise of dual monarchy with Ferdinand of Aragon. Palencia was evidently not the only contemporary to find this state of affairs both novel and threatening.[34]

Alfonso de Palencia was certainly not alone in feeling unease at the exercise of monarchical power by a woman. The tensions of January 1475 had demonstrated significant support in Castile for the male authority of Ferdinand and, inevitably, throughout their life together up to 1504, the marital relations between the spouses were commonly regarded as being of political as well as private interest. Chroniclers who wrote in support of Isabella and Ferdinand loyally presented the royal couple as being in complete 'conformity' one with the other, on the lines agreed at Segovia in January 1475. As for the monarchs themselves, they took care to present themselves, in their official documents and on seals and coins, as completely united because, as Hernando del Pulgar put it, 'if necessity separated the persons, love held the wills together'.[35] In reality, a double standard applied, which allowed Ferdinand to continue fathering illegitimate children, while his wife conspicuously avoided opportunities for infidelity. Thus, according to the German Hieronymus Münzer, who visited Spain in 1494–5, when the king was away in court, his wife slept in a dormitory, with her daughters or with other ladies or maidens of the court, so as not give rise even to the suspicion of scandal.[36] The debate continues over the balance between a fiery temper and religious and marital devotion, in the character of the new Castilian 'proprietary' queen.

Ferdinand's arrival as Isabella's consort inevitably submitted him to the judgement of contemporary Castilian writers. Thus Andrés Bernáldez, parish priest of Los Palacios (Seville), declared his enthusiasm for both monarchs indiscriminately, even though Isabella was proprietary queen. Mosén Diego de Valera and Hernando del Pulgar took a similar attitude, but Palencia, as has been seen, did not. For him, Ferdinand was the true ruler and his 'fortune', in the humanistic definition of the word, was the main determinant of the destiny of Castile, as well as his own 'proprietary' Crown of Aragon. Two Italian humanists at the Spanish court, Lucio Marineo Sículo and Pier Martire d'Anghiera (Pedro Mártir de Anglería), took a similar view, especially in the period after Isabella's death, when her husband's supremacy gradually became more evident, at home and abroad. This was despite their criticism of the king's lascivious nature and their sympathetic treatment of Isabella's jealousy.[37] With a few exceptions, most notably the eulogy of Isabella in Castiglione's *The Courtier*, most sixteenth- and seventeenth-century writers concentrated on the achievements of Ferdinand as a ruler. For example, the chronicler of the Emperor Charles V, Fray Prudencio de Sandoval, described Isabella's husband as 'king of Castile', ignoring the queen altogether. The annalist Zurita, a loyal Aragonese, took a similar line.[38]

In reality, however, as Belenguer has pointed out, it is hard to characterize Ferdinand's personal philosophy and much has to be done by means of analogy and surmise. In terms of international policy, there is no doubting the king's influence, not least in the Italian campaigns. The recovery of Rosselló (Roussillon) and Cerdanya (Cerdagne) from France, in 1493 (see Chapter 5), as well as being a personal triumph for Ferdinand, was the achievement of a longstanding Aragonese objective. The Crown of Aragon had been opposed to France, and to the house of Anjou in particular, ever since the war of the Sicilian Vespers, in 1282.[39] Being, like his wife, a Trastamaran, Ferdinand inherited a strongly pro-French foreign policy, which, in turn, originated in the intervention that had ensured the victory of Henry, the founder of the dynasty, over the legitimate king, Peter 'the Cruel'. Nevertheless, it appears that, at least from the 1480s onwards, Ferdinand dominated the foreign policy of Castile as well as Aragon, drawing it in a traditionally Aragonese and Catalan direction. This meant war for the restoration of Rosselló and Cerdanya from France and active intervention in the central Mediterranean, including the Italian mainland. Foreigners often preferred to deal with Ferdinand and Isabella seems to have resented the fact that diplomatic correspondence from abroad was habitually addressed to him alone. As far as his peninsular territories were concerned, though, however strong the theory on monarchy which Ferdinand inherited from the Castilian practice of the fourteenth century, this had inevitably been mediated through the governance, or attempted governance, of a diverse group of territories, each the jealous guardian of its own laws, political and legal institutions and even language. To this multifarious heritage was added not only the Catalan-speaking Balearic islands, but also the highly individual political entities of Sardinia, Sicily and parts of Italy itself (see Chapter 2). From his own father, John II of Aragon, Ferdinand learned the skills of a patient and frequently unscrupulous manipulator of the diverse and conflicting aims and susceptibilities of the politically powerful or aspiring, whether in his own territories or in Castile. Yet he also had before him the example of his uncle, Alfonso 'the Magnanimous', ruler of Aragon–Catalonia, Sicily and Naples, who successfully combined an 'absolutist'

Trastamaran style of monarchy with ideas gleaned from theorists and practitioners of princely power in the Italy of the Renaissance. In Alan Ryder's words: 'No counsellor, however exalted, however intimate, and no private secretary, however close, entered unreservedly into his confidence.'[40] His nephew Ferdinand, who would eventually also reign in Naples, seems to have learned much from him (see Chapter 5).

Notes

1 Ortí Belmonte, M. A. (1962) 'Exhumación de la momía de Enrique IV', *Boletín de la Real Academia de Córdoba*, vol. 33, pp. 245–6 (report by M. Gómez Moreno and G. Marañon).

2 For an extensive study of this period, see Val Valdivieso, M. I. del (1974) *Isabel la Católica princesa, 1468–74*, University of Valladolid; see also Edwards, J. (2000) *The Spain of the Catholic Monarchs, 1474–1520*, Blackwell, pp. 1–20.

3 Azcona, T. de (1998) *Juana de Castilla, mal llamada La Beltraneja, 1462–1530*, Fundación Universitaria Española.

4 Azcona, T. de (1993) *Isabel la Católica. Estudio crítico de su vida y su reinado*, Biblioteca de Autores Cristianos, pp. 247–8.

5 Jansen, S. L. (2002) *The Monstrous Regiment of Women. Female rulers in early modern Europe*, Palgrave Macmillan, p. 18; Rubin, N. (1991) *Isabella of Castile: the first Renaissance queen*, St Martin's Press, p. 26; Liss, P. (1992) *Isabel the Queen. Life and times*, Oxford University Press, p. 14.

6 Hillgarth, J. N. (1978) *The Spanish Kingdoms, 1250–1516*, vol. 2, *1410–1516. Castilian hegemony*, Clarendon Press, p. 246; Jansen, S. L. (2002) pp. 19, 235.

7 Jansen, S. L. (2002) p. 235.

8 Goldberg, H. (1974) *Jardín de nobles donzellas, Fray Martín de Córdoba: a critical edition and study*, University of North Carolina, pp. 135–41.

9 Ibid. p. 136.

10 Aram, B. (2001) *La reina Juana. Gobierno, piedad y dinastía*, Marcial Pons, pp. 36–8.

11 *Cortes de los antiguos reinos de León y Castilla*, Real Academia de la Historia, vol. 3, pp. 456–94.

12 *Cortes*, vol. 3, 767–9.

13 Nieto Soria, J. M. (2001) 'Los fundamentos ideológicos', pp. 187–8.

14 Pulgar, F. del (1969) *Claros varones de Castilla*, J Domínguez Bordona (ed.), Clásicos Castellanos, p. 150.

15 Nieto Soria, J. M. (2001) 'Los fundamentos ideológicos', p. 192.

16 Nieto Soria, J. M. (2001) 'Los fundamentos ideológicos', p. 194.

17 Pulgar, F. del (1971) *Claros varones de Castilla*, Robert Brian Tate (ed.), Clarendon Press.

18 Nieto Soria, J. M. (2001) 'Los fundamentos ideológicos', p. 205.

19 Palencia, A. de (1973–5) *Crónica de Enrique IV*, 3 vols, Atlas (the Spanish version of A. Paz y Meliá).

20 Palencia, A. de (1970–4) *Cuarta década*, Real Academia de la Historia, vol. 2, pp. 167, 196.

21 Cooper, E. (1991) *Castillos señoriales en la Corona de Castilla*, Junta de Castilla y León, 1 pt. 2, 869.

22 Tate, R. B. (1994) 'Políticas sexuales de Enrique el Impotente a Isabel, maestra de engaños (magistra dissimulationum)', in *Actas del Primer Congreso Anglo-Hispano*, vol. 3, *Historia*, Editorial Castalia, pp. 165–76.

23 Palencia, A. de (1970–4) *Cuarta década*, vols 2, 3, 4.

24 Palencia, A. de (1973–5) *Crónica de Enrique IV*, vol. 2, 155a.

25 Palencia, A. de (1973–5) *Crónica de Enrique IV*, vol. 2, 163a.

26 Cited in Azcona, T. de (1993) p. 251.

27 Anon (1934) *Crónica incompleta de los Reyes Católicos (1469–1476), según un manuscrito anónimo de su época*, Julio Puyol (ed.), Tipografía de Archivo, p. 238.

28 Ibid. p. 238.

29 Palencia, A. de (1973–5) *Crónica de Enrique IV*, vol. 3, 45b.

30 Palencia, A. de (1973–5) *Crónica de Enrique IV*, vol. 3, 70b.

31 Palencia, A. de (1970–4) *Cuarta década*, pp. 38, 48.

32 Palencia, A. de (1970–4) *Cuarta década*, vol. 2, pp. 164, 192.

33 Aram, B. (2001) *La reina Juana*, p. 39.

34 Tate, R. B. (1994) 'Políticas sexuales', pp. 168–74.

35 Pulgar, H. de (1878) *Crónica de los señores Reyes Católicos don Fernando y doña Isabel de Castilla y de Aragón*, Cayetano Rosell (ed.), p. 256.

36 Cited in Aram, p. 40.

37 Belenguer, E. (1999) *Fernando el Católico*, pp. 15–17.

38 Belenguer, E. (1999) *Fernando el Católico*, pp. 17–18.

39 Abulafia, D. (1997) *The Western Mediterranean Kingdoms, 1200–1500. The struggle for dominion*, Longman, pp. 51–6, 67–80.

40 Ryder, A. (1990) *Alfonso the Magnanimous*, Oxford University Press, pp. 358–9.

Chapter 2

_____

❁

Building a Regime

Even before the final defeat of 'La Beltraneja' and her Portuguese supporters, Isabella and Ferdinand had begun to consider reforms in the government of Castile. They inherited what was in theory a comparatively strong royal administration, which supported the monarchs and also supposedly acted in the interest of their subjects. There are some general points to be noted, before the institutions of the respective 'Crowns' of Castile and Aragon are considered in more detail. First, whereas in more recent, post-Enlightenment governmental systems (other than that of the United Kingdom, which is only now, since 2003, being looked at in this way) there has been a concern to separate executive powers from the judicial function, late medieval western European states saw no contradiction here. Second, and deriving from the historically 'personal' nature of monarchy, governmental institutions had an inbuilt personal character, in which it was understood and accepted that the rulers would intervene frequently in both political and judicial matters. Although the notion of the king (or queen) as having two 'bodies', one personal and one institutional, had by the fifteenth century been generally accepted, at least in the monarchies of England, France and Spain, there was certainly no 'statute of limitations' in the Trastamaran monarchies of Castile and Aragon, to restrict the functions of governmental institutions. Instead, these offices and 'departments' might readily be adapted to new activities, as fresh demands faced the sovereigns and the often spectacular incidents of Isabella and Ferdinand's reigns were amply to demonstrate this point, even if resulting governmental problems were to be bequeathed to the Habsburgs.

Crown of Castile

It has often been observed that, despite their somewhat dubious reputation as 'new monarchs' who supposedly moved towards a 'modern' absolutist system of government, Ferdinand and Isabella in fact established very few new governmental and administrative institutions in their respective kingdoms. This was certainly so in Castile, where their main achievement was to use more effectively the institutions that existed in the reigns of John II and Henry IV. The effects of past political instability were still evident up to Isabella's death and even more obvious thereafter (see Chapter 7). Nevertheless, Castile provided the main base for Isabella and Ferdinand's political activity, both in Europe and further afield. One reason for this, apart from the demographic preponderance of Castile over the Crown of Aragon, was the former's strong 'imperial' tradition of monarchy, which dated back to the time of Alfonso X, in the mid- to late thirteenth century. As will be seen, Aragonese and Catalan institutions were largely decentralized and much more open to scrutiny, and in some cases control, by other groups, such as the nobility and the burgesses of the major cities, especially Barcelona and Valencia. One of the main differences between the two 'Crowns' lay in their contrasting parliamentary traditions. In Castile, Isabella inherited a single assembly of the estates (Cortes), while Ferdinand was forced to confront separate assemblies, in the kingdom of Aragon, the principality of Catalonia and the kingdom of Valencia, respectively, with obvious economic and political consequences. When Isabella acceded to the Castilian throne, it had already become traditional, and largely uncontested, except in the case of the 'arbitration sentence' by the nobility against Henry IV, in 1465, that the monarch should be able to govern without any necessity of consulting the Cortes. Yet along with this freedom, which would certainly have been envied by English kings of the period, came a concern that the monarchy should be able to function on a sound legal basis. This explains the huge flow of legislation and administrative directions that emanated from the Castilian chancellery of Isabella and Ferdinand and which has provided much of the basis for modern historical work on the period. During Isabella's reign, sterling, if not wholly successful, efforts were made to collect and organize these documents, as well as those of the preceding three centuries. The most notable compilation of the period was the 'Royal Ordinances of Castile' (*Ordenanzas reales de Castilla*), in which the jurist and civil servant Alonso Díaz de Montalvo collected Alfonso X's major law code, the 'Seven parts' (*Siete partidas*) and Alfonso XI's 'Ordinances of Alcalá [de Henares]' (*Ordenanzas de Alcalá*), Cortes legislation, and numerous administrative documents, such as pragmatics and *cédulas*, which had legal force as though they had been passed by the Cortes. Cortes members had been asking for such a collection since 1433 and it was finally begun after a further petition at the Cortes of Toledo in

1480. First published in 1485, 'Montalvo's laws' (*La leyes de Montalvo*) appeared in further editions in 1488, 1495, 1500 and 1513, this demand resulting from the fact that, although the collection was initially a private project, the monarchs ordered that all places in Castile with over 200 citizens (*vecinos*) should keep a copy, to help settle legal disputes. In 1503, it was supplemented by a new collection of the legislation issued since 1474, which was made by a scribe (*escribano*) of the Royal Council (*Consejo real*), Juan Ramírez. His work, also, was republished, into the reign of Philip II, but Isabella recognized in the codicil to her will (November 1504; see Chapter 7) that Montalvo and Ramírez' efforts were not wholly adequate. This problem was to haunt the Spanish monarchy, as it became, until the end of the 'Old Regime' in the early nineteenth century.

Central government

The historic centre of royal government in Castile was the royal household, together with its surrounding court. Although, as in the constitutional image of the 'two bodies', a theoretical distinction was observed between the personal service of the sovereign and the public service of the Castilian 'Crown', in practice the two functions inevitably overlapped. Thus household officials, especially nobles, commonly carried out political and governmental functions, for which they received special payments from the Royal Treasury of living expenses (*ayudas de costa y mantenimientos*). Also, 200 permanent servants (*continos*) were attached to the household, exercising a wide range of confidential functions on the rulers' behalf. They generally came either from the ranks of university graduates (*letrados*) or from the lesser or middling nobility and the office of *contino* was often a stepping stone to high governmental office. Ladero has described this group as a halfway house between old-style personal servants (*criados*) of the ruler and modern government functionaries.[1] By the late 1470s, when Isabella and her husband began to take a firm grip on the royal administration, the senior offices of the royal household, although they had humble, functional titles, such as 'waiter' (*camarero*) or 'pastrycook' (*repostero*), were in fact honorary and the posts were held by nobles. Those of a more secretarial nature were often held by senior churchmen. Substantial revenues were still attached to such offices and these were often enjoyed, on an effectively hereditary basis, by the great noble houses of Castile. Thus the constable (*condestable*) and 'head waiter' (*camarero mayor*) was traditionally a Velasco, the admiral (*almirante*) of Castile an Enríquez, the chief justice (*justicia mayor*) a Zúñiga, and the head steward (*mayordomo mayor*) a Pacheco. The real work would be done by officials of lesser breeding so that, for example, while the marquis of Villena was *mayordomo mayor*, the two functioning royal stewards (*mayordomos reales*) were Enrique Enríquez and Gonzalo Chacón. The great chancellor (*canciller mayor*) of Castile was the archbishop of Toledo, effectively *ex officio*, and the chief notaries (*notarios mayores*) of Castile, León, Toledo and Andalusia, respectively, were all members of the upper nobility.

It is important to note that, while the contemporary monarchies of England and France had established seats of government, in Westminster and Paris, the Castilian court, like its Aragonese counterpart, remained itinerant in this period. Ferdinand and his wife travelled thousands of miles during their reigns, both together and separately, and they were generally accompanied by a large part of the central government's apparatus (see also Chapter 6). It was still believed that a ruler should be close to his or her people, with the possibility of direct royal intervention in the affairs of even the most humble subject. Nevertheless, although Castile had no official capital in this period, certain cities were especially recognized – Toledo as the capital of the former Visigothic monarchy, Valladolid as the seat of the High Court (*audiencia real*) and frequently the residence of the monarchs – while archives, and other royal goods, were stored in the castles of Segovia (the Alcázar) and of La Mota at Medina del Campo and also in Burgos. As a consequence of the dispersed nature of royal government, considerable sums were spent by the Crown on postal services, both in Aragon and Castile. As the court made its laborious way about the country, the royal quartermasters (*aposentadores*) were kept in almost constant employment.

According to tradition, the main advisory body to the rulers of Castile was the Royal Council (*consejo real*). In common with similar bodies in other countries, the Council had full powers, under the monarchs, to resolve all manner of political and legal disputes, and its written rulings were issued in the form of 'royal provisions' (*provisiones reales*), which were drawn up by one of the Council's official scribes. The Council supervised all senior administrative officials, such as the Crown representatives (*corregidores*) in the major towns (see later) and the investigators (*pesquisidores*) who checked on these officials' conduct in office. It was also, under the ruler and his or her 'viceroys', the supreme judicial tribunal of the kingdom, which inevitably brought it into conflict with the professional High Court (*audiencia*). The Council normally heard judicial appeals on Fridays and, as noted, early in their reigns, the king and queen sometimes attended such sessions. The Council, as a judicial committee, had no jurisdiction over financial and taxation matters, which were the responsibility of the chief royal accountants (*contadores mayores*). Increasingly, the crucial link between the sovereigns and the Council, as well as other organs of the central government, were the royal secretaries. As in other monarchies of the period, notably in England and France, the *secretarios reales* were responsible for drawing up documents to receive the royal signature. For this purpose, they had the use of the 'secret', or court seal, as opposed to the 'great' seal, which was the responsibility of the Chancellery. In Castile, officials who provided such links between the king and his Council had previously been known as 'drafters' (*refrendarios*) or 'reporters' (*relatores*), but the secretaries' role was quickly affirmed by Isabella and her husband in ordinances issued in 1476. These laws did not allude, however, to the political importance of the secretaries, whose constant contact with the monarchs gave them a unique insight into royal desires and an ideal opportunity to implement them by influencing, and on occasions directing, the officers of state. Secretaries formed their own 'cabinets' of advisers and collaborators, as in the cases of Fernán Álvarez de Toledo, up to 1497, and Hernando de Zafra, when he took responsibility for organizing the new administration in Granada, after 1492. These and other royal secretaries constituted the personal staff of the monarchs and their access to the seat of power inevitably downgraded the importance of the Council itself. The danger for an ambitious secretary was that he would misuse or exaggerate his power and influence, in which case his lack of formal status could work to his disadvantage.

One feature of Isabella and Ferdinand's Castile was the survival of ancient offices alongside those that had a real function in contemporary government. This phenomenon has already been noted within the court and household, but it applied equally in the upper echelons of the political administration of the various notional 'kingdoms' of the Crown of Castile. After 1474, the most dynamic of such offices was that of co-ruler or corrector (*corregidor*), which will be discussed more fully later, but many political offices still survived, at least in name, from earlier phases of Castilian history, while others were established to meet particular contemporary circumstances. A case in point is that of governors (*gobernadores*), who began to appear in the last years of Henry IV, and were named temporarily by Isabella, to Ciudad Rodrigo, near the Portuguese border at the time of the threat from the 'Beltraneja', and to the marquisate of Villena, which was a source of internal dissidence during the early years of her reign (see Chapter 1). More permanent *gobernadores* were named to Galicia (Fernando de Acuña in 1480 and Diego López de

Haro in 1484), with the aim of bringing an end to the internecine warfare in that kingdom. The governor, or chief *corregidor* (*corregidor mayor*), also commanded the Galician Brotherhood (*hermandad*), and set up an appeal tribunal in A Coruña, which was later to become an *audiencia* for Galicia. On the frontier with the emirate of Granada, the traditional royal representatives were the 'chief scouts' (*adelantados mayores*), who were normally members of the upper nobility. In Ferdinand and Isabella's time, only the *adelantado* of Murcia retained any practical function, although in western Andalusia the Enríquez de Ribera family retained the title. An entirely new system was set up in Granada after the 1492 conquest (see Chapters 3 and 7). The *adelantamientos* of Castile, León and Galicia had also become titular offices for aristocrats and, as in Murcia and Andalusia, the judicial functions of the *adelantado* had been transferred to professional lawyers, for example to the tribunal of the 'steps' (*grados*) in Seville. Such changes were typical of a more general development.

During the fifteenth century, in common with other western European monarchies, the Castilian Crown had seen a steady increase in the power and influence of bureaucrats with law degrees (*letrados*) or at least some legal training. Some of them were of comparatively humble origin, but more typically they came from the lesser or middling nobility. It has been calculated that, during the reigns of Isabella and Ferdinand, out of a total of 1499 known royal administrators, fewer than 12 per cent were university law graduates, most of them trained in Salamanca. However, in the case of judicial appointments, and posts requiring the practise of the law, the percentage rose to 59.3. In military or governmental appointments, the percentage fell to as little as 5.2, while the royal household contained virtually no law graduates at all. The crucial office of *corregidor* was more commonly filled by knights (*caballeros*) or nobles (*hidalgos*), although about 40 per cent were indeed bachelors or licentiates in civil law. In Isabella's reign, fewer *letrados* seem to have been appointed as *corregidores* than under John II and Henry IV. It should be noted, however, that a *corregidor* who lacked legal training was required to include in his team of officials a chief magistrate (*alcalde mayor*) who was thus qualified. In any case, Castilian, as opposed to Roman, law was not taught in the universities, so that the legal aspects of local administration had largely to be learned on the job.[2]

Taxation

Fundamental to the strength of the 'absolutist' Castilian monarchy was the wealth of the Royal Treasury and, from the very beginning of her reign Isabella, as well as her husband, fully grasped the importance of restoring the Crown's revenues, which had been severely depleted under her half-brother's administration. In theory, this should have been a comparatively easy task since, over the previous two centuries and in contrast with the situation in the Crown of Aragon, Castilian rulers had gained for themselves almost complete freedom to demand taxes and raise revenue. In practice, however, and notably in the reigns of John II and Henry IV, political factors might intervene to prevent this potential from being realized. As in the case of the organs of state, Isabella and Ferdinand made few innovations in the taxation system, which remained in the form it had reached by the beginning of the fifteenth century. As in other late medieval states, the basic ordinary (i.e. regular) revenues of the Crown, its 'regalian' rights, came from duties and imposts on trade, both within the kingdom itself and with other countries, as well as taxes on consumption. Customs duties (*aduanas*) were notionally set at 10 per cent. Those on maritime trade were known on the north coast as 'sea tithes' (*diezmos de la mar*) and in the south as *almojarifazgos*, from the Arabic *almojarife*, an official who supervised such commerce. The movement of livestock, and above all the annual north–south migrations of sheep organized by the association of stockbreeders and shepherds known as the Mesta, were subject to duties known as *servicio y montazgo*, which were collected (and commonly evaded) at strategic points on the established sheepwalks (*cañadas*).[3] In common with other European monarchs of the period, the Castilian rulers had the regalian right to tax salt production (*salinas*). By the end of the fifteenth century, after vigorous efforts by the monarchs and their officials to claw back lost taxes from their subjects, the salt tax provided about 3 per cent of their total revenues, while the *almojarifazgo* and the *diezmos de la mar* produced about 10–12 per cent and the *servicio y montazgo* about 5 per cent. However the great bulk of the Crown's income, up to 80 per cent, in this period and for some decades afterwards, came from a tax on sales and purchases, which was known as the *alcabala*. Notionally set at 10 per cent, this had become general in Castile in 1340s, and applied to virtually all commodities. In Isabella's time, it was farmed by local subcontractors, acting on behalf of a syndicate who bid for the national contract in annual auctions, held at Valladolid, and it functioned in a manner similar to the modern European 'value-added tax'. Finally, in addition to these regular 'ordinary' taxes, Castilian monarchs had the privilege of receiving, on a regular basis, a two-ninths share of the ecclesiastical tithes, the *tercias reales*. This was granted by successive popes in recognition of Spanish efforts in the war against Islam and its value increased spectacularly in this period, from 150,000,000 *maravedíes* in 1480 to 314,000,000 *maravedíes* in 1504.

It is clear that, although Isabella and her husband rarely took direct initiatives in economic matters, their ability to prosecute their political and religious aims depended to a considerable extent on the strength of the Castilian economy and their ability to tap it. As in every other aspect of the kingdom's life, there were great variations between the economies of the regions, which inevitably affected their monetary value to the Crown. Over two-thirds of Isabella and Ferdinand's revenues came from Old and New Castile, which contained the important trading centres of Burgos, Valladolid, Medina del Campo, Segovia and Toledo, and from western Andalusia, with Córdoba and Seville as its main centres. In general terms, the frontier regions adjoining Portugal, Navarre, Aragon and Valencia were less productive, in terms of royal revenues. The rulers paid particular attention to strengthening their authority over Galicia, which helped to compensate, economically as well as politically, for their difficulties in the Basque lordships of Vizcaya and Guipúzcoa. Regular sources of revenue were not, however, the royal couple's only recourse.

All medieval sovereigns claimed the right to make special demands ('extraordinary' in taxation terms) on their subjects, usually in the context of the fundamental duties of governments in the period, which were the defence of the realm and the preservation of law and order within it. In this respect, too, Ferdinand and Isabella were no exception. 'Extra-ordinary' taxes might become extremely ordinary and the *alcabala* is a notable case in point, but, in theory at least, monarchs in Spain, as elsewhere, were required to ask for the specific consent of their subjects, before making such levies, whether of military forces and materials or of cash. This was the origin of the 'parliamentary' tradition in many countries. Both direct and indirect taxes could be raised by this method and in the Castilian case the Cortes was the main traditional vehicle for this purpose. In that kingdom, direct taxes were known as *pechos* ('breast' or poll taxes), and were generally voted by the Cortes as 'aids' (*servicios*), which were notionally a substitute for military service and normally demanded only in time of war. The Cortes of Madrigal, held in 1476 while the war against the 'Beltraneja' and the Portuguese was still in progress, voted a *servicio* in this manner, divided as usual into *pedidos* ('requests') and *monedas* ('cash'), but this was to be the last such grant for over 20 years. Perhaps the most notable constitutional feature of Isabella and Ferdinand's regime in Castile was their downgrading of the Cortes, in favour of extra-parliamentary means of raising revenue. The Castilian Cortes, like other late medieval parliaments, had consisted of three 'estates', which supposedly represented the main sources of power in the kingdom. These were senior churchmen, who represented the first estate, the nobility who formed the second and the 'third estate', which, by the time of Isabella's accession, consisted only of two representatives (*procuradores*) from each of 16 towns (with Granada added after 1492) most of which were the capitals of the notional 'kingdoms' of which the Crown of Castile consisted. By 1480, when the Cortes of Toledo was held, only the *procuradores* of the 16 towns, who were elected by their fellow councillors, functioned in a parliamentary fashion, the Church and the nobility being, by this time, consulted separately, if at all. There was, in any case, a fundamental weakness in the procedure of the Castilian Cortes, which ensured that, even at the best of times, it could only be a feeble check on the royal government. As well as voting funds to the Crown, all late medieval representative assemblies had the duty of raising grievances for the consideration of their rulers, but the crucial point was whether the ruler had to answer parliamentary petitions before receiving the vote of taxation or vice versa. In the case of Castile, the answering of petitions, which were pre-prepared by the members (*procuradores*) in a set form, always followed the voting of funds and there was no tradition of robust parliamentary debate. This, together with the self-evident righteousness and necessity, in the eyes of most Christian Castilians, of the war against the Nasrid emirs of Granada (see Chapter 3), made it relatively easy for the king and queen to bypass the Cortes and obtain their money by other means. The chosen method was to use the fund-raising potential of the Holy Brotherhood (*Santa Hermandad*), which, during the war against Princess Joanna and the Portuguese, had been turned from a set of local, rural police forces into a national network.

As the Granada war progressed, the Hermandad's national assemblies (*juntas*), in addition to funding their own activities, voted significant sums for the war effort. With the help of the campaign's status as a 'crusade', the monarchs were also able to tap other ecclesiastical funds, in addition to the traditional *tercias reales*. On various occasions during the war, successive popes permitted their 'son and daughter' of Castile to collect extra subsidies (*servicios*) from the Castilian clergy and this practice continued after the fall of Granada in January 1492. In addition, the Crown received the benefit of payments made by Christians for the indulgences that were attached to the preaching of the papal bull of the crusade (*cruzada*), which also continued after the conquest of the emirate was complete (see Chapter 4). Castile's Jewish and (ironically) Muslim (*mudéjar*) communities also contributed to the war effort, not only in the form of their regular financial aids (*servicios y medios servicios*) but also, at the beginning of the campaign, by means of a poll tax (*pecho*) of two gold *castellanos* on every male over the age of 16 who possessed property of his own (*hacienda apartada*). Another important addition to the royal income was the administration of the historic 'military orders' of Santiago, Calatrava and Alcántara, which had been set up, at an earlier stage of the 'Reconquest', on the model of the crusading Templars and Hospitallers in the Holy Land. By the late fifteenth century, these orders, which consisted of knights who had taken monastic vows, had become immensely wealthy, even though their role in fighting Islam had greatly diminished. The royal couple took the opportunity of a series of master's elections to put Ferdinand in charge of all three orders, thus effectively annexing them to the Crown. Thereafter, the revenues of the three former masters (*mesas maestrales* or 'masters' tables') were distributed, as estates (*encomiendas*) or in cash, to political allies. Never again would dissident nobles be allowed a power base in one of these orders, as Isabella and her husband had observed to their cost, in the case of the Pacheco, in earlier years.

In the latter part of Isabella's reign, up to 70 per cent of Castilian royal revenues came from 'extraordinary' sources, whereas only 30 per cent had done so in previous reigns. The main financial achievement of Ferdinand and Isabella's regime was to double the revenue from just over a million ducats a year early on to two million by the beginning of the sixteenth century. Nevertheless, the ever growing cost of royal enterprises necessitated increasing recourse to loans, from institutions and individuals. By the end of the Granada war, in 1492, the treasury was having difficulty in paying back this money and resorted to a primitive form of national debt, known as *juros*. Previously, this term had been used to refer to the assignment of parts of the royal revenue to individuals, generally nobles, as favours either for life or in perpetuity (*de heredad*). In the reigns of John II and Henry IV, this practice had seriously damaged the royal finances and one of the laws passed at the Cortes of Toledo in 1480 attempted, with some success, to resume such grants. What happened after about 1490 was somewhat different, however. *Juros* still had the documentary form of grants and favours (*mercedes*) from the Crown to individuals, but in fact they were loans from those individuals to the Crown. As before, each *juro* was assigned to a particular tax, often in a specified locality, for example to the *alcabala* on leather trades in Córdoba, which would be used to pay interest on the loan. As the 1480 law indicated, the monarchs were not keen on hereditary or life *juros*, preferring to issue what were effectively government bonds, known as *juros al quitar*. The treasury might redeem these at any time, paying about 10 per cent on earlier grants and a reduced rate of about 7.14 per cent on newer ones. From these small beginnings would arise the elaborate system of deficit finance later employed by the Habsburgs.

It seems clear that, as Ferdinand and Isabella's ambitious policies unfolded, the burden of taxation on their subjects steadily increased. The flow of satirical verses in Castilian, which had been a feature of the two previous reigns, seems largely to have dried up, but there is an exception. After nearly ten years of costly war in neighbouring Granada, some verses appeared in Jerez de Frontera, an Andalusian town that had sacrificed much in the conflict, sternly criticizing the Crown's fiscal regime:

Open, open your ears.
Listen, listen, shepherd,
Because you are not hearing the clamour
That your sheep were making to you.
Their voices rise to heaven,
Complaining without consolation,
That you fraudulently shear them
So many times in the year
That now they have no wool to cover them.
[. . .]
If you say that your enterprise was
For the benefit of your flock,
And to give savour to your law
And to grow your pasture (*dehesa*) more,
And that what you have sheared
Has been well employed,
Because you flatten the mountains [an allusion to wartime road construction in
    Granada],
Why do you want those lands
Since you're killing the stock?[4]

In Jerez, a town that had been subject to regular Muslim attack earlier in the fifteenth century, when it was closer to the frontier, and therefore had no reason to be fond of the Nasrids, there was something of a tradition of debating the moral aspects of taxation. In 1438, for example, its parish councillors (*jurados*, see later) had (unsuccessfully) protested at the unfairness of the local allocation (*repartimiento*) of royal and municipal taxes and demanded that levels of contribution should be properly related to the ability to pay. The town council was to return to the issue in the fraught conditions of 1508–9 (see Chapter 7). Similarly, in the larger city of Córdoba, which was to be the main base for the Granada war (see Chapter 3), there were protests about the unfair distribution of tax demands, especially as repeated military and financial levies continued to be made after 1492.[5] Although nothing effective was done in response, official circles, both in central government and in the regions, could not claim to be unaware of this discontent.

Out of necessity, however, the Crown was forced, in this period, to continue its relentless search for revenue by all possible means. After 1480, the royal treasurers and accountants (*contadores*) managed to claw back the considerable sum of 35 million *maravedíes* of *juros* 'situated' (*situados*) in royal rents. But, at the end of this process, between 30 and 35 per cent of the total royal income was still being dissipated in this way. There was an ever growing danger that the monarchs' ambitions would outstrip their financial resources. Nevertheless, serious efforts were made in this period to organize the treasury on a more efficient basis and what they did was largely to be copied by the Habsburgs, during Spain's period of imperial greatness. There were two main accountancy departments (*contadurías mayores*), one in charge of making and receiving payments and the other to keep the royal accounts. The chief accountants (*contadores mayores*), for example Gonzalo Chacón and Gutierre de Cárdenas, were among Isabella's closest confidants and their importance was reflected in their pay. While royal secretaries received a salary (*quitación*) of 60,000 *maravedíes* a year, apart from Fernando de Zafra, who received 100,000 and Fernán Álvarez de Toledo, who was paid 200,000, and while members of the Royal Council received 100,000 *maravedíes* a year, the *contadores mayores* were paid between 400,000 and 500,000 *maravedíes* per annum. The *contaduría mayor de hacienda* was subdivided into departments to handle incomings – rents and extraordinary payments – and outgoings, while the *contaduría mayor de cuentas* kept the financial records of all those to whom royal funds were entrusted. One of its most prominent officials was Alfonso de Quintanilla, who had previously served the short-lived Prince Alfonso.

The *contadores mayores* were responsible for organizing the annual auctions of contracts to farm the royal rents and a staff of collectors (*recaudadores*) and treasurers (*tesoreros*) was employed to collect the money from the tax farmers (*arrendadores*). It has already been noted that the most lucrative tax was the *alcabala* and, after 1495, a new system was evolved to collect it. Known as the *encabezamiento*, this involved a global contract between the royal treasury and local authorities, for example town councils, under which the latter would be obliged to provide a single annual sum to cover the whole of this complex rent for the area under their control. It should be noted that local subcontractors for the *alcabala* did not, in any case, aim to tax every individual transaction made by traders, but rather negotiated with them regular payments based on estimated turnover. Both at the national and at the local level, risky calculations had to be made, about the level of trade and about the future value of money.[6] In general, the Castilian Crown's financial record keeping improved greatly from 1476 onwards and it is clear that Isabella, in particular, took a personal interest both in maximizing revenue and in ensuring that it was legitimately obtained. In 1503, as the end of her life approached, she initiated an investigation into the Crown's legal title to its various revenues and this concern was re-emphasized in her will and codicil of the following year (see Chapter 7). If her subjects were to be incorrupt, she expected similar standards of herself. Both parties frequently failed in this respect.

Military expenditure

Inevitably, much of the Castilian royal income was spent on military activity, first in defence of the queen's throne, then in the war to eliminate Islamic rule in Spain and, finally, in a series of further campaigns, within and outside the peninsula, which expanded Spanish influence. At the beginning of Isabella's reign, traditional medieval methods of defending the realm were still in force. In 1474–5, the Castilian Crown maintained 70 fortresses under its direct command, costing between three and five million *maravedíes* a year to maintain, while a further 90 or so were added after the conquest of Granada in 1492, effectively trebling the cost of this type of activity. In the late 1470s, the Castilian standing army was tiny compared with that of France. Part of it consisted of 1000 men-at-arms and a similar number of light cavalry (*jinetes*), who received maintenance (*acostamiento*) from the Crown and were distributed among various towns in the kingdom that were under royal, rather than seignorial, jurisdiction. Attached to the persons of the monarchs themselves were the 'captaincies' (*capitanías*) of the Royal Guard (*guarda real*), which consisted of 1200 *jinetes*, to which were added 1400 more light cavalry, also organized in *capitanías*, who were paid for by the *Santa Hermandad*. When the Granada war started, these troops naturally had to be massively reinforced and the early campaigns against the Nasrids were the last occasion on which a traditional medieval army was sent into the field in Spain. A sign of things to come was the deployment, at royal expense, of artillery, which by the end of the war totalled about 200 pieces. In addition, the Castilian Crown summoned the cavalry and infantry of the royal towns, the seignorial nobility and its forces, the troops of the military orders, knights and nobles who served, in the traditional manner, at their own expense, and the troops levied of the *Hermandad*. Also, it should not be forgotten that the Granada war was a crusade and therefore attracted foreign troops seeking spiritual benefits as well as military experience, although their numbers were never large. As the war went on, the Castilian armies gradually lost the character of a feudal host and became more specialized and professional. Command structures were improved, although traditional noble commanders, such as the marquis of Cádiz, still had a prominent role and troops were organized into battalions (*batallas*), captaincies and units specialized in the use of new weapons such as small cannons and handguns or arquebuses (*espingardas*), as well as naval contingents. All these developments, apart from their military effect (see Chapter 3), served to strengthen the authority of the monarchy.

This process continued with undiminished force after 1492, as the monarchs were determined not to see a large-scale disarmament in Castile. On the contrary, in July 1492 they reminded the wealthier inhabitants of the royal towns (*vecinos cuantiosos*), who possessed goods worth more than 50,000 *maravedíes*, of their historic duty to maintain the horse and weapons of a knight, ready at all times to serve the Crown. From 1495, the renewed war with France (see Chapter 5) created further demand for military forces, the main levies being made in September 1495 and February 1496. The 1495 order specified that, apart from the wealthy 'knights' already noted, men with middling incomes should be required to maintain a crossbow or a handgun, while the poorest needed only a lance. The February 1496 order envisaged the creation of a territorial army, to be organized by the *Hermandad*. One in every 12 Castilian males, between the ages of 25 and 40, should be equipped as an infantryman at the expense of the other 11, and be ready to be called up at any time, in return for some exemption from direct taxes (*pechos*). The hope was that 85,000 men would be armed in this way, but the scheme foundered on logistical difficulties, so that its possible political ramifications were never realized.

Jurisdiction

Isabella and Ferdinand inherited, in Castile, a powerful military aristocracy, which controlled, legally or illegally, the great bulk of the country, was politically ambitious, and continued, at least for a while, to cause them considerable trouble, as it had to Henry IV. Yet, in principle, things should not have been thus, as the Crown had always reserved to itself the jurisdiction over the major towns and cities, each of which governed outlying lands and villages under royal jurisdiction (*realengo*), which might be considerable political and economic assets. In this, as in other respects, the two rulers were traditionalists, yet, as in the case of taxation and revenue, they were concerned to adjust the political and jurisdictional balance between Crown and nobility in the favour of the former. Thus, although the conquest of Granada was to show that further lands and jurisdiction might still, on occasions, be granted to members of the upper nobility (see Chapter 3), the prevailing movement was in the direction of strengthening *realengo*. The main agents in this process were the municipal councils (*concejos*) of the main towns in *realengo*, but these too were politically problematic, from the Crown's point of view. Traditionally, these bodies were supposed, not always accurately, to have consisted of the whole male citizen body, which formed an 'open council' (*concejo abierto*), to consider their community's affairs. Since the mid-fourteenth century, however, the main towns had been ruled, on behalf of the Crown, by councils of *regidores* ('rulers'), whom the monarch appointed for life. In the largest towns, such as Toledo, Seville and Córdoba, there were 24 councillors, who were often known as *veinticuatros*, while smaller towns had councils of 12. Royal towns also had groups of parish councillors (*jurados*), who were traditionally elected by the local citizenry, but might also be appointed by the Crown.

By 1474, however, two major problems had arisen concerning these officers, in whom the Crown had vested a wide range of military, political, social and economic powers. Both arose from the very attractiveness of these powers, the first being a growing tendency towards an effectively hereditary system, particularly in the case of the *regidores*, and the second being the large-scale intervention of local magnates in the affairs of the royal towns. The opportunity for the handing on of urban offices from father to son arose out of the manipulation of the appointments system, which was administered at court. While still fit and in office, a *regidor* might resign his office to his son or another designated individual, such an act being known as a *renunciación*. Alternatively, an officeholder might ask the Crown to ratify the 'expectation' that, in the event of his incapacity or death, the office should be transferred to a named person. In the case of the regional seignorial aristocracies, for example in New Castile, Extremadura and western Andalusia, individual nobles were frequently appointed by the Crown, on an effectively hereditary basis, to senior offices in royal towns, such as those of chief magistrate (*alcalde mayor*) and chief constable (*alguacil mayor*), thus obtaining a base from which to form groupings among the councillors, which they might dominate from houses in the towns themselves, as well as their seigniorial possessions in the countryside. Both these phenomena had become generalized during the reigns of John II and Henry IV and Isabella tackled them at the Cortes of Toledo in 1479–80. By that time, through local enthusiasm for the 'resignation' and 'expectative' system, some councils had been bloated by many excess offices (*oficios acrecentados*) beyond the original 12 or 24. In Córdoba, for example, there were well over 100 *regidores* at the time of the Cortes of Toledo. In the acts of this parliament, the Crown announced its intention to regain control over the appointments system and allow the *oficios acrecentados* to be gradually extinguished, when their holders retired or died. Success was significant, but far from complete, however, and Córdoba still had over 35 *veinticuatros* in post, at Isabella's death.[7]

Crown of Aragon

Although, at the most basic level, all the Christian kingdoms in late medieval Iberia had similar social and governmental structures, there were important differences of political emphasis between them. Ferdinand's inheritance had very much more explicit divisions within it than did Isabella's Castile, in terms of frontiers, powers and institutions and, in simple terms, prevailing Aragonese and Catalan assumptions did not anticipate or desire anything that resembled a centralized, let alone an absolutist, monarchy. Instead, subjects, and not only the politically active, of whom there seem to have been proportionally more in the Crown of Aragon than in that of Castile, saw their rulers as being under contract (*pacto*) with them to deliver good government in return for loyal service. This was the theory behind monarchy in many other medieval states in Europe, but in Aragon and Catalonia the 'constitutional' rhetoric was particularly well developed and unusually effectively applied. In addition, the longstanding cultural and linguistic divisions between the various territories that made up the 'Crown' of Aragon served to accentuate the constitutional divisions between them. Another feature of Aragonese constitutional tradition was the legal exclusion of women from the throne and this was inevitably challenged by Ferdinand II's marriage to the Castilian 'proprietary' queen.

Like his predecessors, Ferdinand had to swear an oath, in Cortes, to uphold the charters (*fueros*) of the kingdom, but whereas Castilian monarchs had traditionally done this just once (and Isabella only summoned the Cortes in 1476, having seized the throne in December 1474), he had to do so three times, in the Corts or Cortes of Catalonia, Aragon and

Valencia. The laws he swore to uphold were entirely distinct in each case. It was inevitable that the king would be absent, for most of the time, from each particular kingdom and his predecessors had traditionally appointed a governor general for each territory, but in Ferdinand's reign the relevant officials had the title of 'lieutenant general' (*lugarteniente general*). Such posts were often held by heirs to throne and, somewhat controversially, Isabella herself acted in this capacity in Aragon, Catalonia and Valencia in 1488. For most of Ferdinand's reign, the lieutenancy of Aragon was occupied by his illegitimate son, Alfonso de Aragón, who had been appointed archbishop of Zaragoza as a teenager. The lieutenant in Valencia was sometimes known as a viceroy, despite local opposition, and had the power to summon the Cortes there. There were also viceroys in Sardinia and Sicily.

There was one Chancellery (*cancillería*) for the whole of the Crown of Aragon. It was headed by a senior churchman, as honorary chancellor, but the main work was done by the vice-chancellor and a group of 'regents' (*regentes*), one for each kingdom or principality, who were assisted by protonotaries, their deputies, and scribes. As in other European states of the period, the Aragonese Royal Council retained a judicial function. In 1493, when he was able to turn his mind from Granadan to Aragonese affairs, Ferdinand reorganized the central administration of royal justice. He set up separate High Courts (*audiencias reales*) for Aragon and Catalonia, the former staffed by five doctors of law and the latter by eight (12 from 1512). Chancellery regents presided over these tribunals and the relevant royal lieutenant also had the power to vote on cases. A similar *audiencia* was set up in Valencia in 1506. Perhaps Ferdinand's most important administrative innovation, however, was the establishment, by a pragmatic dated 18 November 1494, of a 'Council of Aragon' (*consejo de Aragón*), which was intended to provide an organic link between the sovereign will of the king and the various territories of the Crown of Aragon. Its initial president was the vice-chancellor, Alfonso de la Cavallería, and in its final form it consisted of six regents, two for Aragon, two for Catalonia and two for Valencia. It also had its own legal counsel (*abogado*), royal secretaries and a 'general treasurer' (*tesorero general*) to deal with matters concerning the royal patrimony. As well as being the highest judicial tribunal in the Crown of Aragon, the new Royal Council was evidently intended as a mechanism to replicate the more centralized Castilian institutions and bypass the vigorous and constitutionally minded Cortes of Aragon, Catalonia and Valencia. In judicial matters, it intervened particularly actively in Valencia and Majorca, where the powers of older legal and political institutions were less entrenched.

Ferdinand and his advisers adopted a less innovative approach towards local, as opposed to central, government in the Crown of Aragon. Thus, throughout this period, Catalonia retained its 18 'lieutenancies' (*veguerías*) and similar institutions remained in Majorca, while there continued to be 11 'justiciarships' in Valencia and the traditional neighbourhood committees (*juntas*) in Aragon, each with a chairman known as a *sobrejuntero*. Ferdinand inherited numerous royal lands and properties in his various Spanish territories. In Catalonia and Valencia these were administered by bailiffs (*bayles* or *battles*), while in Aragon this function was performed by six regional officials known as *merinos*. All these officials were supervised by 'general bailiffs' (*bayles generales*), except in Majorca, where the job was done by a royal procurator (*procurador real*). These senior bailiffs answered, in turn, to the governors-general and sometimes became intimate advisers to the king, as in the case of Diego de Torres, *bayle general* of Valencia.

As far as royal taxation was concerned, most of the revenue naturally passed to the 'general treasurer' (*tesorero general*), who from 1481 was the *judeoconverso* Gabriel Sánchez. His staff in the royal household included a treasury clerk (*escribano de ración*), the holder of this office between 1478 and 1498 being Luis Santángel, who had an important political as well as economic role and not only in Aragon. In this department there was also a chief accountant (*mestre racional*) for each kingdom of Ferdinand's domain. The fact that the separate Cortes retained control over the taxation of each individual kingdom meant that there was no equivalent in Aragon of universal Castilian taxes such as the *alcabala*. The king could raise neither revenue nor troops without recourse to each individual assembly and, what was worse from the central government's point of view, any money theoretically available was highly fragmented and hedged around with elaborate and fiercely defended charter (*fuero*) restrictions. As the Habsburgs were later to discover, it was seldom worth the trouble of asking for such money. Another problem for the monarchy was that, in the second half of the fifteenth century, the Aragonese royal patrimony had suffered even more severe depredation than its Castilian equivalent. Ferdinand clearly wanted to copy his wife's policy in the Crown of Aragon, but conditions militated against this, especially in Aragon itself and Catalonia. By the time of his accession in 1479, it was evidently quite impossible for an Aragonese king to 'live of his own (resources)' and Ferdinand would have been hard pressed had he not had access to Castilian revenues. Nevertheless, it was on occasion possible for him to obtain revenue from external sources. As in Castile, the Church could be helpful. Earlier popes had conceded to the

Crown of Aragon one-tenth of the rents from ecclesiastical properties within it, as well as handing over to the Royal Treasury the revenues obtained from the preaching of the bull of the 'crusade'. Virtually all of the contribution made by subjects of the Crown of Aragon to the Granada war came by one of these two routes.

Constitutionally, direct taxation had to be granted by the Cortes concerned, *after* the petitions of the estates had been answered by the king. In the fourteenth century, parliamentarians had been willing to make large grants, in the form of financial levies (in Catalonia, *compartiments*) or customs duties and taxes on consumables (in Aragon *generalidades*). The Cortes controlled the collection of these dues, however, and had set up permanent committees (*diputaciones generales*) to organize the process, in Catalonia in 1413, in Valencia in 1419 and in Aragon in 1436. Ferdinand failed to diminish the powers of these bodies, mainly compensating for their strength and obduracy by finding revenue outside the hereditary Crown of Aragon. He did achieve some small reforms, however, mainly at the centre, in so far as such a thing existed in Aragon. He was nevertheless forced to work within the existing 'pactist' system and hence indulge his absolutist tendencies elsewhere. As in Castile, a large proportion of the kingdoms' resources were in the hands of the seignorial aristocracy and its agents, but in Aragonese and Catalan areas the 'royal' towns, which theoretically remained under the Crown's direct jurisdiction, were effectively autonomous as well. Nevertheless, as the councillors of Teruel were to discover in 1484–5 (see Chapter 4), there were constitutional mechanisms whereby a zealous monarch, such as Alfonso V or Ferdinand II, with the help of brute force, might undermine such freedoms. The basic constitution of the towns of the Crown of Aragon had been developed in the reign of James I (1214–76) and generally consisted either of an assembly of citizens, from various social and professional groups, or of representatives of the urban parishes. An example in point is the 'Council of a Hundred' (*consell de cent*) in Barcelona that, from 1455, consisted of 36 'honoured citizens' (*ciutadans honrats*), 32 merchants, 32 artisans and 32 craftsmen (*menestrales*), from a list (*censo*) of qualified individuals that was renewed in 1479. Qualification, in this context, commonly involved descent from fathers and grandfathers who had voted in such elections and thus followed the same criteria as the definition of nobility. The council of the Ciudat de Mallorca (now Palma) had consisted, since 1391, of 12 knights and 24 representatives of each of the estates of citizens, merchants and artisans, while Valencia had a large council of between 60 and 80 members, containing six knights, four 'honoured citizens' (wealthy burgesses), four jurists, two notaries, four representatives from each of the city's 12 parishes and two representatives of each guild (*gremio*). In the Aragonese capital, Zaragoza, by way of contrast, there were no guild representatives on the council and, after reforms in 1414, the *Capitoll y consello* consisted of senior councillors (*jurados*) from the knightly and merchant groups, 24 councillors elected by the parishes and only seven representatives of the rest of the citizen body. Executive power lay in the hands of a tiny group, elected annually by the relevant assemblies – five in Barcelona, six in Valencia and between five and twelve in Zaragoza. In Valencia, a small 'secret council' (*consell secret*) carried out similar functions. Minor officials were appointed annually by the oligarchic councils and, in theory, no official might exercise the same office for two years in succession, although this rule was not always kept.

Nevertheless, although Ferdinand could not legally adopt in Aragon the techniques employed by the Crown in Castile to control municipalities, he did attempt, with some success (and not always violently, as in Teruel) to manipulate the elaborate constitutions of Aragonese and Catalan towns, including Valencia and Majorca, to his own advantage. The prevailing system of election by lots (*sort i sach* in Catalan) appealed to Ferdinand because it could be controlled to a large extent by pre-selecting the list of candidates included, so as to give different factions a fair crack of the whip or ensure that officeholders had a 'safe' pedigree. The king intervened if he could speciously claim that a city council had committed an abuse of power or in some way insulted the royal prerogative. On this basis, he and his agents were able to act in Zaragoza, in 1471 and 1485, in each case having a prominent citizen executed and obtaining the formal 'submission' of the city, which lasted until 1506. Even after that, Ferdinand continued to vet all the names that went into the lots for election to municipal office. In Barcelona, he used the corruption of the old patriciate, the *Biga*, as a pretext to intervene in the municipal government, but his 'reforms' still tended to favour the 'safest' and most prosperous citizens. As a result, the number of *ciutadans honrats* on the *Consell de Cent* rose from 32 to 48, forming an overwhelming power bloc. In 1498, the procedure for drawing lots was finally settled and 16 knights were permitted to enter the council, with one post of *conseller* reserved for them. Thus the military and mercantile elites of Barcelona began to be openly fused, bringing to the city the concept of a council of nobles, which already prevailed in many of the larger towns in Castile, where nobility (*hidalguía*) came to be required for higher urban office. In Valencia, the tradition of royal intervention was better established, in any case, and the system of lots would not be introduced there until the seventeenth century.

Overall, it was the power of the nobility that played the main part in frustrating Ferdinand's attempts at reform in the kingdom of Aragon itself. As in Castile, attempts were made, in 1487, to revive the concept of the *Hermandad*, the initiative coming from the Pyrenean town of Huesca. Its first attempt to arrest a 'robber baron' failed, however, because of aristocratic solidarity and the problem of public order continued. There also continued to be occasional uprisings among the rural labour force, but these never approached the seriousness of the *remença* wars in Catalonia. To the end of his reign, Ferdinand never secured the co-operation of the Aragonese nobility, within or outside the Cortes. He was more successful in obtaining social peace and economic recovery (*redreç*) in Catalonia, where, after the Cortes of Barcelona in 1481, he successfully co-operated with the Catalans themselves, notably in the 'Arbitration Sentence' of Guadalupe, in April 1486.[8] On some occasions, at least, Isabella and her husband were successful in bringing some kind of peace, rather than conflict.

Notes

1 Ladero Quesada, M. A. (1999) *La España de los Reyes Católicos*, Alianza Editorial, p. 161.

2 Ibid. p. 171; Lunenfeld, M. (1987) *Keepers of the City. The corregidores of Isabella I of Castile (1474–1504)*, Cambridge University Press, pp. 158–9; Edwards, J. (1982) *Christian Córdoba. The city and its region in the late Middle Ages*, Cambridge University Press, p. 33.

3 Gerbet, M-C. (1999) *L'élevage dans le royaume de Castille sous les Rois Catholiques (1454–1516)*, Casa de Velázquez.

4 Ladero, M. A. (1999) p. 177.

5 Edwards, J. (1995) 'The morality of taxation: the burden of war on Córdoba and Jerez de la Frontera, 1480–1515', *Meridies. Revista de Historia Medieval*, vol. 2, pp. 109–20.

6 Edwards, J. (1982) pp. 74–7.

7 Ladero, M. A. (1999) pp. 207–18; Edwards, J. (1982) pp. 34–43; Highfield, J. R. L. (1965) 'The Catholic kings and the titled nobility of Castile' in Hale, J., Highfield, R. and Smalley, B. (eds) *Europe in the Late Middle Ages*, Faber & Faber, pp. 358–85.

8 Hillgarth, J. N. (1978) *The Spanish Kingdoms, 1250–1516*, vol. 2, *1410–1516. Castilian hegemony*, Clarendon Press, pp. 517–40; Ladero, M. A. (1999) pp. 61–77, 187–99; Belenguer, E. (1999) *Fernando el Católico. Un monarca decisivo en las encrucijadas de su época*, Ediciones Península, pp. 128–40, 158–75.

Chapter 3

The War against Islam

Isabella and Ferdinand's war for the capture of the Muslim kingdom of
Granada, which was eventually to complete the Christian 'Reconquest' of
the Iberian peninsula in 1492, began in a remarkably obscure way. Probably at the very end of 1481, the frontier castle of Zahara fell to Muslim
forces under the command of Emir Abu'l-Hasan Ali, the news reaching
the king and queen, in Valencia, early in the following year. The *converso*
chronicler Fernando del Pulgar blamed the governor, Gonzalo de Saavedra,
for allowing the Granadans to scale the walls, one dark night, and take
the population away into captivity.[1] Such frontier incidents had not been
infrequent, in earlier years, but this time the response was unusually
rapid and strong. On 1 February 1482 the king and queen reached Medina
del Campo, evidently with war in mind, but the first military reaction
came from the Andalusian nobles, with the marquis of Cádiz, Rodrigo
Ponce de León, in the lead.[2] Even before they received royal instructions
he, together with the royal governor (*asistente*) of Seville, Diego de Merlo,
had set off in secret, with the aim of retaliating with a surprise attack on
Muslim-held Alhama. This is generally held to be the beginning of the
series of campaigns known as the Granada war.[3] The Nasrid emirate of
Granada dated from the mid-thirteenth century, when most of western
Andalusia, including the great cities of Córdoba and Seville, fell into
Christian hands. In 1246 Ferdinand III of Castile made a pact with
Muhammad ibn Nasr, in which a 20-year truce was agreed and the latter
became a vassal of Castile. It seems probable that Ferdinand did not
intend the Muslim state to be a permanent phenomenon and, although
Muhammad and his successors were able to pursue a more or less in-
dependent foreign policy, there was never a stable or permanent peace
between Castile and Granada.[4]

Inevitably, on a frontier that remained fairly stable between 1250 and
1482, despite the Castilian capture in that period of a band of territory
that stretched from Tarifa in the west to Riquena in the east, complex

48

relationships evolved between Christians and Muslims. Apart from being the focus of periodic warfare, as well as treaties and truces, the border, which was largely open and invisible, acted as a conduit for traffic in people and goods, the sea being even more important than land routes in this context. Until the early years of Isabella and Ferdinand's reign, when internal difficulties and the war with Portugal made such demands impractical, truce terms normally included the payment by the emirs to the Castilian Crown of monetary vassalage tributes, known as *parias*. Such vassalage was clearly essential for the survival of the emirate, but the Nasrid rulers must always have been conscious that, by becoming the subordinates of Christian rulers, they were going against every principle of Islamic law (*sharia*). What is more, under the terms of a series of a dozen truces, concluded between 1406 and 1481, the emir was required to attend the Castilian Court when requested and, in order to pay the *parias*, he was forced to tax his subjects at a higher level than was permitted by *sharia*. López de Coca notes that, when such agreements were made, Muslim rulers found it much easier to deliver this money than to surrender captives. Yet the terms for handing over money and prisoners were not included in the formal truce or treaty agreements and were always described, in the relevant private memoranda, not as tribute but as 'gifts'. This was to make such transactions more acceptable to Islamic jurists, who generally disapproved of any transfer of resources, whether human or monetary, from Muslim to non-Muslim rulers.

The king and queen's personal involvement in the war against the Muslim emirate was evident from the start. Alhama, a town of 4000 people that was only 55 km from Granada itself, on the main road to Málaga, fell to Andalusian forces on 28 February 1482 and, as soon as she heard the news, Isabella left Medina del Campo and headed for the frontline. According to a councillor (*conseller*) of Barcelona, Joan Bernat Marimón, writing from court to his colleagues on 13 March, 2000 lancers had already left for the front and an unprecedentedly large feudal levy (*alarde*) of troops was underway. The next day, Ferdinand departed, with more troops, to take command of the campaign and, after a fortnight of hard riding, his advanced guard was at La Rambla, south of Córdoba, entering the city itself on 31 March. Reinforcements were quickly sent to Alhama, the first contingent being led by Andalusian nobles and the second by the king himself, who left troops and provisions in the castle there. Alhama presented a strategic threat to the heart of the emirate and Ferdinand soon came up with the scheme of using it as a base from which to besiege Loja, to begin the expedition, if possible, on 25 June. Its capture would have opened the way to the Vega, the fertile plain around

Granada. Meanwhile, Isabella, anxious not to be left out of the action despite being in an advanced stage of pregnancy, had by 23 June arrived in Córdoba, which was to be the rear base for most of the war. Only six days later, Princess Mary was born. The siege of Loja did not instantly reveal military genius on the part of her father. There were not enough troops, supplies were inadequate and Ferdinand had to beat an ignominious retreat and wait for the next campaiging season, in the spring of 1483. The 'Granada war' seemed to have come to an immediate halt although, by September 1482, a further seven or eight months' supplies had reached Alhama, which had been unsuccessfully besieged by Muslim forces in the previous July. This was not enough for Isabella, whose vocabulary did not contain the word 'failure' and who, as after the defeat by the Portuguese and Castilian rebels at Toro, seven years earlier (see Chapter 1), made her husband feel the lash of her tongue. No doubt to show her determination as well as to recover from the birth of her third daughter, the queen stayed in the royal castle at Córdoba until the end of October 1482, working on military and financial plans for the following year. Pope Sixtus IV aided the cause, at this time, by making a further grant of the tithe and the crusade tax (*cruzada*) for the war against the Muslims of Granada.

What followed Isabella's stay in Córdoba was a lengthy tour of the north of Castile and the Basque country and this journey set a pattern that was to be followed by the couple for the rest of the war, in which campaigning in Granada was balanced by travels aimed at securing and keeping control of other parts of her and her husband's realms. In December 1482, before Isabella returned from the north, Ferdinand was in Córdoba to prepare the next campaign. In the meantime, the *junta* of the Holy Brotherhood (*Santa Hermandad*), held at Pinto, had voted the funds to raise 6000 infantrymen (*peones*) and provide 16,000 pack animals. Once again, however, the king's plans met with disaster, in the Axarquía, an area of mountains and valleys to the north of the port of Málaga. By March 1483 the troops stationed in Andalusia were keen for action and one of their commanders, Alonso de Cárdenas, master of the military order of Santiago, proposed to capture this militarily significant area, which, because of its mulberry trees and silk industry, was also an important economic target. On the Muslim side, the loss of Alhama damaged the prestige of the emir, Abu'l-Hasan, who was portrayed, grief stricken, in a famous Castilian ballad, reciting the refrain, 'Oh, my Alhama!' (*¡Ay de mi Alhama!*).[5] At this time, a rival Granadan clan, the Abencerrajes (Banu Sarraj), exploited his weakness by forcibly releasing his son, known to history as Boabdil, from imprisonment in the Alhambra and proclaiming him emir, as Muhammad XII. Boabdil and his supporters took control of the capital, while his father and his uncle Muhammad al Zagal went to Málaga. Abu'l-Hasan had apparently been willing to give Zahara, all the Christian prisoners held in Granada and 30,000 Castilian *doblas* to Ferdinand and Isabella if they would return Alhama, but the political split put an end to all attempts at conciliation, as the rival factions sought to gain power through military victory over the Christians. Thus, by March 1483, the level of localized violence on the frontier had risen and the main armies on both sides were spoiling for a fight. In the event, the master of Santiago and the marquis of Cádiz led 3000 cavalry and 1000 infantry into the Axarquía of Málaga, but they were ambushed by a much smaller force of Abu'l-Hasan's troops, who killed about 800 and captured another 1500. Contemporary accounts indicate that self-doubt now broke out on the Christian side, as this disaster was added to the failure at Loja in the previous year. A few days later, on the eastern front, there was another disappointment, when the port of Almería, which was on the point of being surrendered to Murcian forces by its governor, Yahya al-Nayyar, declared for Boabdil, drove Yahya into the mountainous Alpujarras and vowed to fight on.

It was now time for the 19-year-old Boabdil to prove himself militarily and, buoyed up by his father and uncle's victory near Málaga, he led 700 cavalry and up to 9000 infantry into Christian territory to the south of Córdoba. Disaster struck, however, when, on 21 April, he was ambushed at Lucena by a much smaller army led by local magnates, the count of Cabra and his relative, the 'governor of the royal pages' (*alcaide de los donceles*). Most of the Granadan cavalry, including one of the finest, Ali Atar, were killed and, worse still, Boabdil was captured. Once again, local Andalusian initiative had achieved success without royal intervention, but Ferdinand was quick to grasp the opportunity provided by Boabdil's unexpected capture. He signed a treaty with the young 'emir' and released him, hoping thereby to isolate the 'war party' of Abu'l-Hasan and Al Zagal and confine the Christian war effort to defeating them and holding on to Alhama. Before taking this course, however, Ferdinand returned to the region as commander. In June, he launched a violent, 'scorched-earth' raid (*tala*) in the Vega of Granada and he also captured the tower of Tájara, which was halfway between Loja and Alhama, as well as re-supplying the latter. Finally, in July, he signed the desired treaty with Boabdil, who thereby became a vassal of Isabella and Ferdinand, offered a two-year truce and agreed to pay *parias* of 12,000 gold *doblas* a year, to serve the Castilian Crown with 700 'lances' (*lanzas*) of cavalry, to assist in the war against his own father and to free 400 Christian captives immediately and 60 more in each subsequent year. Boabdil handed over as hostages his own son, his eldest brother and the sons of ten Granadan nobles. In making this agreement, Ferdinand was following a traditional method of Castilian–Granadan diplomacy but, in this case, although most of the rural population and part of the aristocracy favoured peace, the Granadan religious leadership (*alfaquíes*) quickly issued a pronouncement (*fatwa*) that Abu'l-Hasan, the leader with Al Zagal of the war party, was the legitimate ruler and Boabdil fled to Guadix.

During the summer and autumn of 1483, skirmishes and raids continued, in which the marquis of Cádiz, rather than the king, took the lead, the main incidents being a victory over the Granadan cavalry between Utrera and Lopera and the highly satisfying recapture of Zahara. At the time, the monarchs were at Vitoria, in the Basque country, and Ferdinand, who was still thinking traditionally, appears to have felt that it was time to rest on his laurels. He seems to have regarded the capture of Alhama, the treaty with Boabdil and the latter's becoming a Castilian vassal as equivalent to his grandfather Ferdinand I of Aragon's achievement of capturing Antequera, in 1410, and as a sufficient expression of his personal interest in the Granadan enterprise. He was also increasingly preoccupied with the recuperation of the Catalan counties of Rosselló and Cerdanya. Louis XI, who had promised to return these historic possessions of the Crown of Aragon, had recently died and Ferdinand called the Aragonese Cortes to Tarazona, among other things in order to authorize the transfer. At this point, however, the latent tension between the Castilian queen and her Aragonese husband exploded to the surface. As 'proprietary queen' of Castile, Isabella insisted, in her customary forceful manner, that all the couple's resources should be devoted to wrapping up the Granadan war as soon as possible. Not for the first or last time, Ferdinand duly gave way, although the Tarazona Cortes were still to meet in February–March 1484 and travelled back to Córdoba to re-enter the fray. Before he did so, but this time on royal orders, the marquis of Cádiz and the master of Santiago mounted a major *tala* into the Axarquía of Málaga. This took place in late April and early May 1484 and appears to have been aimed at avenging the defeat of the previous year. Naval support was involved, apparently for the first time in the war, and this raises important points about strategy and tactics in the effort to end the Nasrid state's independence.

When the Granada war began, as in so many conflicts before and afterwards, there seems to have been no thought either that it would take nearly ten years to bring the Muslim emirate to its knees or that traditional fighting methods would prove inadequate. Raiding parties, consisting largely of horsemen, carried out most expeditions and when more forces were required, reliance was placed on feudal levies, from royal and seigniorial towns. Despite the coastal nature of much of the enemy's territory, there is little sign in the first two years of conflict that the king, or the local Andalusian commanders, understood the value of combining land and naval forces. There was, however, one exception to this rule. When the war began, the prominent *converso* soldier and writer, Diego de Valera, was living in retirement in the small royal town of Puerto de Santa María, on the Atlantic coast of Andalusia, having relinquished the governorship (*alcaidía*) there to his son, who went by the French name of Charles. During his career in the royal service, Diego had participated in the debate about the nature of monarchy and nobility that absorbed so much intellectual and political energy in Castile during the reigns of John II and Henry IV. On 10 February, the old soldier and courtier wrote a letter to Ferdinand. He had heard about the fall of Zahara to the Muslims and although El Puerto was not immediately adjacent to the frontier, he had clearly given much thought to methods for ending the independence of the Nasrid state, thus bringing about the restoration of Christian monarchy to all 'the Spains'. This had been his cause for many years and he assumed that his king (the letter was not addressed to Isabella) shared his enthusiasm for the completion of the Reconquest. This was probably not the case at this stage, but Valera outlined an extraordinarily comprehensive plan, which foretold much of what was indeed to happen during the next ten years, involving an economic blockade and combined military operations by land and sea, with the capture of Málaga as the main focus: 'With Málaga taken, Granada is yours.' At this stage, Ferdinand seems not to have been focused on such ambitious plans and Valera wrote to him again, on 10 April, amplifying the contents of his earlier letter with references to historical precedent. He argued that traditional *talas* would not defeat the Nasrids and pointed out that previous advances in the Reconquest, especially in the reigns of Ferdinand III, Alfonso IX and Alfonso XI, were achieved by combined operations of land and naval forces. It was crucial to focus not on raids but on *conquest*.

The first positive response that he received from the king and queen concerned naval warfare. Apparently at their request, the old soldier and naval man provided an additional memorandum, in which he outlined methods for organizing the fleet that should patrol the straits of Gibraltar and the coast of the emirate. Diego specified the number and types of ships to be used, the level of manning, the command structure and rates of remuneration for personnel.[6] During 1484, Diego de Valera may well have felt that his advice was being ignored. Yet, while large raiding forces were unbeatable in the field, his insistence on conquest as the only goal could not and would not ultimately be evaded. By the summer of that year, it must have been obvious to many that the traditional operational pattern, of periodic *talas* and attacks on frontier castles, would not force the Nasrids to surrender. The raids were extremely destructive, but the Granadans were able to use truce periods to rebuild their resources and had rarely lost an important castle, let alone a major town. By avoiding pitched battles, they were able to keep their forces largely intact. Historians have noted an increased awareness in royal circles, after more than two years of fairly unsuccessful campaigning, that the war against Islam was not a diversion for bored aristocrats but a matter of vital concern, especially as the Turkish threat was becoming ever more visible in the central and western Mediterranean. The idea of native Spanish Muslims as potential 'fifth columnists' had been born.

Nevertheless, there was no immediate change in tactics. Thus, in June and early July 1484, Ferdinand led a new campaign, during which Alhama was again re-supplied and Álora captured, while there was another *tala* in the Vega of Granada. In Álora, the Christians followed their customary practice of raising the banner of the Cross (the war was, after all, a Crusade), proclaiming Castilian rule and consecrating the main mosque as a church. After this, Ferdinand and his entourage returned to Córdoba, spending the hottest part of the summer there and allowing his Andalusian troops to attend to the harvest. During this time, an embassy arrived from Boabdil, reaffirming his vassalage and, at last, serious attention was paid to Valera's advice on naval matters. As he had predicted, troops and supplies were being smuggled into Granada on a large scale, by sea from North Africa, so an expansion of the Castilian fleet was ordered. Another indication of a new commitment to the war against Islam was the king and queen's decision, apparently taken at this time, to remain in Andalusia during the winter of 1484–5. Before that, there was to be further significant military action, before the 1484 campaigning season came to an end. In September, Setenil, a small fortified town with 200 inhabitants and just 10 km from the strategically significant mountain town of Ronda, was besieged and captured. Here, as earlier in Álora, considerable use was made of artillery, in order to breach otherwise easily defended walls. The combination of heavy bombardment and the offer of fairly generous surrender terms, which was employed in these towns, would prove equally effective in the future. The fall of Álora and Setenil placed heavy pressure on the Muslim defenders of Ronda, which was now largely isolated from the rest of the emirate to the east. Towards the end of September

1484 Ferdinand's forces made incursions into the outlying territory of Ronda, before sending his artillery train to Écija for the winter, which the Court was to spend in the royal palace at Seville, planning final victory over the Nasrids.

It was in 1485 that drastic changes began to appear in the prosecution of the war. The priority was no longer a combination of *talas* near Málaga and Granada, frontier skirmishes and the provisioning of Alhama, but rather a direct assault on the emirate's major military and economic centres, with the aim, as advocated earlier by Diego de Valera, of complete conquest. As more and more resources, in manpower and supplies, were assembled from all over Spain, diplomacy was relegated to secondary importance, political developments on the Muslim side effectively forcing this change. At the beginning of 1485, the war party, under Al Zagal, succeeded in expelling Boabdil not only from his base in Almería but from the emirate as a whole, forcing him to flee over the border to Castile. By this time, Al Zagal was the effective ruler of Granada, on behalf of his brother, but in June 1485, first Boabdil's uncle was proclaimed vizier by the militants and shortly afterwards Abu'l-Hasan died. Between then and 1487 the Castilians evidently had a three-pronged strategy: first to seize Ronda and its surrounding mountains (*serranía*), which were the main centre of frontier warfare at the time, second, to capture Málaga and its hinterland, which were the economic heart of the Nasrid state, and finally to gain control of the Vega of Granada, the fall of which would leave the capital isolated and without supplies.

These three objectives were not necessarily pursued in sequence. By mid-April 1485 troops had assembled in Córdoba and at Antequera for the season's campaign and by the end of the month Benamaquiz, Coín and Cártama had been captured, along with other places close to Málaga. Al Zagal had had warning and time to strengthen the port's defences, however, and Ferdinand decided to withdraw to Antequera once again, being influenced in this decision by secret surrender offers which had been received from Ronda by the marquis of Cádiz. The withdrawal was achieved with enough concealment to lead Al Zagal to keep the main body of his troops in Málaga and even plan a counterattack against Loja. In fact, Ferdinand headed at full speed towards Ronda, and started to besiege it on 8 May 1485. The extramural suburb (*arrabal*) was first bombarded on 17 May, surrendering the next day. On the 20th the town's water supply was cut off and it surrendered just two days later, without further resistance and on relatively favourable terms. All the smaller places in the Serranía gave up at the same time, accepting Isabella and Ferdinand's authority, and the port of Marbella followed suit on 15 June.

For the first time, a major portion of the emir's territory, complete with its Muslim population, had fallen into Christian hands and this situation was duly contemplated when the monarchs were reunited in Córdoba. As in 1484, an autumn campaign was planned, the target being Moclín, with its castle that controlled the road passage from Alcalá la Real to Granada. This time, however, forces under the regional command of the count of Cabra were thwarted by Al Zagal, with the deaths of about 1000 Castilian troops. After this, Ferdinand settled for the less ambitious objective of capturing two castles nearer to Jaén, Cambil and Alhabar, which fell after a massive artillery bombardment, much to the delight of the nearby Christian inhabitants, who had long suffered from the activities of their Muslim garrisons. Meanwhile, on the diplomatic front, things had improved from the Castilian point of view. In September 1485, Boabdil returned to the eastern part of the emirate with Castilian support, under the terms of the 1483 treaty and began to widen his influence, helped by the fact that many Granadans still did not recognize his uncle, Al Zagal, as emir. In March 1486 even the Albaicín, in Granada itself, rebelled in his support and street fighting in the capital continued for two months at which point the two factions decided that the Castilians and their allies were the real enemy and called a truce. Under the resulting agreement, Boabdil recognized Al Zagal as emir and in return was granted devolved authority over his former inland stronghold in the east, including Guadix, Baza, Vélez Blanco, Vélez Rubio and Vera. He was also allocated the task of defending Loja and this may have been the ultimate provocation in the eyes of Ferdinand and Isabella. They regarded the Granada agreement as treachery, which invalidated their own treaty of 1483 with Boabdil.

It had already been planned that 1486 would see Castilian attacks on Loja and in the Vega of Granada. Forces were once again assembled in Córdoba, in April of that year, while the artillery was prepared in Écija. The campaign began in mid-May, by which time Ferdinand had learned, to his disgust, that Boabdil was in Loja to defend it against him. His troops first cut the road from Loja to Granada to prevent reinforcement and then surrounded the town with trenches and siege fortifications. On 22 May the suburbs were attacked and the main town was bombarded by artillery, this being repeated on the 26th and the 28th. The following day Loja surrendered and Boabdil was captured, although the inhabitants were allowed to go free. In this way, the road to Granada was opened and during June 1486, as no reinforcements emerged from the capital, its defending castles, Íllora, Moclín, Colomera and Montefrio duly fell to artillery bombardment and, in the case of Moclín, an explosion of gunpowder in the castle itself. Contemporaries noted that before the advent of the big guns, lengthy sieges and the starvation of the defenders would have been necessary before such sites could be secured. Ferdinand and Isabella's sense of righteous zeal seemed to be growing day by day. Almost all the inhabitants of these small towns fled to Granada, adding to the burden of the increasingly beleaguered population there and Ferdinand and Isabella placed strong garrisons in their most recent conquests, to defend them against a possible counterattack. On this occasion, Isabella came to the front with her ladies, to raise the morale of the troops and gain a personal impression of the efforts that they were making. The queen's party, including the infant Princess Catherine, who had been born in the previous December, was escorted from Córdoba to the front by troops from the marquis of Cádiz's contingent and inspected his main force at Archidona. They then continued to Loja, visiting its main church and castle and the next day went on to Íllora, where a spectacular and noisy concert was put on. Boabdil remained to be dealt with.

In the event, having captured Loja, Ferdinand and Isabella decided to forgive their former ally for his agreement with Al Zagal and made a new treaty with him, on terms even more favourable to themselves. Boabdil once again swore to be their vassal and was promised that, if he succeeded in recovering Guadix, Baza, the two Vélez, Vera and Mojácar within eight months, he would be given the Castilian title of duke or count over them. In the event, Boabdil achieved even greater success, although not entirely as planned, thanks to the internal conflicts that afflicted the last years of the Nasrid emirate. He failed to secure Baza, Guadix or Almería, which remained loyal to Al Zagal, but in September 1486 he managed to return to the Albaicín, overlooking Granada itself, and managed to hold it against his uncle's supporters until the following year, with the help of the Castilian governors of the castles in the Vega, who supplied him with crack troops and military provisions. As a result, in the early months of 1487, the war entered the streets of the capital. In February, Isabella and Ferdinand once again recognized Boabdil as emir, renewing the treaty for a further three years and authorizing him to receive supplies via Loja or the Christian possessions in the Vega. During the next 12 months, faction fighting in Granada was extremely violent, with Boabdil occupying the Albaicín and Al Zagal the city itself. It was clearly vital, from the Castilian point of view, that Boabdil should gain complete control of the capital but, in parallel to this, the king and queen decided to attack Málaga. The omens were good, since Boabdil's supporters, led by his representative, Yusuf ibn Kumasa, had gained control of the government of the port and declared their support for Castile's ally. This did not, however, save them from attack, in what proved to be one of the most bloody and cruel episodes in the entire war, the siege of Málaga.

Ferdinand began by focusing on Vélez Málaga and set up camp to the north-east of Málaga itself, cutting communication with Granada and awaiting the laborious arrival of his artillery, over rough and mountainous terrain, from Écija. At this time, he was receiving supplies by sea, organized by his Muslim supporters within the port. Already, however, developments among the Nasrids were making a peaceful outcome increasingly unlikely. First, the fortress of Gibralfaro, next to Málaga, was garrisoned by North African Berber troops (*gomeres*), commanded by Hamet al-Zegri or Hemete Zeli (Ahmad al-Thagrif), who was loyal to Al Zagal. Then the emir made an agreement with his nephew, Boabdil, under which the latter, although supposedly a vassal of Castile, would refrain from any action while Al Zagal attacked the Christian forces that were besieging Vélez Málaga. His loyalist troops reached their destination on 22 May 1487, just as Ferdinand's artillery train was finally arriving, but after four days Zagal had to admit defeat by superior forces and on the 27th the governor of Vélez surrendered, giving up all his Christian prisoners. The Muslim population was allowed to leave freely and did so on 3 May. At this time, it looked as though the war would be over quickly, since Al Zagal did not attempt to return to Granada, going to Almería instead, thus allowing Boabdil, at the end of April, to take control of the city of Granada and the Alhambra. 'Muhammad XII' immediately proposed negotiations with Isabella and Ferdinand, aimed at a new treaty, which was duly concluded in May 1487. The agreement enshrined the legal 'conquest' of the emirate. Under it, Boabdil surrendered his title of emir, in return for a Castilian lordship (*señorío*), which would include areas that had been loyal to him during the war, including Guadix, Baza and Vera. Various properties would be granted to Boabdil's main collaborators and the people of the Albaicín, who had sustained him while his uncle controlled the rest of the city, were to be exempt from taxes for ten years. The rest of the Granadans, however, would have to leave their homes. In the event, the third treaty between Castile and Boabdil was not to end the war, which would continue for a further four years and more.

When news of the treaty emerged, the situation in the emirate quickly deteriorated, from the Castilian point of view. In his base at Almería, Al Zagal prepared to defend the eastern part of the Nasrid territory, where his nephew hoped to have his new lordship. In Málaga, the news that Boabdil would not after all be emir of the city and protect its trade undermined his supporters among the mercantile community there. A Christian attack now seemed inevitable and defeat was likely to lead to exile, as in other conquered towns, including nearby Vélez. Hamet al-Zegri took advantage of the situation to seize the Alcazaba, the main fortress of Málaga, as well as the walls and other fortifications, with the apparent intention of fighting to the death. As well as his Berber *gomeres*, it seems that Hamet's army included Jewish *conversos* who had escaped from the initial activity of the Inquisition in Andalusia and Christians, known as *elches*, who had arrived in Muslim territory in order to convert to Islam. Bandits from the Serranía de Ronda also fled to Málaga and supported those in the city who wished to fight. The dilemma for both sides was acute and one that occurs so often in human conflict. For Ferdinand and Isabella themselves and the rest of the 'Old' Christian population of their realms as well as those *judeoconverso* courtiers and writers who sought their salvation in a strong Castilian monarchy, the issue was simple. Málaga was a rebel city, which owed allegiance to Castile, both because of its rulers' claims as supposed successors to the Catholic Visigothic monarchs who preceded the Muslim invasion of 711 and because even its current ruler, Boabdil, was a Castilian vassal. According to the recognized laws of war in late medieval Europe, these legal factors entitled Ferdinand and Isabella, if there were any further resistance from the city, to besiege it and, in the event of victory, to deal with the inhabitants in any way they wished. For Muslims, contrariwise, no Islamic territory should ever be voluntarily conceded and in this case the potential defenders included people from the Castilian side of the border, both Jewish and Christian in origin, who had reason not to wish their former king and queen well. As so often in such cases, the result was violence and tragedy, followed by a pyrrhic victory.

Once some commanders and troops inside the city had decided to fight to the death, the siege of Málaga was bound to end, not in peace pacts such as had hitherto prevailed in the Granada war, but in the most severe sanctions. The action lasted from May to August 1487 and reached new levels of violence in this particular war and possibly greater cruelty than had occurred in any previous conflict between Christians and Muslims in Spain. Ferdinand and Isabella, with their Andalusian commanders, had finally grasped the nettle that had been offered to them five years earlier by Diego de Valera. As a result, both they and their opponents were to enter new territory, in the terms of warfare. Málaga was the first large city to be besieged during the war and the first to be defended by artillery, as well as some highly motivated troops. Also, for the first time, it was clear to those in command that, as Valera had predicted, short-term campaigns, followed by tactical withdrawal, would no longer be sufficient and the Andalusian economy in particular began to feel the strain of unprecedented royal demands for men and war materials. By July 1487 the Castilian state and economy were virtually at breaking point and, if Ferdinand and his commanders had not finally taken Diego de Valera's advice and set up a proper naval blockade, so that the people of Málaga could no longer be provisioned from sea, it is likely that the 'manifest destiny' of the Christian Reconquest would have had to be postponed for many years. In any case, once Ferdinand and Isabella's initial peace over-tures had been rejected, a strategic debate took place in their camp, between those who advocated a long-drawn-out blockade, leading to starva-tion and surrender and those who favoured a close siege and violent assault. The king did not trust wholly in a naval blockade and ordered immediate military action. This was bound to be difficult and bloody, thanks to Málaga's geographical situation, on a narrow strip between the mountains and the sea, and the fact that its fortifications, including the multilevel complex of the Alcazaba and the lofty castle of Gibralfaro, potentially blocked all east–west communication on land. In addition, the defenders had adopted a ruthless strategy in preparation for the initial Christian assault on Gibralfaro, demolishing properties near the walls so that any attackers who scaled them would find themselves in a lethal open space below the Muslim-held castle. Christian writers stress the particular violence of this combat, the official chronicler Pulgar claim-ing that: '[The Muslims] seemed to have a greater desire to kill Christians than to preserve their own lives.'[7] Ferdinand's troops managed to take the hill of Gibralfaro, with heavy casualties, the defenders withdrawing into the castle itself, and then followed one of most remarkable technical achievements of the entire war. The Castilian engineers built up earth-works opposite the castle, placing on them a huge wooden fort which reached the same level as the castle battlements themselves. In addition, the whole walled and fortified area of Málaga was surrounded by smaller forts on the same pattern, modelled on the contemporary Italian *stanza* (*estança*). A static artillery battle then ensued, during which the king's tent had to be moved to safety, but the Christian naval guns were brought ashore and artillery reinforcements were even acquired from Flanders, in addition to a stock of old cannonballs from Algeciras.

At this point, one of the periodic differences of opinion seems to have occurred between the king and queen, concerning the wisdom of con-tinuing what looked likely to be a bloody action, especially as plague had broken out in places near Málaga, clearly threatening the besiegers. Isabella, in the rear base at Córdoba, became worried about future losses and began to urge abandonment of the siege, but Ferdinand reacted by asking her instead to come to the front, as she had done at Loja and Íllora in the previous year. The queen and her ladies duly headed south from Córdoba in June 1487, but while their appearance may have encouraged their own side, morale remained high inside the walls and Ferdinand was in danger of running out of gunpowder. The artillery was not proving effective, as besiegers were not allowed by the defenders to take advantage of breaches in the walls and a new debate on tactics took place. As a result, it was decided that mining under the walls should be tried, but this too proved unsuccessful. News then arrived from Boabdil, which provided some relief. The Málaga siege was now evidently being regarded by Muslims, both within and outside Spain, as a *jihad* for the Faith, and the first sign of this had been the despatch from Granada, by Al-Zagal, of a column of suicide troops who, in Pulgar's words: 'Believing that if they did manage to enter Málaga, it would be a mighty deed, and if they did not they would [nevertheless] save their souls, thus resolved to die or enter the city.'[8] Boabdil was able to report to Ferdinand and Isabella that the force had been ambushed and cut to pieces by fellow Muslims. Tension was evidently increasing on both sides and resulting in extreme human reactions.

One sign of the increasingly desperate atmosphere was the decision of a Muslim called Ibrahim al-Jarbi (Abraen to Pulgar), from Djerba in Tunisia but then living near Guadix, to raise a force, not only for the relief of Málaga but also to kill the king and queen. In Pulgar's words:

This Moor gave out that he was holy, and that God had revealed to him through an angel what was going to happen. In this way he knew the Moors were to be saved and Málaga would be victorious against the Christians who were besieging it.[9]

Ibrahim's force of 400 Granadans and Berbers crossed country mainly by night, eventually reaching the eastern edge of Málaga, where they attacked one of the temporary forts (*estanças*) at dawn. Half were killed and half got into the fort, but Ibrahim himself had a different plan, which was to be taken prisoner and try, by means of his evident charisma, to reach his royal targets. After the fort action, he hid in a gully, his hands in a prayerful attitude, and he was duly arrested by Castilian troops who were engaged in mopping-up operations after the battle. As he had prayed earlier, he was not killed, but taken to the marquis of Cádiz, who seems to have regarded him as a religious negotiator, who might bring nearer the end of the campaign. While under interrogation, he claimed that he had received a secret revelation, but could only divulge it to the monarchs in person. Amazingly, he was brought to the royal tent, not only wearing the burnous in which he had travelled, but also with his dagger still in his belt. Crowds gathered to see the 'holy man', who seems not to have been associated by them with his 400 martyr fighters, but, when he entered the tent, Ferdinand was sleeping off a large lunch and the queen decreed that he should not be woken. Thus Ibrahim was taken to wait in the tent of two of Isabella's ladies-in-waiting, the marchioness of Moya and Felipa, wife of Alvaro de Portugal, son of the duke of Bragança. It seems that Ibrahim spoke no Castilian and, seeing Alvaro and Felipa in their fine clothes, he appears to have thought that they were the king and queen. He nearly killed the unfortunate Alvaro with a dagger wound in the head and tried to stab Felipa, but in his excitement he missed and was quickly overpowered by Ruy López de Toledo, a treasury official, and killed by indignant Christians, before he could reach the sovereigns. At this point, events took another unpleasant turn, which further raised the heat of the Christian–Muslim conflict. With or without royal authority (the Christian sources are silent), the decision was taken to propel the pieces of Ibrahim's dismembered corpse into the city. Once within the walls, the parts were sewn together with silk thread and the reintegrated body was washed, perfumed and given a pious and emotional Muslim funeral and burial. It was hard, in these circumstances, to see what paths diplomacy might follow in the future and harder still when, in indignant retaliation, the Malagans selected a Christian captive, presumably of some rank, killed him, mounted him on an ass, as Jesus had entered Jerusalem before his Passion, but facing backwards, and steered the animal towards the Castilian lines.

In this climate of overwhelming mutual bitterness, starvation began to threaten the besieged population and a split developed between the North African garrison, which was away from its own lands, isolated and determined to fight to the death, and a 'peace party' of native Andalusians, led by 'Ali Dordush and Amar Benamar. Eventually, these two leaders left the city to negotiate, asking to become Muslim (*mudéjar*) subjects of Ferdinand and Isabella, but were told that the time for pacts was passed and the choice before them was captivity or death. This rebuff caused a last burst of defiance, with the Malagans threatening to hang all their Christian prisoners from the battlements and burn their city to the ground, rather than hand it over to such merciless enemies. The monarchs threatened in turn to kill all the inhabitants if a single prisoner were harmed, but eventually they relented sufficiently to allow the 'peacemakers', including 'Ali Dordush, to leave unmolested. Thus, on 18 August 1487, the Castilian standard flew from Gibralfaro castle and the Alcazaba of Málaga, and a new government was set up, which served as a prototype for the subsequent conquest of Almería and Granada. Six hundred haggard Christian captives were released, but the Muslim population, both male and female, was evicted from its dwellings and concentrated in 'enclosures' (*corrales*), to await distribution as spoils of the victors. Crown officials kept back some of them to be exchanged for Christian prisoners held in the Muslim states of North Africa, 3000 were given as rewards to nobles and knights who had fought in the siege and the Crown kept for itself up to 8000, together with their property. In theory, under the surrender 'agreement' of 4 September 1487 the Malagan Muslims were allowed to ransom themselves, but they were evidently in no position to do so, their value as captives, together with their goods, being estimated in total at the astronomical sum of 150 million *maravedíes*. One hundred Berber troops were sent as a gift to Pope Innocent VIII, 50 Muslim maidens to the queen of Naples and 30 maidens to the queen of Portugal. Parallel negotiations took place for the Jews who had found themselves trapped in Málaga during the siege. They left the emirate and so did the port's Muslim population, many of whom were despatched to Seville, Córdoba, Jerez de la Frontera and Écija, thus, paradoxically, increasing the Muslim population of those towns. Those Muslims who were not able to leave Málaga immediately were entrusted to the care of the city's new *corregidor*, García Fernández Manrique.

The length and bitterness of the siege of Málaga had had the side-effect of affording some respite to Al Zagal, in Almería, and the fact that the war lasted for four more years was due to Granadan political skill as well as the technical and economic limitations of the Castilian war machine. Although the lack of any prospect of external Muslim reinforcement, despite a Granadan embassy's visit to Ottoman Istanbul in 1487, meant that a Christian victory was more or less inevitable, 1488 proved to be a somewhat fallow year in terms of military action, one reason for this being Ferdinand's growing embroilment in foreign affairs, particularly in Italy (see Chapter 5). The bind was that adventures abroad could not be effectively undertaken unless the conquest of Granada was first completed. Orders for the new season's campaign were issued from Valencia and envisaged limited activity in the eastern part of the emirate. The troops and artillery, mostly from Andalusia, were to be concentrated at Lorca, under the command of Ferdinand, the marquis of Cádiz, and the *adelantado* of Murcia. In June 1488, their relatively limited forces succeeded in subduing a remarkably large proportion of the eastern emirate, including Vera and Huéscar. It has been thought that the relative gentleness with which this part of the Nasrid territory was treated was due to the longstanding relationship between the Spanish monarchs and Boabadil. It now appears, however, that an important influence was Yahya al-Nayyar, a relative of Al Zagal, who had tried to surrender Almería to Castile as early as 1483. In December 1485, Yahya had made a second pact under which he would surrender all the territory under his command, including Almería and Vera, in return for the Valencian duchy of Gandía, which was potentially in Ferdinand's gift, and the grant of the eastern part of the emirate to his son, who would marry the daughter of the Christian commander on the Murcian–Granadan frontier, Juan de Benavides. In 1488, this scheme seemed likely to be implemented, but the diehard resistance of Al Zagal in Almería put an end to it and 1489 was planned to be the year of his destruction.

During the winter of 1488–9, Al Zagal sent out raiding parties into Christian territory and it was decided that Baza, rather than Almería, should be the first target. Not surprisingly, in view of recent experience at Málaga, it was felt that an inland town would be easier to besiege than a seaport. The attackers could be supplied by land from Quesada, in the upper Guadalquivir valley, and by sea via the beaches south of Murcia. Al Zagal stayed in Almería and, although it may seem strange that he sent Yahya to take command in Baza, the young man was surrounded by faithful Zagal henchmen, in order to prevent treachery. A now conventional siege operation began in the middle of June. First, a *tala* was carried out around the small, fortified town, to destroy its fields and gardens, while a new road was built to allow the artillery to reach the best positions. This process proved difficult and preparations lasted until October 1489, these including the road from Quesada and Jaén and the construction of trenches and siege fortifications, as previously at Málaga. When autumn came, the decision was taken not to withdraw, in accordance with tradition, but to bed down for the winter. Thus tents were replaced by permanent camps, crops were sown, further reinforcements were sent in and the artillery finally arrived. Also, the queen made her third appearance at the front, arriving at the camp (*real*) on 7 November. There was general astonishment, among Muslims as well as Christians, that Isabella should do such a thing in the winter months and Yahya rightly concluded that the guns would soon open up. By 4 December he had negotiated the surrender of Baza, after a siege of nearly six months. No doubt in view of Yahya's past links with Castile, as well as the need to encourage quick (and cheap) surrender by other Granadans, the terms of the pact were generous. The desired effect was achieved, with the rapid surrender of other, smaller places in the neighbourhood, but before the end of December the big prize was won, with the surrender by Al Zagal of all his territory, including Almería and Guadix, in return for the lordship (*taa*) of Andarax, in the Alpujarras.

These events obviously had a considerable effect on Boabdil who, during 1488 and 1489, had remained in Granada, receiving economic aid from the Castilians, and even being allowed to placate a generally hostile population by cultivating part of the Vega. As soon as he heard of his uncle's surrender, Boabdil sent his constable, Abu'l-Qasim al-Mulih, to meet Ferdinand and Isabella, by then back in Córdoba. The Muslim was accompanied by the two Christian captains who had responsibility for the Vega of Granada, Gonzalo Fernández de Córdoba (the future 'Great Captain'; see Chapter 5) and Martín de Alarcón, and the aim was to open surrender negotiations for Granada. However, when the king and queen announced their intention to despatch an army, early in 1490, to receive the surrender of the city, together with the remaining Nasrid territory, further difficulties emerged. For one thing, having expended so much treasure (if not blood) on the capture of Baza, Isabella and Ferdinand were not keen to hand it, or Guadix, over to Boabdil, as the 1487 treaty stipulated. The main problem, however, was that the people of Granada itself had no intention of allowing their emir to surrender the city without a fight. Thus 1490 saw a renewal of the war, but at first on a limited scale, which suited both sides at this stage. Boabdil had support for his peace efforts from many ordinary people in Granada – merchants, artisans, peasants – but was under heavy pressure from nobles and religious leaders to fight on.

Ferdinand and Isabella needed to re-gather their forces and their economic resources before launching a new military effort. In 1490 and thereafter the sense of honour, on both sides, was to lead to much human misery and upheaval, which affected all levels of Granadan society, from Al Zagal, who fled to Tlemcen, in North Africa, rather than see the consequences of his policy of resistance to the Castilians, to the general Muslim populations of towns such as Guadix, Baza and Almería, who faced forced local migration or expulsion, as a result of Christian attack and the negotiations of their own leaders. The rest of 1490 and the early months of 1491 saw the last episodes of old fashioned 'frontier warfare', with its localized violence and destruction, which had been a feature of Spanish life for so many centuries. In April 1491, however, a massive new Castilian army was assembled between Loja and Alcalá la Real. Boabadil tried vainly to negotiate, but, by the 26th of that month, Ferdinand and Isabella's forces were encamped in El Gozco, only a few miles from Granada itself. They would not leave until the city surrendered, on 2 January 1492. From that base, and in order to confirm their complete control over the surrounding territory, the Castilian forces began to construct what was, in effect, a new fortified town in the Vega, which was to be named Santa Fe ('Holy Faith'), after the Christian faith for which they claimed to be fighting. The site was carefully chosen, to provide good communications with Loja, and the new highroad back to the supply bases in the Guadalquivir valley. More locally, it was surrounded by irrigated and cultivated land, which would both sustain the Castilian army and obstruct any Muslim counterattack. It could also remain as a base, as Córdoba had done earlier in the war, if other commitments called Ferdinand away. In addition, Santa Fe obstructed the links between Granada and Boabdil's remaining supporters in the Alpujarras. Various military episodes took place in these months, including chivalric combats between small groups of Muslims and Christians and individuals from either side, but there was no repetition of the massive artillery bombardments and desperate engineering and raiding tactics that were characteristic of earlier episodes in the war.

Negotiations were now the main priority and it was clearly desirable, from Isabella and Ferdinand's point of view, that Granada should be taken intact and thus become a jewel in their crown. Some Castilian troops were even discharged in June and July 1491 and this relaxation seemed to have been justified when, in September, Boabdil duly began to negotiate, some said on the advice of his mother, Aisha. Finally, on 25 November at Santa Fe, terms were agreed for a surrender, which was planned for May 1492. The terms granted to Boabdil's Granadans, and to his supporters in the Alpujarras, were quite generous, but no such mercy was shown to the Jewish *conversos* and the voluntary Christian converts to Islam (*elches*), who had taken refuge under his sovereignty (see Chapters 4 and 7). Even at this stage, however, some of the relevant documents envisaged a surrender in January 1492 and, from the beginning of December 1491, negotiations were underway to bring the date forward. At the same time, many Castilian troops who had served in earlier phases of the war were summoned back to Santa Fe, in order to witness the impending triumph. They would not have long to wait.

On 1 January 1492 500 Granadans emerged from the city to act as hostages for Boabdil's compliance with the peace terms. There were violent protests from the Muslim population, which brought about the final dénouement. On the pretext of the riots, and probably in genuine fear of his life, Boabdil asked for Castilian troops to occupy the Alhambra, which they did that same night. At dawn on 2 January, in that same palace, the last emir of Granada surrendered the keys of the fortress to one of Isabella's most longstanding retainers, Gutierre de Cárdenas, chief commander (*comendador mayor*) of the order of Santiago. After this, the new governor of the Alhambra, Don Iñigo López de Mendoza, count of Tendilla, entered the fortress with more troops, while the bulk of the Christian army moved in formation towards the city walls. In their sight, Fray Hernando de Talavera, the queen's confessor and bishop of Ávila, raised the banner of the Cross and the Castilian banner, on a tower, while the emir Muhammad (Boabdil) and his entourage went out to welcome the king and queen, handing over the keys of the city. The official entry to Granada of the monarchs and their court took place on 6 January, the Christian feast of the Epiphany, the 'showing of Christ to the Gentiles'. They spent the next few months consolidating their hold over the former emirate, while Boabdil retired to his new 'lordship' in the Alpujarras.[10]

Notes

1 Pulgar, H. de (1943) *Crónica de los Reyes Católicos*, J de M Carriazo (ed.), Espasa Calpe, p. 3.

2 Azcona, T. de (1993) *Isabel la Católica. Estudio crítico de su vida y su reinado*, Biblioteca de Autores Cristianos, pp. 635–7.

3 Ladero Quesada, M. A. (2002) *Las guerras de Granada en el siglo XV*, Ariel, pp. 134–5.

4 Ibid. pp. 12–14; Harvey, L. P. (1990) *Islamic Spain, 1250–1500*, University of Chicago Press, pp. 37–40.

5 Ibid. pp. 80–1.

6 Valera's *Epístolas*, cited in Edwards, J. (1985) 'War and peace in fifteenth-century Castile: Diego de Valera and the Granada war' in Mayr-Harting, H. and Moore, R. I. (eds) *Studies in Medieval History presented to R.H.C. Davis*, Hambledon Press, pp. 283–95.

7 Pulgar, H. de (1943) *CCE*, vol. 6, p. 286.

8 Ibid. p. 307.

9 Ibid. p. 314.

10 Among the best of numerous accounts of the Granada war are Harvey, L. P. (1990) pp. 275–323 and Ladero, M. A. (2002) pp. 83–170.

Chapter 4

Defenders of the Faith

Jews, converts and the Inquisition

When, in 1667, the annalist of Seville, Diego Ortiz de Zúñiga, attempted to describe the introduction of the 'Spanish Inquisition' to his native city, he placed the primary personal responsibility for the policy on Isabella and Ferdinand.[1] Given that his analysis has been followed, in general outline, ever since, through many religious and methodological changes, it is important to look more carefully at the events that surrounded the introduction of the new foundation of the Inquisition, first to Seville and then to the rest of the Crown of Castile and to the Crown of Aragon. As Ortiz noted, Isabella and Ferdinand could not establish such a tribunal without authorization from the pope and thus the formulation used in the text of the relevant bull, which was issued by Sixtus IV on 1 November 1478, is of considerable interest. This was the foundation document of an organization that was to last nearly 400 years. In it, the pope refers to a petition he had recently received from Isabella, in which she alleged that, in various parts of her kingdoms, there were people who, having been 'regenerated in Christ by the holy bath of baptism without having been coerced into it, and adopting the appearance of Christians', had reverted to Judaism, both in belief and practice. As is customary in documents issued by the Roman See, earlier precedent is stressed, and it is stated that converts who thus 'Judaized' were subject to the penalties formulated for such cases by Boniface VIII (1294–1303). Having repeated the terms of the Spanish petition, Sixtus first responds by praising Isabella's zeal for the Catholic faith and then accepts her request. He delegates to her the power to appoint to each city or diocese three, or at least two, inquisitors, who are to be:

[B]ishops, or of superior rank, or other men of probity, secular priests or religious from orders, mendicant or non-mendicant, forty years of age, of good conscience and praiseworthy life, masters or bachelors in Theology, or doctors in Canon Law, or licensed after rigorous examination, fearful of God.

They were to have full inquisitorial and episcopal jurisdiction over both heretics and those who aided and abetted them (*fautores*), regardless of any earlier papal privilege or ruling that might contradict this bull. Remarkably, given past Roman practice, Isabella was to be allowed to remove and replace her appointees if they proved unsatisfactory, and the pope exhorted her:

Exert yourself to choose and appoint for the aforesaid tasks such people as, stimulated by their own probity, integrity and diligence, may ceaselessly gain the fruits of the exaltation of the Faith and the salvation of souls.[2]

Did the responsibility for the establishment of the new Inquisition really lie as completely with Isabella as Sixtus's bull suggests?

In order to understand Isabella and her husband's role in the establishment of the new Inquisition in Castile, it is first necessary to go back in time, to earlier attempts to set up tribunals there, to match those already existent in the Crown of Aragon. It is also essential to note the pre-existent conditions that put such an issue on the agenda both of the Spanish monarchies and of the papacy. Between 1390 and about 1420, tens of thousands of Castilian and Aragonese Jews were baptized as Christians, apparently as a result of violent attacks on Jewish quarters in the major towns, in the summer of 1391, and subsequent social, legal and missionary pressures. A generation later, the 'Old' Christian majority, as it had begun to style itself, started to be conscious of the arrival in its midst of the 'New' Christians, or converts (*conversos*), and, in its resentment, to doubt their orthodoxy in their new faith. Given that this was a Spanish problem, and that the 'Spanish Inquisition' is primarily known to history as an instrument of the Spanish Crown, it may surprise some to know that the first suggestion of such a tribunal in Castile came from the papacy, in 1442, when Pope Eugenius IV issued a bull to Henry IV of Castile, aimed at protecting the position and rights of converts from Judaism, who were evidently under pressure from some sectors of the 'Old Christian' majority, but also stating that, if any *conversos* did indeed return to the Jewish religion, they should be investigated by the relevant inquisitorial tribunal and duly punished. At this stage inquisitorial duties in Castile were not in the hands of specialized tribunals, as in the Crown of Aragon, but remained with diocesan bishops. In any case, however, the notions that there was a *converso* 'problem', and that an inquisition would 'solve' it, had been injected by the pope into Castilian consciousness, where they were to remain for several centuries. The 1449 rebellion in Toledo inevitably focused attention on 'Judaizing' converts and how to deal with them. Once again, the main initiative came from the papacy. Nicholas V intervened to protect the rights of *conversos*, both in Toledo and elsewhere, but he also issued a bull, dated 20 November 1451, in which he granted to the bishop of Osma and to the vicar-general in the diocese of Salamanca the power to act as inquisitors in cases involving supposed 'Judaizing'. In the event, the Toledo rebellion ended and the bull was not put into effect, but the theoretical foundation had been laid, on papal rather than royal initiative, for what was eventually to occur in 1478.[3] A climate of hostility towards *conversos* continued to develop and, at some time between 1458 and 1464 (the latter being the date of the first known manuscript), an Observant Franciscan friar, Alonso de Espina, completed a lengthy work entitled *Fortalitium Fidei* ('Fortress of the Faith'), attacking heretics in general and 'Judaizers' in particular. Taking many details from the Catalan Nicolau Eymerich's manual for inquisitors, the *Directorium inquisitorum* ('Directory for inquisitors', c.1377), Espina outlined a then unparalleled 'solution' to the 'problem' of Castile's *conversos*, writing:

I believe that if, in our time, a real inquisition was to be made, innumerable people would be despatched to the fire, who really will be found to be judaizing. These people, if they are not most cruelly punished here for publically being Jews, will have to be burned in the eternal fire.[4]

All efforts, in Henry IV's reign, to introduce the Inquisition to Castile were unsuccessful, but clearly, the princess and future queen could not have been unaware of the continuing potential of conflict between non-Jewish and Jewish Christians to cause instability in the kingdom. There was renewed violence in Toledo, in July 1467, during which, in contrast to the events of 1449, *conversos* took the initiative, invading the cathedral on Sunday 14th, and fighting a pitched battle with 'Old Christians' on the following Sunday. The *conversos* lost and agents for Prince Alfonso (see Chapter 1), who had lordship of the city at the time, attempted to restore order, but tensions did not disappear. There were fights between Old and New Christians in Sepúlveda, in the following year, and riots in Córdoba and Jaén in 1473. Just before Henry's death, in 1474, there was violence of this type in Segovia, and once again in Córdoba.[5] Isabella, of course, came to the question on a basis of deep and active Christian piety. Yet the involvement of political factors was equally inescapable and it is impossible to see the queen and her husband's petition of 1478, to Sixtus IV, outside the context of the war for the Castilian succession. Azcona argues reasonably that the monarchs could not have tackled the question of integrating Jewish Christians into Church and society until Alfonso and Joanna had been defeated. It was to deal with political disorder and to identify dissidents that Isabella voyaged, in 1477, through Extremadura to Seville and in that sense the religious issue came second.[6] In the most general terms, involving all the themes in this chapter, and not only the question of the Inquisition, it is wise to bear in mind Luis Suárez Fernández's observation that:

It is difficult to establish a difference between the conduct of Ferdinand and that of his wife in relation to this matter [of religion]: it seems that they coincided completely.[7]

Seville in the late fifteenth century had approximately 40,000 inhabitants. It contained a small Jewish community, of a few hundred at most, who were descended from the survivors of the robbery and massacre of Jews in the city in 1391, and also considerable numbers of *conversos*, who were active in many professions and trades, both in Seville itself and in outlying towns, such as the duke of Medina Sidonia's port of Sanlúcar de Barrameda. Juan Gil characterizes thus the situation in the city at this time:

It is very far from being by chance that the first tribunal of the Holy Office found its base in Seville, a city pullulating with heretical depravity [sic], yes, but also where some lofty heads had to be brought low, beginning with that of the eternal protector of the New Christians, the [duke of] Medina Sidonia.[8]

Gil argues that it was because of the link between so many prominent local *conversos* and the duke that Seville, rather than, for example, Toledo or Burgos, where there were also numerous economically and politically active *conversos*, was chosen for the establishment of the first tribunal. There are, however, other reasons for this choice.

First, it should not be forgotten that, in 1478, Seville was the scene of a national synod of the Castilian Church (see following section), which had the reform and 'purification' of the Body of Christ at the top of its agenda. It was during this gathering, which had been called on the initiative of Isabella and her husband, that, as Ortiz de Zúñiga noted, Fray Alonso de Hojeda, prior of the Dominican convent of San Pablo in the city, told his tales of 'Judaizing' atrocities, supposedly perpetrated by Seville's *conversos*. Cardinal Pedro González de Mendoza, who had been archbishop of Seville since 1474, was not, at first sight, a likely enthusiast for Hojeda's claims. A member of the aristocratic Mendoza clan, one of his female relations had married into the *converso* Arias Dávila family.

Yet not only did the cardinal relay Hojeda's concerns to Ferdinand and Isabella, but he also initiated a campaign to evangelize the *conversos*, assuming, along with so many of his contemporaries, that their supposed reversion to Judaism was based at least as much on ignorance of Christianity as on hostility towards it. A new Inquisition should not be introduced until the Faith had been properly taught. To head the new missionary effort, which was initially confined to his own archdiocese and the neighbouring diocese of Cádiz, Mendoza chose the Jeronymite Fray Hernando de Talavera, who was to work alongside the cardinal's deputy (*provisor*), Pedro Fernández de Solís, also bishop of Cádiz. Already influential at court, Talavera seems to have been chosen partly for his own *converso* ancestry and partly for his willingness to avoid the theological innovations of some of his New Christian predecessors who gave high status to Jewish Christians. He preached the traditional message, that all the Old Testament prophecies had been fulfilled in Jesus, that the Mosaic Law had been made redundant by Jesus' incarnation and that the Church was the new Chosen People, the New Israel, outside which there was no salvation, so that full conversion to Christianity was the sole correct option for Jews. Not only did Talavera rail in his sermons against the sin of 'Judaizing' apostasy, but he also, in co-operation with Bishop Solís and the Seville cathedral chapter, drew up a set of ordinances, 'in order that Christian religion and life may grow and be practised in that most noble city and in its monarchs', who were thus directly associated with the enterprise.[9] In this code, which prefigured the later concerns of the Inquisition, *conversos* were instructed to keep a crucifix and images of Mary and the saints in their houses, to act as a focus of Christian devotion and they were forbidden to wash their dead before burial or to eat kosher meat, because these were Jewish customs. The cardinal ordered that notice boards should be placed on the door of every church in the diocese, displaying these rules ('the form which the Christian must keep from the day he is born') together with edicts threatening the disobedient with dire penalties. He also ordered the parish clergy to teach this code, as well as enforcing it.[10]

During 1478, while Mendoza's 'missionary' campaign was still under way, lobbying continued for a permanent Inquisition to be set up. Among those involved was a figure who would soon achieve considerable resonance: Fray Tomás de Torquemada, who wrote a memorandum to the king and queen, entitled 'The things which the kings must remedy', which coincided with the growing pressure on *conversos* in Seville. In it, half of Jewish descent himself, he attacked both Judaism and Jews, advocating the policy of separation (*apartamiento*) between the Jewish and Christian communities, which was already on Isabella and Ferdinand's agenda, together with the wearing by Jews and Muslims of distinctive badges, as had been ordered by the Roman Church ever since the Fourth Lateran Council of 1215. This text makes no explicit mention of an Inquisition, perhaps out of deference to Cardinal Mendoza and his 'conversion' policy, which had, after all, received royal sanction. Nevertheless, even if Torquemada cannot properly be described as the 'creator' of the Spanish Inquisition, by advocating draconian measures against the Jews, and also, on Espina's model, 'against blasphemers, [and] deniers of God and the saints', as well as 'witches and diviners' (*hechiceros y adevinos*), he clearly mapped out the course that would very soon be followed.[11] Although the monarchs did not use their power to appoint inquisitors until September 1480, further moves were made, during 1478–9 that threatened the security of Castilian *conversos*.

Talavera continued to prefer exhortation to arrest and trial, but he nevertheless affirmed, in his sermons in Seville, that relapsed heretics 'in some cases must die'. It appears, from the Jeronymite friar's testimony, that he and Bishop Solís did undertake an 'inquisition' of the traditional kind, which led to some convicted heretics being handed over to the secular authorities ('relaxed to the secular arm') for burning. It seems probable, but is not absolutely clear, that this was a precursor of the new, permanent tribunal. By the beginning of 1480, however, *conversos* were beginning to flee, some seeking refuge in Muslim Granada. In that year, an anonymous pamphlet appeared in Seville, avowedly written by a Christian cleric and asserting the genuine Christian fervour of the *conversos*. The tract reaffirmed the earlier theology of Alfonso de Cartagena and, ironically in view of what was soon to follow, of Juan de Torquemada, in which the Jewishness of Jesus was asserted. Preachers such as Talavera, who condemned the Law of Moses as outmoded, were accused of seeking honours out of vainglory. In fact, the messianic kingdom was soon to arrive, under the leadership of the Spanish Crown, but it would, it seems, have more Jewish than Christian characteristics. By the time Talavera refuted this work, in a treatise published in 1481, what Juan Gil calls the 'soft' Inquisition had come to an end. The king and queen had indeed acted, but not in the manner envisaged by the anonymous cleric of Seville.[12]

At Medina del Campo, on 17 September 1480, Ferdinand and Isabella appointed two Dominican friars, Juan de San Martín and Miguel de Morillo, under the powers granted to them by Pope Sixtus IV (his bull of 1 November 1478 being included in the document), to act as inquisitors throughout the Crown of Castile.[13] In practice, however, they were to begin work in Seville and, on 2 January 1481, San Martín and Morillo themselves issued an edict to the ecclesiastical and secular authorities of Seville, Córdoba, Jerez de la Frontera, Toledo and all other parts of the Castilian Crown stating that, with the assistance of Dr Juan Ruiz de Medina, a member of the Royal Council, they had begun an inquisition in Seville. They had found, however, that numerous people had fled from the city, many of them taking refuge in the lands of the second most prominent magnate in Andalusia, and future hero of the Granada war, Rodrigo Ponce de León, marquis of Cádiz and count of Arcos de la Frontera. The inquisitors naturally wished these escapes to stop and de-manded that all the region's authorities co-operate fully with their work.[14] From this time onwards, it is easy enough to document the activities of the new Inquisition, as its tentacles spread, first through Castile and then into the Crown of Aragon. It is much harder directly to discern the personal roles of the queen and her husband in the build-up to their request to Sixtus IV to issue the bull of 1 November 1478. Nevertheless, their unstinting support for Tomás de Torquemada, who was appointed by Sixtus IV as an inquisitor, along with six other Dominicans, on 11 February 1482, gives a good indication of their views, and further evid-ence was soon to accumulate. On 4 September of that year, for instance, inquisitors were appointed to set up a new tribunal in Córdoba and, over the next ten years, further Castilian tribunals were established in Jaén, Ciudad Real/Toledo, Ávila, Segovia, Medina del Campo, Valladolid and Sigüenza. It is estimated that, between 1481 and 1488, inquisitors in Castile handed over about 700 convicted 'Judaizing' *conversos* to the secular authorities to be burned, in person if present, and in effigy if they had fled before trial. Many others were imprisoned for long periods, and received various financial and spiritual penalties. There is no sign that Isabella and her husband did not fully support this action and Ferdinand's personal attitude was clearly revealed when the decision was taken, in Spain not Rome, to extend the new Castilian Inquisition to the Crown of Aragon.[15]

On 17 October 1483, Pope Sixtus issued a bull appointing Torquemada as Inquisitor-General of Aragon, Catalonia and Valencia. In the preceding two years, Ferdinand had made efforts, through his ambassadors in Rome, to gain more power over the existing inquisitorial tribunals in his hereditary lands, in order to bring them into line with what his wife was doing in Castile, but more drastic measures were evidently called for. Yet he and the pope must have known that there would be complica-tions, because there was no legal way in which a Castilian institution, even an ecclesiastical one, could be extended into Aragonese territory.

In addition, it was clearly going to be necessary to wind up the existing tribunals, in Zaragoza, Barcelona and Valencia, in order to allow Torquemada and his officials to function. Ferdinand's initial revival of the old papal Inquisition had, of course, threatened the *conversos*, many of whom occupied prominent positions in local and national government, but had not raised constitutional issues. Torquemada's appointment, however, defied the much cherished Aragonese and Catalan charters (*fueros* or *furs*), which forbade non-native officials to function within the relevant boundaries. Thus, as Ferdinand, in 1484–5, pushed forward the introduction of the new-style tribunals in his kingdoms, he met resistance on two fronts, constitutional revolt being added to the natural fears of the *conversos*, and ensuring that the latter would receive much wider support, among those who were not of Jewish origin, than their Castilian equivalents. On 14 April 1484, Torquemada held a meeting (*junta*) in the Aragonese town of Tarazona, where the kingdom's cortes were then meeting under Ferdinand's presidency. There the new Inquisitor-General announced the forthcoming appointment of inquisitors 'of heretical depravity' to Zaragoza, Huesca, Teruel, Lleida, Barcelona and Valencia. In May 1484, a start was made with the naming of two Dominicans, Fray Gaspar Juglar and Fray Pedro Arbués de Epila, as inquisitors in the Aragonese capital, Zaragoza, which had prominent *converso* and Jewish communities. Juglar and Arbués immediately faced strong opposition from an alliance of *conversos* and constitutionalists and their troubles were soon to be repeated, when a young Basque Dominican, Fray Juan de Solibera, was appointed inquisitor of Teruel.

Since the twelfth century, when it had been on the frontier with Muslim territory, this small Aragonese town had jealously guarded its legal autonomy, under the overall authority of the king. When Solibera arrived outside its walls, on 23 May 1484, Teruel's representative (*procurador*) at the Cortes of Tarazona had already warned his fellow councillors of the inquisitorial threat. After a secret night-time session with their lawyers, they formally refused the inquisitor entry to their town, on the grounds that he was only 24, and therefore well below the age of 40, which was required by papal legislation and that, since he was not Aragonese and was a subject of Isabella of Castile rather than Ferdinand, any action he took as inquisitor would be a *contrafuero*, against their hallowed charter. The good friar retired, angrily and ignominiously, to the neighbouring town of Cella, where he attempted to start investigating cases of supposed 'Judaizing', with the help of his fellow inquisitor, Martín Navarro, who was vicar there. Ferdinand's personal responsibility in the crushing of Teruel's resistance is clear and unequivocal. Apart from issuing their own legal objections (*exceptiones de jure*), the councillors rallied the population of their outlying territory (*comunidad*), as well as sending appeals for help to Daroca and Calatayud. They also appealed directly to the *Diputación General*, the standing governmental committee for Aragon, in Zaragoza, sending ambassadors there on 10 June 1484. Finally, on 23 June, in a last desperate throw, they sent a further delegation south to Córdoba, to appeal directly to the king. Ferdinand had to make a clear decision and did so forcefully, insisting, as he did in other such cases, that, if the people of Teruel were as innocent of heresy as they claimed, they had nothing to fear from Solibera and Navarro. The king instructed his 'captain' in Teruel, Juan Garcés de Marcilla, to suppress all rebellion and enable the inquisition to function, which he succeeded in doing within a matter of months (by 25 March 1485), although the troubles there did not end entirely until 1487.[16]

When Ferdinand introduced Torquemada to the Crown of Aragon, the Catalan capital, Barcelona, had had Juan Comes in place as inquisitor, under the old regime, since 1461. The city councillors therefore felt no need to send a representative to the 1484 Cortes of Tarazona, but this did not save them from Fray Tomás's new appointees. Although there was no violence, Barcelona refused to accept either the revocation of Comes's powers or the commissions of his successors but, as in Teruel, Ferdinand personally forced them to submit. Thus, during 1485, many *conversos* fled the city and, on 3 February 1486, Innocent VIII cleared all legal obstacles by formally revoking the powers of all the Castilian, Aragonese and Catalan inquisitors, both old and new. This measure gave Torquemada full powers to appoint whom he wished under the new rules, or 'instructions', which he had formulated in 1484.[17] The Inquisitor-General duly replaced Comes with a Dominican, Alonso de Espina (not the author of the 'Fortress of the Faith'; see earlier), but, as in the case of Seville, many of Barcelona's *conversos* fled rather than face trial. In Valencia, to the south, two inquisitors under the old foundation, Juan Cristóbal de Gualbes and Juan Orts, had been appointed by Sixtus IV as recently as 1481. Here, too, Torquemada introduced Martín Iñigo and Juan de Epila as inquisitors for the new tribunal, in 1484, but the latter was Aragonese rather than Valencian and protests were made against his appointment on the basis of the local *fuero*. However, the most spectacular incident connected with the introduction of Ferdinand and Isabella's Inquisition to the Crown of Aragon took place in Zaragoza, in 1485. As noted earlier, in the previous year, Pedro Arbués de Epila had been appointed as inquisitor in the Aragonese capital, under the new foundation, and his vigorous action against supposed 'Judaizers' had provoked a bitter dispute with the city's influential *converso* community. By September 1485, Arbués felt that his life was in danger and had taken to wearing a coat of mail under his clerical robes and a steel helmet under his cap. Nevertheless, on the night of 15–16 September, he was stabbed to death while praying in Zaragoza cathedral, thus becoming the Spanish Inquisition's first 'martyr', a victim of royal policy who was eventually to be canonized as a saint. The eight conspirators were quickly identified, the *conversos* were inevitably, and apparently rightly, blamed and the new tribunals were reaffirmed in their work of investigation and punishment. Between 1480 and 1492, hundreds of *conversos*, in both Castile and Aragon, were arrested, imprisoned and interrogated, dozens of them being burned, either in person or in effigy, while the confiscation of their property ruined both them and their families. In this process, there is absolutely no sign that the king and queen disapproved of any aspect of 'their' inquisitors' activities.

Thus the personal initiative of both Ferdinand and Isabella in the foundation and initial work of the new Inquisition, mainly among the *conversos*, can easily be demonstrated. Yet the central question of their perception of Judaism and its relationship to Christianity requires further consideration. In recent decades, many scholars, in Spain itself and abroad, particularly in the United States, Israel and Western Europe, have returned to the extensive archives of the Castilian and Aragonese tribunals for the period 1480–1520. The results have tended to concentrate on two main areas, the first being the organization and procedures of the tribunals, and in particular the ability of inquisitorial methods correctly to identify the religious beliefs and practice of individuals, and the second, as a consequence, being the question of the 'true' religious identity of the *conversos*. The estimation of the value of the evidence obtained by inquisitors, both from accused persons and from witnesses, remains controversial. Some scholars, and most notably Benzion Netanyahu, totally reject the surviving documentation as an indication of the *conversos*' religiosity, because of the bias and secrecy of the methods whereby it was collected. Netanyahu goes further, in asserting that the converts were basically sincere Christians, rather than secret Judaizers, and were therefore cruelly and unjustly persecuted by Ferdinand and Isabella's Inquisition.[18] The political and social reality was, however, that both the monarchs and their agents believed that secret Judaism did indeed exist within their realms and worked from the assumption, common in that period, that the Jewish faith was both outmoded and thoroughly and actively wicked. Relativism in the matter of religion was not unknown in late medieval Spain, where, at least up to 1492, Jews and

Christians lived alongside one another and Christians continued to co-exist also with Muslims thereafter. But the notion that salvation could be obtained legitimately through full and sincere adherence to any of these three faiths, though it was sometimes expressed by ordinary people, was always rejected in official circles and, in this respect, the views of the king and queen were entirely conventional. To them, the Inquisition's methods were wholly legitimate, entirely desirable and necessary in order to remove a genuinely mortal danger from Spanish society – that of Jews masquerading as Catholic Christians and destroying the Church from within. Their support for the inquisitors lasted throughout their lives, but their passionate anxiety to remove the perceived threat of Judaism, from Church and society, also expressed itself in two important policy initiatives, which were developed during and after the Granada war.

First, one night in June 1490, Benito García, a *converso*, was staying at an inn in Astorga, on the frontier of Old Castile and Galicia. After an altercation, some 'Old Christian' revellers claimed to have discovered in his luggage a stolen Host, the consecrated unleavened bread of the Mass. In medieval Europe, those who removed such wafers from churches were believed to be inspired by the Devil, an accusation which was commonly made against Jews, in Spain and elsewhere.[19] In this case, the vicar-general for the bishop of Astorga was quickly involved and the case was then placed in the hands of the Inquisition in Valladolid, which subsequently transferred it to the tribunal in Ávila, Torquemada's home town. Over the following months, inquisitors attempted to unravel what they claimed to be a conspiracy, involving about ten *conversos* and Jews, in which not only had the Eucharistic Host been stolen for nefarious purposes, but a young boy from La Guardia (Toledo) had been kidnapped from his parents, taken to a cave near his home town and made to suffer the same torments, such as scourging and crucifixion, as had been inflicted on Jesus in his Passion. From the technical point of view, the difficulty of reconciling the contradictory testimony of the accused led the inquisitors to abandon their normal procedure, as formulated by Torquemada in his 1484 instructions. Instead of being imprisoned and interrogated separately, the accused were confronted with each other and, eventually, a supposedly 'authentic' and cohesive narrative emerged. Although no dead and tortured child was ever found and no distraught and bereaved parents were produced, the 'Holy Child of La Guardia' (*Santo Niño de La Guardia*) acquired the name 'Cristóbal' (Christopher, or 'Christ bearer') and was said to have been spirited away in Toledo, during a fair held to celebrate the Assumption of the Blessed Virgin Mary

(15 August, the year in question being unspecified). Eventually, in November 1491, the inquisitors found all the accused guilty, the Inquisition's external assessors (*calificadores*) confirmed the verdicts and sentences and an *auto de fe* was held in Ávila on the 16th of that month. The cult of the 'Holy Child' has still not completely disappeared from view, at least in La Guardia itself, but the feature of immediate interest is the effort which was made by the Inquisition to publicize the case, in the Crown of Aragon as well as Castile.

The message to be spread among Ferdinand and Isabella's 'Old Christian' subjects was that, just as the inquisitorial tribunals had been claiming since 1480, the 'New Christians' were secret Judaizers, but, worse still, the 'Holy Child' case was made to demonstrate that these *conversos* were still playing a full part in the anti-Christian conspiracies of Jews.[20] At this point, the political spotlight began to fall on those Spanish Jews who had not been baptized. At the time of the *auto de fe* in Ávila, the Granada war was, of course, coming to its climax, but Torquemada and his fellow members of the 'Supreme Council of the General Inquisition', known as 'La Suprema', continued their campaign to persuade Isabella and Ferdinand to expel 'their' Jews, or else force them to convert. As Christians, they would no longer be able to attract *conversos* back to Judaism and they too would be subject to inquisitorial discipline. By no means all Spanish Jews had succumbed to conversionary pressures, between 1390 and 1420, and, in the 1470s, both Castile and Aragon contained surviving Jewish communities, mostly located in small towns and villages, under either royal or seigniorial jurisdiction. Despite the active opposition of certain prominent courtiers and writers, for example the royal chronicler Fernando del Pulgar, himself a *converso*, during the 1480s a political orthodoxy had been created in which all New Christians (and the term was increasingly applied to the descendants of converts, who had been Catholics all their lives) were regarded as potential or actual secret Jews, insidiously undermining Ferdinand and Isabella's regime. The fact that some of the rulers' most faithful retainers, such as Andrés Cabrera, marquis of Moya, and Gonzalo Chacón, were *conversos* seems not to have deflected them from this belief and its result in policy.[21] Indeed, the case of the 'Holy Child of La Guardia' appears to have convinced them of the validity of the Inquisition's case and there is evidence that the edicts for Castile and Aragon, which were dated 31 March 1492, had in substance been drafted by inquisitors. These epoch-making documents were not, however, Isabella and Ferdinand's first involvement with general policy towards the Jews and in particular with the plan to force them to convert or be expelled.

When the two monarchs inherited their respective thrones, the legal status of their Jewish subjects had remained largely unchanged for several centuries. Jews, like Muslims, were treated as separate communities (*aljamas*), although they were not necessarily confined to separate quarters. They were allowed religious freedom and their own leadership, which was responsible for collecting the taxes which they owed, but their religion excluded them from many of the essential institutions of late medieval Spanish society, such as national and local government, the Church, the legal system, trade guilds and the universities. They were also forbidden to bear arms and hence excluded from highly prized military careers. In a manner of compensation for these disabilities, they were placed under the protection of the Crown, which should have guarded them against attack, but had clearly failed to do so in 1391. It remained to be seen how first Isabella, and then her husband, would interpret the status quo, in which, despite severe losses to Christianity, there were still over (and perhaps well over) 100,000 Jews within the two realms. The new queen first turned her attention to her Jewish subjects during the wartime Cortes of Madrigal, in 1476. Even while Isabella was fighting for her throne, the members of this parliament found time to re-enact old legislation, which ordered Castilian Jews to wear distinguishing red or yellow badges, not to dress in precious materials or wear jewels and to lower their interest rates for loans. Also, the powers of Jewish community judges were reduced in favour of their Christian colleagues. These measures, demanded by urban members, were not new, having been asked for and enacted at every Trastamaran Cortes in Castile since 1369, so that the queen's role in the matter cannot be identified.

It would be after the end of the war with Portugal, in the Toledo Cortes of 1479–80, that royal policy would began to appear more clearly. In the meantime, and indeed almost up to the eve of the 1492 expulsion order, the Crown would continue to issue documents protecting the legal and financial interests of individual Jewish *aljamas*.[22] At Toledo, Isabella and her husband ordered the segregation of these communities from the rest of their subjects and work soon began in various towns to create, or re-create, enclosed quarters which later, first in Venice, would come to be called 'ghettos'. This, too, was not a new measure, but simply the enforcement of a law which dated back to the Cortes of Valladolid in 1411. Nevertheless, it indicated that life was about to get harder for Castilian Jews, as they faced increasing tax demands for the Granada war, enforcement by municipalities of social restrictions and often the upheaval involved in moving from one part of town to another. It is worth noting also that, although unbaptized Jews were not subject to the jurisdiction of the new Inquisition, Jews, and especially rabbis, were often forced to testify against *conversos*, in order to confirm that their supposed religious practices were indeed Jewish.[23] In May 1484 Isabella and Ferdinand obtained confirmation from Pope Sixtus IV of their restrictive measures against Jews, including the policy of segregation (*apartamiento*). By the end of 1491 the monarchs seem to have become convinced that unbaptized Jews, even when subject to these laws, were having such a bad influence on converts that they should either become Christians themselves or leave.[24]

On 31 March, in newly conquered Granada, two documents were dated, one by the Castilian chancellery, in Ferdinand and Isabella's name, and the other by its Aragonese equivalent in the king's name alone. Although their main thrust was the same, their exact wording differed. The Castilian version referred to an earlier episode in which, in 1483, Jews had been expelled from Andalusia at the request of the Inquisition, although they had later been allowed to return.[25] The Aragonese version omitted this episode, instead launching an attack on Jewish usury, as well as Jews' 'corruption' of Jewish converts to Christianity. In each case, however, Jews were given four months to decide whether or not to leave, although in practice they only had three months, because of a delay in the issuing of enforcement orders to local authorities, possibly caused by the attempts of Jewish leaders, especially Abraham Seneor and Isaac Abravanel, to buy off their rulers.[26] In any case, Isabella and Ferdinand seem to have been happy both to precipitate and to witness the painful voyage of Jewish families, by land and sea, into exile, taking with them only what they could carry and even that subject to the depredations of local officials, customs officials and sea captains. No revisionism can disguise the horror of these episodes, which are graphically recorded in both Jewish and Christian sources and tens of thousands departed, on land to Portugal and Navarre and by sea to North Africa, Italy and the Eastern Mediterranean.[27] In this very real sense, the experience of Spain's Jews in 1492 has rightly been described as an 'expulsion', and the new Jewish diaspora of the 'Sephardim', the 'Spanish' Jews, that it created continues to have demographic and cultural resonance today.

Yet it may still be asked whether this loss of skilled and educated citizens was really the intention of sovereigns who sensed themselves to be on the brink of a world mission of conquest and evangelization. The clue to the answer may lie in the word 'evangelization', on the analogy of what had happened in Spain in the early fifteenth century. Certainly, the issue of conversion seems subordinate to that of expulsion in the edicts of 31 March 1492, issued in fact at the end of April, but the same cannot be said for a subsequent document, issued by Ferdinand on 15 May of that year, which instructed Torquemada and his subordinates to ensure that Jews who decided to convert, and remain in Spain, were not deterred from seeking baptism by fear that they would subsequently be investigated for their previous links with *conversos*.[28] This explicitly inclusive measure went to the very heart of the work of the tribunals that the king and queen had set up and cherished and was accompanied by other edicts and actions that spoke of conversion rather than expulsion. On 10 November 1492 Ferdinand issued a further document, addressed to those Jews who had recently left Castile and Aragon, inviting them to return as Christians. Jews who could produce certificates of baptism would not only be allowed to return to their former places of residence, but would be given back their former property, which they had been forced to sell, generally for very low prices, during the previous spring and summer. The buyers would be compensated for improvements that they had made as well as the purchase price, but the message was clear. The 'Catholic monarchs', as they were soon to become, wanted to retain their Jewish subjects and not lose them, but baptism was the unavoidable condition. It should also be noted that alongside this measure, which was clearly used as a 'law of return' by numerous former Jews, there was another form of transaction, again explicitly authorized by the Crown, in which *conversos* might make payments, according to their means and to the Royal Treasury rather than the Inquisition, which would, as it were, 'wipe out' their previous religious offences or remove any charges that the inquisitors wished to make against them.[29] It remains to be seen what kind of Church the newly baptized Jews were expected to join.

Christianity and the Church

In December 1496 Pope Alexander VI granted Ferdinand and Isabella the title of 'Catholic Kings' (*Reyes Católicos*). Like the later concession by Clement VII, to their son-in-law, Henry VIII of England, of the designation 'Defender of the Faith', this had to be seen as a recognition of the recipients' loyalty to Catholic Christianity in general and to the Roman papacy in particular. At the time of the grant, with the evangelization of the Americas about to begin, the pope regarded the establishment of the Inquisition, the expulsion of Jews who refused to convert to Christianity, the conquest of Granada and the prospect of further expeditions of conquest against Muslim North Africa, as clear signs of the Spanish rulers' Christian piety. These were external observations, however, and it remains to be seen how much can be known of Ferdinand and Isabella's personal religion and of their notion of how the Church should be and function. Most, if not all, of their individual Christian practice took place in the court and particularly in their respective chapels (see Chapter 6), but the main concern here will be the ways in which their personal beliefs or other motives were reflected in their relations with the Church in their own territories and with the papacy.

These issues arose as soon as Isabella made her contested bid for the Castilian throne. Henry IV's death, in December 1474, turned the papal Curia, within a few weeks, into the centre of international negotiations concerning the succession. First out of the blocks, understandably, was Afonso V of Portugal, who sent a letter to Louis XI of France, asking for his support in claiming Henry's throne. This speed was advisable, since, as soon as he heard the news from Castile, John II of Aragon began to organize an embassy, with the aim of persuading Pope Sixtus IV to support his son, Ferdinand, and Isabella. The Franciscan pope greatly respected the diplomatic prowess of the elderly king of Aragon, who had not offered personal allegiance to Sixtus, since his acquisition of the tiara in 1471. When this finally happened, in July 1476, the master of the military order of Montesa making submission on behalf of the Crown of Aragon, at the same time as the dean of Burgos on behalf of Castile, Sixtus effectively recognized the validity of Isabella's claim, although his speech on this occasion was hardly fulsome. The outbreak of hostilities between Castile and Portugal was already testing the pope's resolve, as well as the political judgement of other Western European rulers. An immediate problem arose with the Castilian military orders, since the ratification of the election of their masters was a papal responsibility. Between 1378 and 1415, during the 'Great Schism' of the Western Church, European rulers had been faced by two rival candidates for major Church appointments, named by different 'popes'. Now, in 1475, the position was reversed in the case of Castile, with Afonso and Joanna on the one hand and Isabella and Ferdinand on the other requiring Sixtus IV to adjudicate between their nominations to important posts. The problem first manifested itself when Afonso proposed the marquis of Villena, by now an enemy of Isabella, to be master of Santiago, while she and Ferdinand successfully proposed Rodrigo Manrique. More fundamental, however, was another decision that the pope had to make, this being whether or not to grant the necessary dispensation of consanguinity for Afonso to marry Joanna. The entire Portuguese claim to Castile rested on this decision, which, partly as a result of pressure from France and the Empire, went eventually, on 3 February 1476, in favour of Afonso, although other evidence suggests that Sixtus at least tacitly supported Isabella's claim to the throne. In any case, the Ligurian Franciscan was worried about the developing situation in the Iberian peninsula and decided to send a legate to represent him there. First, however, he gave the master of Montesa a formal reply to John II of Aragon. In it, he bemoaned the outbreak of renewed civil strife in Castile, a kingdom that had a history of fidelity to the Roman See and that was essential to the confrontation with militant Islam, all round the Mediterranean. On 1 August 1476 Sixtus appointed, as his plenipotentiary legate (*legatus a latere*) to Castile, Nicolao Franco, then a canon of Treviso but soon to become bishop of Parenzo. The documents issued to him by the papal chancellery appear to indicate genuine doubts about how the papacy should tackle the situation in Spain and Portugal. Franco was an apostolic notary and a diplomat and, as well as being a legate, with the job of dealing with the political situation, he was also appointed as a collector of papal revenues, with implications for the Spanish Church as a whole.

Given their precarious legal and political situation, the monarchs were keenly aware of the importance of papal support, but they also rated highly their own role in controlling the Church within their domains, being supported in such a stance by both Castilian and Aragonese monarchical tradition. As they faced the Portuguese threat, their willingness to entertain papal diplomats was paralleled by an acute need for finance. Those who have, in recent times, attempted to plead Isabella's cause of Catholic sainthood, must take account of her action in financing the defence of her throne by seizing the liturgical plate of the Castilian Church. The facts are well enough documented. In the early stages of the war, Ferdinand and Isabella's main economic resource was the royal treasure in the Alcázar at Segovia, which was guarded for her by her faithful *converso* steward, Andrés Cabrera. This was not large, however, and she soon had to resort to pawning precious objects, including her personal jewellery. Ferdinand also pawned royal property, thus obtaining 3 million *maravedíes* from the Jeronymite friary of Montamarta. These transactions involved obtaining money from the Church in return for royal goods, but a very different kind of demand was soon to be made on the churches and religious houses of Castile.

Efforts to recoup lost royal revenues were still in their early stages so, in 1476, the demand went out, apparently with the approval, in some cases but certainly not all, of senior clergy, for silver, silver-gilt and gold objects to be handed over to the Crown. Dioceses within, or close to, the areas of conflict were natural targets, but the requisition seems to have been general. The monarchs instructed officials of the treasury and High

Court, as well as supporters in individual dioceses, to collect the plate from sacristies and have it inventoried before notaries. Expert valuers (*tasadores*) were then called in to establish the metal content of each item – chalices, bowls, dishes, etc. – and, in most cases, the metalsmiths took charge of the vessels, paying the Crown at the rate of 2300 *mrs* per mark of silver, with appropriate rates for other metals. The Crown undertook to repay the recorded value in due course. It is important to note that this was not an exercise in melting down liturgical objects and also that repayments continued to be made, into the 1480s, despite the subsequent financial demands of the Granada war. The sums raised could be considerable, for example over 1.3 million *mrs* being obtained from the cathedral and parish churches of the diocese of Zamora.[30]

Nicolao Franco came to Spain with instructions to support John II of Aragon and Isabella of Castile in efforts to reform the Church and the queen moved in this direction in 1478, summoning an assembly or 'Congregation' of the Castilian clergy to Seville in July of that year. Both Aragon and Castile had a strong tradition of active royal intervention in ecclesiastical matters and Isabella, in particular, was scarcely in need of Pope Sixtus' bidding. The notable feature of the Seville assembly is that it was not a conventional provincial or diocesan synod but an irregular body, called together purely on royal initiative. The argument that Isabella and her husband were moving in the direction at least of a 'regalist' if not a 'national' Church in their territories is strengthened by their adoption of this type of body, which bypassed the conventional mechanisms of Catholic Church government. Before 1492, when a new province of Granada was added, the Castilian part of the Church was divided into three ecclesiastical provinces or archdioceses: Toledo, which had the primacy, Santiago de Compostela and Seville, each province consisting of several dioceses. The Crown of Aragon contained the provinces of Zaragoza, Tarragona and Valencia, which were similarly subdivided. There was, however, a complication from the respective Crowns' point of view, this being that provincial boundaries did not entirely correspond to the frontiers between the various Iberian kingdoms. Thus, among Castilian dioceses, Astorga and Ourense, in the north-west, were included in the Portuguese archdiocese of Braga; Calahorra, in the north-east, was part of the archdiocese of Zaragoza and Cartagena, on the east coast, was under the oversight of the archbishop of Valencia. In addition, three important Castilian sees, those of León, Burgos and Oviedo, were not part of any Spanish ecclesiastical structure, being directly subject to the pope. This situation, which had arisen as a result of many centuries of unsystematic development, would not assist the rulers in creating a coherent 'Church of Spain', to parallel their policies in the secular sphere. They were well aware of this fact and, where possible, attempted to rectify it, although most of the relevant diocesan changes took place after Isabella's death, in 1504. In the meantime, however, she and Ferdinand took full advantage of their conquests, in Granada and the Canary Islands, to establish ecclesiastical structures that were more firmly under their own control (see following section and Chapter 5).[31] The 1478 Seville assembly provided them with a platform for the enunciation of their personal policies in Church matters. The electoral system for the assembly paralleled that of the secular Castilian Cortes, in that the representatives who attended it were chosen by the various cathedral chapters, who empowered them to debate and decide on resolutions. It was clear, however, that, in the situation of emergency which prevailed in the kingdom, the Seville meeting would bypass the long-established clerical or first Estate of the Cortes. Convocations of the first Estate had traditionally been summoned by a papal legate, or else on the initiative of individual bishops or cathedral chapters, both to take part in general Cortes debates and to defend the liberties of the clergy. The dynamic at Seville in 1478 was to be very different and, not only that, but the assembly was to be the precedent for more such gatherings, thus further marginalizing the traditional governing structures of the Castilian Church. Before examining Isabella and Ferdinand's innovations, however, it is necessary to look at their existing powers over the Castilian Church. It was not until the following year that Ferdinand would have the chance to act similarly in the Crown of Aragon.

As in other medieval European kingdoms, the Church in Spain was an essential part of the social and economic structure of the peninsula. Having been the beneficiaries (hence the term 'benefice' for a permanent clerical post) of centuries of lay Christian giving, with the added impetus, in the Spanish case, of the permanent Islamic threat, bishops, cathedral chapters, colleges of canons, religious orders and military orders possessed, in 1474, huge estates, as well as jurisdiction, on behalf of the Crown, over dozens of towns and villages, together with their inhabitants. Thus, as rulers elsewhere in Europe were to find in the sixteenth century, any attempt at major religious change would have immense legal and social implications. At the top of the seigniorial tree among churchmen were, of course, the bishops. Many of them had resources equivalent to those of the secular upper nobility, but monarchs could not treat them in the same way, because of their ordained allegiance to God and the bishop of Rome and because they were not dynasts, but temporary stewards of corporate possessions, who constantly claimed the 'liberty' of the Church against any governmental onslaught. These constraints did not prevent Isabella and her government from seizing episcopal possessions in specific circumstances. The temporalities of the see of Toledo were thus occupied by the Crown, with permission from Sixtus IV, at the time when Archbishop Carrillo was an opponent of Isabella's accession and the Crown took over the castle attached to Segovia cathedral, when that city was a vital base for her regime, in the early years of her reign. For the same reason, the bishop of Palencia effectively lost jurisdiction over his cathedral city to the Crown. Apart from these more extreme cases, the supposed boundary between royal possessions and ecclesiastical temporalities was inevitably blurred in the case of taxation and other revenues, including tithes and the proceeds of the sale of bulls for the 'crusade' (see Chapter 2).

Isabella and Ferdinand were, of course, zealous in such matters, but they concentrated much of their energy on an attempt to choose appropriate people, from their point of view, to lead the Church in their domains. From the very beginning, in 1475, they tried to enlist the aid of the papacy in this process, but who was 'appropriate' could be a controversial matter. Ferdinand's insistence, apparently with his wife's support, that his teenage bastard son, Alfonso, should be named by Sixtus IV as archbishop of Zaragoza did not augur well for future 'reform' in this area. Sixtus initially aimed to appoint a curial cardinal, who would be non-resident, but at least had the proper qualifications in other respects. Yet, paradoxically, it was precisely this apparent epitome of the corruption of the 'old' Church, so castigated by reformers both at the time and later, which seems to have whetted Isabella and Ferdinand's appetite for greater or, if possible, complete control over the appointment of bishops and other major benefice holders in Aragon and especially in Castile. There followed a series of very public rows over nominations to Castilian bishoprics, which lasted well beyond Isabella's death and into the 'governorship' of Ferdinand. The monarchs never weakened in their determination to choose, as far as possible, the bishops in their Church, but what were their criteria in searching for suitable candidates?[32]

Thanks to the vigour of Isabella and Ferdinand's action in the question of episcopal appointments, it is not hard to see which qualities in a leading churchman were most important to them and the resulting list begins, at least, to suggest what Christianity actually meant to them, beyond the obvious economic and political interests of the kingdoms they governed. The first point, constantly repeated in the case of all senior Church appointments, was that successful candidates should be native Castilian or Aragonese subjects. The arguments deployed, in correspondence and negotiation with Rome, to justify this insistence were similar to those used by other rulers at the time, particularly in France and England. It was essential that senior churchmen, who might have responsibility, as in the cases of Toledo, Seville and Valencia, for numerous towns, vassals and revenues, as well as control over private armies and major castles and fortresses, should owe allegiance to the Spanish rulers and not to potential enemy powers abroad – including the papacy itself. There was also a moral argument, which would acquire increasing topicality in the sixteenth century. This was the question of bishops' residing in their dioceses, rather than leaving pastoral oversight to permanent deputies ('suffragans') or to 'flying' bishops, the latter having no diocese of their own but possessing the power to carry out the sacramental functions of a bishop, such as confirmations and ordinations. After 1517 the demand for resident senior clergy would become insistent in both Protestant and Catholic lands, but already, in their battles with Sixtus IV and Innocent VIII, Ferdinand and Isabella were raising the issue. 'Their' bishops should be in Spain, at their sovereigns' beck and call, but this should not be a matter only of political and administrative convenience, but also of pastoral care. There was an evident contradiction here, since bishops and other senior churchmen were frequently appointed by the Crown to 'secular' administrative and political posts that inevitably took them away from their dioceses or religious houses. In addition, popes often pointed out that it was actually necessary and desirable for bishops, both Spanish and Italian, to work for the Spanish rulers' interests in Rome and, in practice, the latter accepted the point, sometimes acquiescing in the grant of Castilian and Aragonese sees to foreign curialists. Indeed, from 1475 onwards they spent a great deal of time and effort in establishing and maintaining a religious and political presence in Rome, in particular supporting the reformed Franciscan community of San Pietro in Montorio (see later) and paying for the rebuilding of their church. Nevertheless, Isabella, in particular, does seem genuinely to have cared about the moral quality of her bishops. All Christian rulers, in the late medieval and early modern periods, seem to have believed in the 'top-down' principle of leadership and teaching, in which the people in general should be nurtured in the faith by educated and devout pastors, who led moral lives. These pastors should also be well educated and the senior ones should not necessarily be noblemen. Thus a great deal was said, in documents issued both by Isabella and by the apparently less morally zealous Ferdinand, about the need for bishops and other Christian leaders, such as cathedral canons, parish priests, abbots and friars, to set a good moral and devotional example. Yet although these concerns were evidently shared by many Christians, and not least by satirists, throughout late medieval Europe, they had never been easy to satisfy. Even so, Isabella and Ferdinand's programme for Church reform always had a moral as well as an institutional dimension.

Inevitably, however, given the high proportion of human and economic resources in Castile and Aragon that were in the hands of Church institutions ('dead' hands in the sense that such property, once acquired, did not normally find its way again on to the market), much attention had to be paid to matters of law, property and taxation. As far as royal control over provisions to bishoprics was concerned, the sovereigns and their lawyers based their case on Roman canon law, as well as the laws and traditions of their own kingdoms. The twelfth-century collection of papal legislation, known as the 'decretals', allowed a ruler to reject the pope's choice for a bishopric in their territory, if the candidate or his family were suspected of crime or disloyalty and this criterion was indeed deployed against Meléndez Valdés, as a candidate for the archbishopric of Seville. As far as native legal tradition was concerned, Isabella and her husband returned frequently to the claim, as expressed in a document of 1503, that:

Thus it is an immemorial custom that the kings of Castile and León present prelates, who are provided by the Holy Fathers [popes] to archbishoprics and bishoprics and other dignities [senior Church offices] in these kingdoms.[33]

The same could certainly be said for the Crown of Aragon and this claim provided, in each case, ample scope for negotiation with the papacy about specific posts. Yet the pragmatic power of the Spanish monarchs over the Church had always to face the basic fact that whatever gains they made would inevitably appear, in Rome, as concessions from the Apostolic See, however weak the pope's bargaining position may have been at the time. To counter papal claims, lawyers in the Spanish court, and notably Montalvo (see Chapter 2), followed the example of 'imperialist' predecessors all over Europe, in trawling through earlier legislation for evidence of monarchical primacy over the Church. Lay patronage, the power of non-clergy to make appointments to clerical posts, had a long history in medieval Europe and Ferdinand and Isabella were certainly not the only late medieval rulers anxious to maintain and even revive it. In these circumstances, Spanish bishops were often prepared to support their sovereigns against papal claims, although it would be simplistic to characterize such attitudes as 'nationalistic' in the modern sense. Nevertheless, the roots of later Habsburg and Bourbon 'regalism' were already in the ground.[34]

Similarly, ideas of reform that would be further developed in the sixteenth century drove much of Isabella and Ferdinand's activity in ecclesiastical matters, and herein lies a paradox. In Spain as elsewhere, the fifteenth-century Catholic Church possessed immense but unequally distributed wealth. Even among bishops, diocesans in poorer regions, such as Galicia, could only dream of the riches that came the way of archbishops of Toledo or Seville. Cathedral chapters might be wealthy but many were not and there was a rigid set of social and economic distinctions within the whole of the vast clerical body. Yet there was also ample awareness that, in many respects, things should not be like this. The quest for the 'primitive Church', the supposed apostolic and evangelical purity of the first century after Christ, touched the king and queen as much as any hermit or prophet and also affected some of the Crown's most senior ecclesiastical advisers. Such ideas lay behind royal efforts to raise the quality of the episcopate, but they also affected other Church institutions such as parish churches and monasteries and convents, these last to be powerhouses of prayer for the whole people of God, the Christian faithful. It should always be remembered, however, that the primary aim was to change the morality and customs, and hence, it was thought, the spiritual state of the entire population, including Jews and Muslims who should ultimately be baptized.

In Spain, as elsewhere in the western Church, the clerical 'Estate' had expanded, by the late fifteenth century, to include categories of people who would not be regarded as 'clergy' in later times. A minority of 'clerics' had been given the 'major orders' of deacon, priest or bishop, these being acquired cumulatively, but the clerical 'proletariat' was mainly to be found in the 'minor orders' of porter (or doorkeeper), sacristan, acolyte and sub-deacon. These lesser offices, which were nonetheless essential to the complete performance of Catholic liturgical worship, did not demand the same level of commitment and discipline as the higher orders, but their holders still enjoyed the protection of Church courts that, in Spain as elsewhere, were generally held to be much more lenient than their royal or seigniorial equivalents. The cutting of a man's hair in a 'tonsure' (*corona*) visibly demonstrated his clerical status and Isabella and Ferdinand were greatly preoccupied with the scandal caused by those, such as the minor clergy of cathedrals and other churches, as well as university students, who did not live up to their calling or keep their vows. The queen is recorded as attacking senior clergy, for example the diocesan administrator (*provisor*) of Cuenca, in 1503, for not sufficiently examining candidates for either minor or major orders. Like other frustrated rulers, elsewhere in Europe, she and her husband on occasions attempted to make examples of particularly gross offenders, by transferring to transfer their cases from Church to royal courts, but the legal basis for doing so was dubious and the effect was often to increase rather than reduce public scandal. More commonly, they worked through ecclesiastical assemblies, including that at Seville in 1478, asking that clergy should keep the tonsure and not attempt to disguise their clerical status. Another problem was the ordination of reluctant boys and the monarchs asked that those ordained under the age of the 14 should be vouched for by the sworn oath of their parents. At least some bishops began to implement the Seville measures in their diocesan synods but, much later, Ferdinand and Isabella still felt it necessary to seek papal authority, in the form of Alexander VI's bull *Romanum decet*, of 27 July 1493. During these years, Isabella regularly intervened in the enforcement of clerical discipline, sometimes goading diocesans into action. The conquest of Granada, as well as the colonization of the Canary Islands, provided further impetus for this longstanding policy.[35]

For many centuries, some Christians, both men and women, in Spain as elsewhere, had set themselves apart, often physically as well as spiritually, to lead a life of prayer, austerity and complete devotion to the worship of God. By the fifteenth century, however, the generosity of lay Christians, from kings to peasants, towards those who had come to be known specifically as the 'religious' had caused many monasteries, convents and even friaries that were supposed to live by begging to accumulate wealth and power. Yet their original spiritual function had not been forgotten and Isabella, in particular, sought to restore it to its former glory. Given the current focus on the religiosity of the two sovereigns it is inevitable that much of what follows will concern the various Franciscan orders, including the male friars ('First Order'), the nuns of St Clare ('Clarisas' or 'Second Order') and the lay Third Order, or 'Tertiaries'. Isabella and Ferdinand's activity in relation to religious orders took place in a context which has traditionally been seen as a conflict, in the fourteenth and fifteenth centuries, between 'conventual' and 'observant' forms of monastic life. These were international phenomena and, as the two terms appear so frequently in discussions of the activities of monks and friars in this period, particularly in the context of Spanish reforms, it is necessary first to consider their meanings and implications. The word 'conventual' has commonly been used to describe the rather lax form of observation of the 'rule' that governed the life of each order. The archetypical rule of western monasticism was that of St Benedict, dating from *c*.540 and still applicable in the late Middle Ages, in monastic houses of the Benedictine tradition. In the early thirteenth century, Francis and

Dominic were allowed, subject to papal examination, to produce new rules for their respective orders, while the Augustinian and Jeronymite friars (the latter a native Iberian order) were governed by medieval rules which were notionally ascribed to Saints Augustine and Jerome respectively. The slackening of discipline among monks and friars in the late Middle Ages has commonly been attributed to the effects of the social and economic crises of the mid-fourteenth century, which were connected, in Spain as elsewhere in Western Europe, with successive outbreaks of the bubonic plague, known as the 'Black Death'. As a reaction, partly to these social upheavals and partly to the splitting ('Great Schism') of the Roman Papacy into two, and briefly three, rival camps (1378–1415), a new 'Observant' movement developed in the religious orders, first in Italy and then elsewhere, including Spain. In each order, the main claim made by the 'Observants' was that they alone 'observed' their rule, in contrast to the laxer 'Conventuals' who, they claimed, had allowed corrupt religious and economic practices to creep into their community life and, in many cases, dominate it. Ferdinand and Isabella inherited the pro-Observant bias shared by many fifteenth-century rulers, but were to develop it with particular force, as an instrument of state policy.[36]

At the Assembly of Seville in 1478, with war in progress and the spotlight on either potentially or actually disloyal bishops and parish clergy, it was natural that the king and queen would not pay much attention to the more quiescent religious orders and the subject was not mentioned either in their early embassies to Rome. Nevertheless, the religious had not been forgotten and it was hardly likely that Isabella and Ferdinand would pay less attention to them than their two immediate Castilian predecessors had done. In fact, they gave their full moral backing to the vicar-general of the Dominicans in Spain, Fray Alfonso de San Cebrián, and supported similar efforts among the Franciscans, and especially the Clarisas, whose official visitors were in dispute over how to proceed. At their request, Sixtus IV introduced as arbitrator the bishop of Segovia, Juan Arias Dávila. Once the war with Portugal was over, however, the monarchs were able to turn more of their attention to the matter. Early in 1479 Isabella sent an embassy to Rome, headed by the bishop of Tuy, Diego de Muros, himself a Mercedarian friar and one of its instructions was to ask the pope for an unusual type of bull, which would authorize them, rather than Church officials, to reform all the religious houses in their kingdoms. The monarchs would act as 'royal vicars' for the pope and, although Sixtus did not oblige, such a concession was eventually obtained from Alexander VI. The issue was not as simple as the king and queen sometimes made it appear. 'Observance', as opposed to 'Conventualism', was not only about the issue of faithfulness to a rule of religion, but also concerned the role of academic work in the life of friars. Thus Observants tended to oppose the involvement of friars in university life, this issue even affecting the Dominican order, which had had an intellectual preoccupation ever since its foundation in the early thirteenth century.

Ferdinand and Isabella petitioned successive popes that they should be allowed to appoint the churchmen who, as visitors, would pursue the reform of the religious orders within their territories. They also asked that abbots, priors and other heads of religious houses should be elected directly by the communities concerned and not appointed by collation from Rome, thus keeping the relevant revenues within Spain, rather than allowing them to the Curia. Eventually, on 11 December 1487, Innocent made a partial concession, allowing a committee of Castilian bishops to take charge of the reform of Benedictine and Cistercian monasteries, and chapters of Augustinian canons, in Galicia. This did not, of course, satisfy the king and queen, who pursued the matter further, until Alexander VI took a more sympathetic attitude. Inevitably, progress was slow in the meantime and the main successes took place after 1500. In any case, there was little sign of warmth in relations between the Borja family and the Spanish rulers, but, in return for concessions to his son Cesare in the family fief of Valencia, Alexander issued a series of bulls, between 1493 and 1499, which opened the way for them and their henchmen, in particular Cardinal Cisneros, to pursue long-desired reforms.[37] What, though, did 'reform' really mean in this context?

The institutional aims of the 'Catholic monarchs', in the reform of religious houses as of other ecclesiastical institutions, seemed clear enough. The Observant version of the religious life was by definition regarded as superior to any other and the best way of introducing and enforcing it seemed to be to increase royal control, both economic and disciplinary, over Castilian and Aragonese monasteries, friaries and convents, thus reducing opportunities for papal intervention, by means of the heads of the religious orders. The nature and content of the Christianity practised, or at least aimed at, by the monarchs is less easy to characterize at the internal level. The records of Ferdinand and Isabella's chapels (see Chapter 6) provide ample evidence of their concern for a rich and complete 'observance', to use their preferred word, of the forms of Catholic devotion. Their reform programme seems to have been aimed at a 'restoration' of its completeness, within entirely traditional institutional frameworks, and their most serious quarrels with popes seem never to have gone quite as far as a serious intent to sever relations. The most complete version of their ideas, however, would appear in answer to the opportunities afforded by the former emirate of Granada, after 1492, and later in the New World.

Islam

When Bishop Fray Hernando de Talavera raised the banner of the Cross on the battlements of the Alhambra in Granada, on 2 January 1492, he signalled the determination of his sovereigns to establish the Catholic Christian faith in the newly conquered emirate (see Chapter 3). Thus the terms of the final surrender agreement, made with Boabdil in November 1491, had inevitably to co-exist with the Christian fervour which had been shown throughout the war and with the daily confrontation between militant conquerors and sullen conquered. Also, throughout the war, the monarchs had shown a preoccupation with those of their Christian subjects who had, for whatever reason, converted to Islam in Nasrid territory. Wartime agreements stated, moreover, that such individuals should not be forced to re-convert to Christianity.[38] It remained to be seen what would happen to these generous policies in practice, with the Castilians in largely undisputed control.

The man responsible for re-introducing the Catholic Church to the 'kingdom' (reino) of Granada was Fray Hernando de Talavera, whose record as a spiritual leader and counsellor of the queen has already been noted. Work to introduce a full Church structure, alongside what remained of the fabric of an Islamic society, began immediately after the conquest and was to remain an important personal commitment and preoccupation of the king and queen and their administration. Newly conquered Granada was to be a laboratory for the development of what would become a 'national' Church in Spain, albeit still under nominal papal control. Work to set up such a structure in the emirate had begun during the war. As early as 1485 Ferdinand and Isabella had approached Pope Innocent VIII, first through their ambassador in Rome, Francisco de Rojas, and then through the future captain-general in Granada, the count of Tendilla. In his bull, Dum ad illam, dated 4 August 1486, Innocent delegated to the archbishop of Toledo, Cardinal Pedro González de Mendoza, and the archbishop of Seville, Diego Hurtado de Mendoza, the power to establish in the newly conquered territory any ecclesiastical benefices that they thought necessary, funding them from the tithes that would be paid by the relevant Christian inhabitants and also, because initially these were likely to be few, from any goods granted to them by the Crown. Quite soon after the conquest, on 21 May 1492, this bull was finally put into effect, when Cardinal Mendoza established senior offices (*dignidades*), canonries and other benefices in the new cathedrals of Granada, Málaga, Guadix and Almería and the collegiate churches of Santa Fe and Baza. The new parish structure for the kingdom was not to be put into legal effect until 15 October 1501. On 13 December 1486, Innocent VIII had issued a second bull, *Orthodoxae fidei*, which made various important concessions to the Castilian rulers, giving them effective control of patronage in cathedrals, collegiate churches and the more prosperous monasteries (with rents worth 200 gold florins or more) in Granada. This bull came into effect once Boabdil surrendered and the boundaries of the dioceses of Granada, Málaga, Guadix and Almería were fixed by Alexander VI in a further bull dated 11 April 1493. In order to fund the new ecclesiastical establishment, and to ensure royal control over it, the monarchs, and particularly Isabella, in support of her former confessor, Talavera, were generous with personal gifts of liturgical objects to Granadan churches, as well as allocating captured lands and goods as endowments. The outcome of all this activity was to depend, however, on whether the new Christian population (see Chapter 5) would be able to co-exist with the Muslim majority.[39]

When they took control of the entire territory, the monarchs and leading churchmen already had a religious strategy, which had evolved during the earlier stages of the war. This was, in the long run, conversion of the Muslims, although supposedly without coercion. On a personal level, the royal accounts for this period show that Isabella made dozens of payments to Granadans who did convert.[40] The Church, by the same token, for some years before 1492, was already selecting the most able (male) converts to act as a missionary advance guard among their former co-religionists. As he travelled through wartime Granada, in the royal entourage, Talavera was constantly on the lookout for such people and he is said personally to have converted over 100 people. Once he was installed as archbishop in the city itself, the Jeronymite friar seems to have avoided forcibly converting Muslims but he nonetheless undertook from the start an active evangelistic campaign in his archdiocese. In accordance with the spiritual preoccupation of so many churchmen in this period, he seems to have regarded his appointment to this new see as a unique chance to build a 'primitive' Church, on the lines described by the New Testament – unique because Granada had previously been a confessional Islamic state and was therefore, unlike the rest of Europe, effectively 'virgin' territory for Christian mission.

The traditional view of Talavera's work in Granada, between 1492 and his death, in 1507, when he was a suspected Judaizer in the eyes of the

Inquisition (see first section), is that he was not only holy but gentle, a model prelate, but also respectful of Muslims. Talavera certainly built at least 100 parish churches in his diocese, to add to the mosques which had been taken over in 1492, as well as male and female Franciscan convents. He personally funded one each of these in Granada, to be burial places for his parents. Fray Hernando was keen to bring more people into church and is said to have tried to popularize the normally clerical office of matins by bringing it forward from the customary monastic hour of midnight or later and turning it into an evening service, with Spanish devotional songs as commentaries on the scriptural readings. He also anticipated a measure later implemented by the Council of Trent, when he established a diocesan seminary in Granada to train priests for the pastoral care of the new Christian population and for mission to Muslims. The seminary was intended to be the equivalent of the universities, teaching arts courses such as grammar and logic, as well as theology. Talavera required all his ordinands to learn by heart Paul's epistles to Titus and Timothy, which are full of instruction to pastors. Mission to Muslims was always his concern and he clearly understood that an ability to use Arabic was essential to this task. He made limited progress himself, but his main aim was to nurture an Arabic-speaking clergy, preferably including enthusiastic native converts. The archbishop set up a refuge for orphaned and unwanted children, whom he is said to have 'indoctrinated' personally and to have opened two houses of women converts, one for those who intended to become nuns and the other to provide both food and work for the rest. His servants were sent out to bring in vagabond children (no doubt a common feature in the post-war period) so that they could be cared for and instructed. In his mind, knowledge of Christianity had precedence over any other form of education and he is even said to have locked converts out of their houses from Palm Sunday to Easter, so that they would attend the Holy Week liturgy.[41] It remained to be seen how effective these techniques would be.

Up to 1499, Talavera's approach seems to have prevailed, but from the end of that year until the spring of 1501, the initiative seems to have moved to the archbishop of Toledo, Cardinal Cisneros. This phase was followed by a third, in which the Crown took the lead. Most of Talavera's converts seem to have come from Boabdil's wartime stronghold, the Albaicín, and at least some of them were apparently genuine. Being of Jewish *converso* stock himself, the friar was evidently sensitive to the nuances of a transfer from one 'faith of Abraham' to another. Writing to 'his' converts in the Albaicín, the archbishop speaks of a once-for-all and life-transforming turning to Christ. He urges his new flock to abandon and forget completely everything to do with the 'Mohammedan sect': prayers, fasts, festivals, rites associated with birth, marriage and death, ritual bathing. Male converts, together with their whole households, should learn the rudiments of Christianity that were required of all Catholic believers at the time: how to cross themselves, how to behave correctly in church, about the veneration of the Cross, the reverencing of images (such a culture shock for ex-Muslims), as well as the recitation of the Lord's Prayer, the Ave Maria and the Creed (usually the Apostles'). New-born children from convert (*morisco*) families should be baptized within eight days of birth, marriages among these families should always take place in church and those who died should always be buried in con-secrated Christian cemeteries. Not only should they fulfil the normal Catholic obligation of attending mass on Sundays and major festivals, but the whole family should attend vespers in their parish churches, or the cathedral, as well. During the week, the men should go to church each day to pray and take holy water to bless them in their work. The *moriscos* should organize themselves into confraternities for mutual support in life and death. This suggestion appears to indicate that Talavera, with his *converso* background, recognized the difficulties the converts would experi-ence in becoming integrated into mainstream church life, although, in the case of Granada, Old Christian structures were brand new as well.

Morisco children should be sent to classes held in the churches, to learn to read and sing, or at least to recite, the major prayers. One or two hospitals should be set up for the converts, to care for the sick and aged. Finally, the archbishop turned to social and cultural matters, stating that the Old Christian population would not believe in the true conversion of these former Muslims if they did not adopt Spanish Christian dress and dietary habits. They should also abandon Arabic completely and effect-ively undergo a complete change of identity, going far beyond doctrinal assent to Christianity. This memorandum was printed and distributed to all the convert families, but it also inevitably put pressure on the unconverted Muslim population. Such prescriptions clearly threatened the long-term survival of Islamic identity in Granada, whatever may have been said in the *capitulaciones*. Another obvious problem, which had occurred up to 1492 in the Jewish context, was that *moriscos* continued to live among their *mudéjar* relatives and neighbours, who were continu-ing, as far as possible, to practise Islam. It was at this point that Cardinal Cisneros intervened.

In the summer of 1499 the king and queen returned to Granada for the first time since the conquest. Although their goal was still to extend the war against Islam into North Africa and Melilla had been captured, affairs elsewhere in Europe, notably in Italy, had diverted them (see Chapter 5). It seems that, when they saw the situation for themselves, Ferdinand and Isabella felt that progress in conversion was much too slow and hence called in the archbishop of Toledo, who was now the queen's confessor and one of their closest spiritual advisers. It has generally been suggested that Cisneros' arrival marginalized Talavera and led to the introduction of far more drastic and brutal missionary techniques. Yet the Jeronymite recorded his welcome to his Franciscan brother and it has been seen that the undermining of the cultural, as well as the religious identity of Granada's Muslims was already in progress before the cardinal's arrival. As for the monarchs' responsibility in this matter, Cisneros states categorically, in a letter to his Toledan chapter, dated 4 January 1500, that:

[T]heir Highnesses, like most Christian princes, have so much taken [the conversion of the Moors] to heart that we hope the resulting fruit will be everything that our Christian religion desires.[42]

The inquisitors had entrusted Cisneros with the task of reconciling the renegades (*elches*), baptized Christians who had converted to Islam, and the archbishop acted with vigour, pressurizing the adults and often secretly baptizing their children. His campaign lasted for some months until, on 18 December 1499, he sent a constable into the Albaicín to arrest an *elche*, a riot broke out and the law officer was killed. The streets were barricaded and hidden weapons were produced to start a full rebellion. The consequences were drastic, since not only did the count of Tendilla, as captain-general, quickly restore order, but Cisneros initiated a mass conversion campaign, claiming to have achieved 3000 baptisms on 23 December, ready for Christmas, including those of two muezzins, whom he planned to send back to Toledo as trophies. By January 1500, the conversion campaign appeared, at least to its author, to be going extremely well, in a festive spirit and much to the delight of the king and queen, and to be spreading to the rural districts outside Granada, but violent resistance was already developing, to follow on from the efforts of the pioneers of the Albaicín. According to Cisneros, the revolt in Guájar, near Granada itself, was quickly suppressed, with 3000 prisoners requesting baptism and much booty taken, but things were not to be so easy in the austere mountains of the Alpujarras. When rebellion broke out there, Ferdinand and Isabella, who were wintering in Seville, offered an amnesty to any Muslims who agreed to convert, but it was decided that the king needed to take charge himself. He came to Granada, called for reinforcements, and began negotiations with the rebels, Cisneros commenting that they should have been imprisoned, in which case they would be better Christians. In the event the rebellion was crushed by a two-pronged assault, by the count of Tendilla and Gonzalo Fernández de Córdoba from Granada and Pedro Fajardo from Almería, and the king went back to Seville in March.

The revolts that began in the Albaicín, in December 1499, appear to have been precipitated by the Inquisition's aggressive pursuit of *elches*, who as apostates were its legitimate targets. The whole situation of the former emirate was problematic and a particular difficulty was created for the queen by the fact that her two archiepiscopal confessors were, at least to some extent, at loggerheads. Ferdinand tried to solve the Granadan problem by setting up a committee, which included Talavera, Cisneros, the count of Tendilla, Gonzalo Fernández de Córdoba, the *corregidor* of Granada (Andrés Calderón) and two others. Cisneros was apparently over-ruled and a non-aggressive conversion campaign was approved, Isabella summoning him to Seville and leaving Talavera in sole charge of ecclesiastical matters in Granada. The elderly Jeronymite was evidently tired, however, and, towards the end of July 1500, the court returned to Granada. After this, effective control over the policy towards Muslims and *moriscos* seems to have passed to the sovereigns themselves. At this point, more severe measures began to be taken, very much on the lines of Cisneros' earlier efforts. Further clergy were summoned from all over Castile, to provide better Christian instruction for converts, but the arrival of the monarchs certainly did not produce peace. On the contrary, in the early months of 1501, further revolts broke out in Ronda and the Sierra Bermeja and once again Ferdinand was forced to intervene personally. Meanwhile the queen remained in Granada, supervising the conversion effort and her writings at this time indicate that she had arrived at a 'solution' for unrepentant Muslims, which had been imposed ten years earlier on Jews – conversion or expulsion.

The first public sign of the new policy was an order to her whole realm, issued by Isabella from Granada on 12 October 1501, that all copies of the Koran in the former emirate, as well as some other Muslim religious books, should be assembled and burnt. The argument of the document was the same as that used in the case of Jews, ten years earlier. *Moriscos* would not become genuine and faithful Christians as long as they lived among unconverted Muslims. Also, if the sacred texts of Islam were removed, the religion would die out. The relevant books were to be handed over to the authorities within 30 days. This destructive order, which completely undermined the relevant provisions of the 1491

Granadan *capitulaciones*, was followed by a further pragmatic, issued in Seville on 12 February 1502. This stated that, in order to protect the faith of the *moriscos*, all Muslims in the Crown of Castile (but not the Crown of Aragon) aged 14 or more if male and 12 or more if female, except for prisoners, whether born in Castile or elsewhere, should either convert to Christianity or leave by the end of April that year. As in the case of the Jews ten years earlier, departing Muslims were allowed to take goods that they could carry, but not gold, silver, potential war materials or other 'forbidden goods' (*cosas vedadas*). The restrictions on Muslims were much tighter than those that had been applied to Jews. Perversely, departures could only take place through the ports of Vizcaya, in the Basque country, where royal customs officials would be on duty to deal with the exiles. This would, of course, force those who came from Andalusia and Granada to traverse the whole length of Spain. Established Muslim communities in many Castilian towns would, for the first time for centuries, be forced either to convert or to leave their familiar surroundings. There were also restrictions on the refugees' places of destination. Those expelled should not go to obviously Muslim countries such as the kingdoms of North Africa or the Ottoman empire and neither should they move into the neighbouring kingdoms of Navarre and Aragon. This appeared to leave the lands of the sultan of Egypt, which were specified, and Portugal, which was not. After the end of April 1502, no Castilian subject was to harbour an unbaptized Muslim, on pain of the loss of his goods.

As in the case of the edicts for the expulsion of Jews from Castile and Aragon, no mention was made in the document of conversion, although this was surely the main aim, to judge by a further pragmatic, issued in Toledo on 17 September 1502, the main provision of which was that converted Muslims (*moriscos*) should not leave the kingdom within the next two years. Evidently, Muslims in Castile and León, as well as Andalusia, had been converting in numbers, but some were apparently becoming disillusioned with their new religion and were attempting to leave for a country where they could return to Islam. Proclaiming her concern for their souls' welfare, Isabella announced that *moriscos* who lived elsewhere in her realm were not to be allowed to travel to the kingdom of Granada, although they were to be permitted limited, and individually licensed, business trips to Aragon and Portugal. She did not, in this pragmatic, enter into the questions of the mechanisms or sincerity of these conversions.[43] These problems were soon to surface in Spain as a whole and eventually to lead to the expulsion of all *moriscos* in the early seventeenth century.

Notes

1 Ortiz de Zúñiga, D. [1667, 1796] (1988) *Anales eclesiásticos y seculares de la muy noble y muy leal ciudad de Sevilla*, Ediciones Guadalquivir, pp. 103–4.

2 Martínez Díez, G. (1998) *Bulario de la Inquisición española*, Editorial Complutense, pp. 74–9.

3 Valdeón Baruque, J. (1994) 'Los orígenes de la Inquisición en Castilla' in *Inquisición y conversos. III curso de cultura hispano-judía y sefardí (Toledo, 6–9 septiembre, 1993)*, Cromograf, pp. 36–7.

4 Espina, A. de (*c.*1459) *Fortalitium Fidei*, cited in Azcona, T. de (1993) p. 489.

5 Ibid. pp. 494–5; Edwards, J. (1999) 'The "massacre" of Jewish Christians in Córdoba, 1473–1474' in Levene, M. and Roberts, P. (eds) *The Massacre in History*, Berghahn Books, pp. 55–68.

6 Azcona, T. de (1993) pp. 495–6.

7 Suárez Fernández, L. (1996) 'El máximo religioso' in *Fernando II de Aragón, el rey católico*, Institución Fernando el Católico, p. 47.

8 Gil, J. (2000–1) *Los conversos y la Inquisición sevillana*, Universidad de Sevilla and Fundación El Monte, vol. 1, p. 42.

9 Talavera, F. de (1961) *Católica impugnación*, Flors, p. 69 (letter to Ferdinand and Isabella).

10 Ibid. pp. 186, 218, 222; Gil, J. (2000) vol. 1, p. 46.

11 Huerga Criado, P. (1996) 'Fernando II y Torquemada' in *Fernando II de Aragón, el rey católico*, pp. 66–7; Azcona, T. de (1993) pp. 499–500.

12 Gil, J. (2000) pp. 45–9.

13 Martínez Díez, G. (1998) pp. 80–3.

14 Ibid. pp. 84–7.

15 Edwards, J. (1999) *The Spanish Inquisition*, Tempus, pp. 58–9.

16 Edwards, J. [1984] (1996) 'Religion, constitutionalism and the Inquisition in Teruel, 1484–5' reprinted in *Religion and Society in Spain, c.1492*, Variorum, no. XIII.

17 Martínez Díez, G. (1998) pp. 168–71.

18 Netanyahu, B. [1995] (2001) *The Origins of the Inquisition in fifteenth century Spain*, New York Review Books.

19 Po-Chiah Hsia, R. (1992) *Trent 1475. Stories of a ritual murder trial*, Yale University Press; Rubin, M. (1999) *Gentile tales. The narrative assault on Late Medieval Jews*, Yale University Press.

20 Fita, F. (1887) 'La verdad sobre el martirio del Santo Niño de La Guardia, o sea el proceso y quema (16 noviembre 1491) del judío Juce Franco en Ávila', *Boletín de la Real Academia de la Historia*, vol. 11, pp. 7–134; Edwards, J. (1999) 'Ritual murder in the Siglo de Oro: Lope de Vega's *El niño inocente de La Guardia*' in *The Proceedings of the Tenth British Conference on Judeo-Spanish studies, 29 June–1 July 1997*, Benaim, A. (ed.), Queen Mary and Westfield College, Department of Spanish, pp. 73–88.

21 Rábade Obrado, M. del P. (1993) *Una elite de poder en la Corte de los Reyes Católicos. Los judeoconversos*, Sigilo.

22 Suárez Fernández, L. (1964) *Documentos acerca de la expulsión de los judíos de España*, Universidad de Valladolid.

23 For an Aragonese case, see Edwards, J. [1984] (1996) 'Jewish testimony to the Spanish Inquisition: Teruel, 1484–7' in Edwards, J. *Religion and Society in Spain, c.1492*, Variorum, no. XII.

24 Azcona, T. de (1993) pp. 774–807.

25 Beinart, H. (1986) 'La Inquisición española y la expulsión de los judíos de Andalucía' in Beinart, H., *Andalucía y sus judíos*, Monte de Piedad y Caja de Ahorros de Córdoba, pp. 49–81.

26 Edwards, J. (1994) *The Jews in Western Europe, 1400–1600*, Manchester University Press, pp. 49–52 (translation of the Castilian edict).

27 Raphael, D. (1992) *The Expulsion 1492 Chronicles. An anthology of medieval chronicles relating to the expulsion of the Jews from Spain and Portugal*, Carmi House Press.

28 Edwards, J. (1994) pp. 52–3.

29 Edwards, J. (1996) 'Jews and *conversos* in the region of Soria and Almazán: departures and returns' in Edwards, J. *Religion and Society in Spain, c.1492*, Variorum, no. VI; Edwards, J. (1999) *The Spanish Inquisition*, pp. 85–90.

30 Azcona, T. de (1993) pp. 301–2.

31 Ibid. p. 546.

32 Ibid. pp. 556–66.

33 Ibid. p. 577.

34 See Hermann, C. (1988) *L'Église d'Espagne sous le patronage royale (1476–1834)*, Casa de Velázquez.

35 Azcona, T. de (1993) pp. 589–608.

36 Ibid. pp. 711–14.

37 Azcona, T. de (1993) pp. 714–70.

38 Ladero Quesada, M. A. (2002) *Las guerras de Granada en el siglo XV*, Ariel, p. 174.

39 Azcona, T. de (1993) pp. 680–6.

40 Torre, A. de la and Torre, E. A. de la (eds) (1955–6) *Cuentas de Gonzalo de Baeza, tesorero de Isabel*, CSIC, vol. 1, p. 17, vol. 2, pp. 11–12.

41 Azcona, T. de (1958) 'El tipo ideal de obispo en la Iglesia española antes de la rebelión luterana', *Hispania Sacra*, vol. 11, pp. 21–64; Meseguer Fernández, J. (1980) 'Fernando de Talavera, Cisneros y la Inquisición' in Pérez Villanueva, J. (ed.) *La Inquisición española. Nueva visión, nuevos horizontes*, Siglo XXI de España, pp. 371–400.

42 Biblioteca Nacional Madrid MS 13020 fol. 110, cited in Azcona, T. de (1993) p. 691.

43 Harvey, L. P. (1990) pp. 324–39; Azcona, T. de (1993) pp. 680–702; García Oro, J. (2002) *Cisneros, el cardenal de España*, Ariel, pp. 111–23.

Chapter 5

Diplomacy and Expansion

Conquest

Whatever ventures of conquest were to be undertaken by Ferdinand and Isabella outside their own kingdoms, after 1492, would inevitably have before them the precedent of their successful war in Granada. As was noted earlier, it was not entirely clear, in the earlier campaigns, that the aim had become conquest, rather than the traditional one of raiding Muslim territory (*talas*) and demanding cash tribute (*parias*). When the war began, no new places had been permanently captured by the Castilians since Jimena in 1456, but although Isabella's half-brother Henry had largely restricted himself to the *tala* approach, she and her husband did have before them the Castilian and Aragonese precedents of the thirteenth century.[1] Ferdinand and Isabella's strategy for the conquest, and where appropriate the settlement, of the Nasrid emirate gradually emerged in the agreements (*capitulaciones*), between Christians and Muslims, which normally ended each campaigning season. Such documents existed in various types, the first being, as Ladero puts it, 'their very absence' (*su misma ausencia*).[2] In such cases, towns and castles surrendered unconditionally, which meant that all the inhabitants went into captivity and all their property was confiscated. This was simply a development of the traditional practice, on both sides, of taking and ransoming prisoners and it reached its most extreme manifestation in the aftermath of the siege of Málaga, in which 11,000 Muslims were seized (see Chapter 3).

Normally, however, some form of agreement was reached in which, in return for surrender, the existing inhabitants would have their lives guaranteed, as well as their property, which they could take with them if they were forced to leave. If they were allowed to remain, they would be guaranteed religious freedom and allowed to retain their existing social organization, their community tax regime, based on Islamic principles, and the ability to carry on their previous work, with proper remuneration.

The generosity of the terms offered by Castile in such agreements varied as the war went on. In the earlier phase of Christian successes, from 1484 to 1487, the Muslim population normally had to leave captured towns, if it had put up armed resistance, taking whatever goods people could carry with them. They might be allowed by the Crown to emigrate to other parts of Castile, to North Africa or even, as in the case of the inhabitants of fortresses in the Vega of Granada in 1486, to the unconquered city of Granada itself. Initially, the wealthy and powerful among the Muslim population were encouraged to emigrate to North Africa, but later they had to pay a toll and give a proportion of their property for the privilege. Up to 1487 the new Castilian regime adopted the policy of re-employing existing local officials, in towns that had freely surrendered, and allowing them to retain their property. Pacts made in this period normally required the immediate and unconditional release of all Christian prisoners.

More is known about the surrender agreements made in 1488–9. These allowed Muslim inhabitants to retain their freedom and property, even in cases where they had put up armed resistance, but the reason was probably that the places in question were destined, under treaty, for Boabdil's lordship. When there was an armed conspiracy in the summer of 1490, in various towns including Baza, Guadix and Almería, the Muslim inhabitants lost their property and were expelled. In normal conditions, however, the agreements made in 1488–9 allowed conquered Muslims to retain their horses and even light weapons and offered partial or full compensation to the former owners of liberated Christian captives. Christians, in turn, were compensated for their Muslim prisoners, who, if born in the emirate, were allowed to return home.

The November 1491 *capitulaciones*, like their predecessors, offered honourable treatment to the existing Muslim authorities. Throughout the emirate, where communities continued to exist and had not emigrated, religious leaders (*alfaquíes*) and judicial authorities remained in place, interpreting the Islamic faith and law (*sharia*). Constables (*alguaciles*) and local municipal authorities also remained in office and even military chiefs (*arraeces*) and governors (*alcaides*) of fortresses were paid to continue, sometimes in cash but more commonly in raw and woven cloth, which better retained their value during the high inflation of the immediate post-war period. During the war, the leaders too, including Al Zagal and Yahya al-Nayyar, had been allowed to retain their former dignity and standard of living and the same applied to Boabdil and his henchmen in 1491–2. It is impossible to calculate exactly how many Granadan leaders emigrated under the terms of such agreements, but over all, by 1502, it is likely that the emirate had lost about half its former population, leaving 120,000 or so. It is known that about 10,000 people left the city of Granada itself in 1492–3.

The failure on the Castilian side to observe the terms of the 1491 *capitulaciones* has already been noted (see Chapter 3). The same happened with other aspects of the agreement and it is hard to avoid the conclusion that Isabella and Ferdinand must bear much of the responsibility for this. In general, the events of 1499–1502 replaced a climate of at least limited co-existence (*convivencia*) with one of confrontation, which inevitably affected the Islamic religious, social and cultural structures that had survived the military conquest. For the Castilian Crown, the pacts (*capitulaciones*) were not rights but privileges, which were graciously but only provisionally granted by sovereigns to their legal subjects. These agreements did not have the status of international treaties, made with other European powers, because the agenda of the 'Reconquest' dictated that Isabella and Ferdinand, in conquering the Nasrid emirate, were doing no more than coming into their own inheritance. In their view, they were not fighting a war against another sovereign power, but putting down a rebellion in their 'own back garden'. This perception does much to explain the outcome of events in Granada between 1492 and 1516. In any case, furthermore, the violent counterattacks of some Muslims would render the paper agreements largely irrelevant. Technically speaking, the rulers undertook, by 'their faith and royal word' (*su fe y palabra real*) to observe the terms of the agreements that had been arrived at, but the documents concerned were 'royal letters of privilege' (*cartas reales de privilegio*), which were always controlled by the high Trastamaran doctrine of royal 'absolutism' (see Chapter 1), and simply gave legal force to agreements made elsewhere. Historians have debated whether the Granada *capitulaciones*, and especially that of November 1491, were primarily contractual pacts of a 'feudal' kind or rather the absolutist precursors of a 'modern' Spanish state. What is undoubted, however, is that, in January 1492, the former subjects of the emir of Granada became Ferdinand and Isabella's 'vassals and subjects and natives and under their protection and security and royal defence' (*vasallos y súbditos y naturales, e so su amparo e seguro e defendimiento real*). This legal situation added to the difficulties that were already being suffered by the conquered Granadans and made it so unlikely as to be virtually impossible that the terms of the surrender would be observed over any period of time.

Sometimes at least the superficial appearance of self-determination might be allowed. When, in February 1492, the Muslims surrendered most of their weapons, they did so supposedly 'voluntarily', but the threat of starvation was the determining factor. Later, in 1498, Muslims 'agreed' to evacuate the central quarter (*medina*) of Granada and retire to suburbs such as the Albaicín and Antequeruela, but a year later an order was issued (no pact here) that Muslims should no longer be allowed to live in the city at all. During this period, a puppet Muslim town council (*concejo*) remained in place, but its position became increasingly uncomfortable and untenable as the political and military situation deteriorated. Even in cases where Muslims were allowed by agreement to retain their property, this concession might be turned into another form of subjection. In the Serranía de Ronda, for example, the relevant *capitulación* required all Muslims to live in their official places of residence and nowhere else, effectively like serfs in Christian law. More significantly, in the Vega of Granada, Muslims were allowed to dispose of their properties, but the purpose of this measure was clearly to enable a new Christian population from north of the border to settle there. Conquered Muslims might also be subjected to extraordinary demands for taxation, for example in 1495–7 and again in 1499. Such demands were, of course, made of Castilians in other regions, but not only were the Muslim Granadans royal vassals, but they had no buffer to protect them, in the form of a local municipal council, which in Castile would often be dominated by powerful members of the aristocracy (see Chapter 2). After the uprisings of 1499, taxation demands on the Muslim population increased steadily. In addition, on 31 October 1499, a new royal edict was issued concerning inheritance law. According to the 1491 *capitulaciones*, inheritance among those who remained Muslim was to continue under Islamic law, but a problem arose with those who had become Christians, when a transaction involved one person of each religion. The sovereigns hereby ordered the judges in their kingdoms to deal with such cases under Christian law. The same measure removed an anomaly of the 1491 agreement, by which Muslims who had been imprisoned in Christian territory, during the war, might now return freely to Granada. Confusion had been caused by the fact that some of them had meanwhile converted to Christianity and thus rendered their legal status uncertain. The October 1499 document offered these individuals the same 'right of return' as their Muslim fellow Granadans.[3]

The other main pressure felt by the Muslim population of Granada in these years was the influx of immigrants and settlers from Christian territories. It is estimated that between 35,000 and 40,000 people, often in family units, moved into the emirate to settle during the years 1485–98. The majority of them were Andalusians, the next largest contingent coming from Old Castile and León, followed by those from New Castile and Extremadura, as well as Murcians and Valencians in the eastern territories and some Basques on the coast. It was royal policy to exclude from this opportunity all those who were not already regarded as solid citizens, with established families and property in their regions of origin. In accordance with earlier practice, in Spain and elsewhere in Christian Europe, suitable 'citizens' (*vecinos*) were offered tax concessions as an incentive to displace themselves and their families into what was, especially in the early years after the conquest, an unstable society full of rebellion and resentment. However, as well as encouraging archetypal 'settlers', Isabella and Ferdinand's government did not resist the temptation to make large grants of lands and jurisdiction to absentee landlords, in the form of wealthy and powerful individuals and institutions, the latter both secular and ecclesiastical. A case in point is that of the nobility of Córdoba and its region, many of whom had fought bravely in the campaigns and whose capital city had been the main rear base for the war. The senior Cordoban magnate, Don Alonso de Aguilar, who was to perish during the rebellion in the Sierra Bermeja in 1501, received the lordship of Almena and El Cerro; the count of Cabra, head of the second branch of the Fernández de Córdoba family, who had been active in the battle of Lucena in 1483, was granted jurisdiction over Canillas de Aceituna, Archez and Corumbela; while the *alcaide de los donceles*, who was also responsible for the capture of Boabdil in that action, received Sedella and Comares, the latter as a marquisate in honour of his particular achievement in netting Castile's main ally for the rest of the war. As a general rule, such important grants of Granadan lands and jurisdiction were made to existing members of the middle or upper nobility, thus serving to confirm the status of those who were already the leaders of local society in Andalusia, as well as that of the most powerful families elsewhere in the Castilian realm.[4] The settlers, along with the existing Muslim population, were placed under the new administrative hierarchy, headed by Iñigo López de Mendoza, count of Tendilla, as captain-general. It would be many years before Castile would see a return on its massive investment in the war and conquest.[5]

Diplomacy

In political terms, however, Ferdinand and Isabella tried to exploit their victory in Granada by returning to earlier agendas in Europe. It is sometimes forgotten that the 'superpower' of fifteenth-century Europe was

France. Although the French Crown, having finally expelled the English in 1453, did not control all the territories which were subsequently to be included in that kingdom, notably Savoy and the Rhineland, its king ruled over approximately three times as many people as his married neighbours to the south. The Trastamaran dynasty, from which both Isabella and her husband were descended, owed virtually everything to French support of Count Henry's seizure of the Castilian throne in 1369. Yet Ferdinand, as king of Aragon, inherited a very much less positive attitude towards the northern neighbour, which had expelled his predecessors from their hereditary lands in Languedoc, notably Montpellier. During the reign of his father, John II, the main bones of contention were the counties of Cerdanya and Rosselló and Ferdinand had early experience of action in this conflict, at the siege of Perpinyán (Perpignan) in June 1473. The immediate context of this conflict was a dispute between Louis XI and John II of Aragon which had lasted more than a decade and also involved the politics of Catalonia. During the successive years of war, both Louis XI and Henry IV of Castile intervened in Catalonia, with the intention of annexing the principality to their respective kingdoms, so that, as Ferdinand grew up, he found himself in the paradoxical position, as a Trastamaran, of pursuing a largely, although never wholly, anti-French policy. The young prince's intervention to assist his father at Perpignan, in April 1473, followed John II's exploitation of Louis's involvement in other areas of policy to re-enter the city, on 1 February 1473. The French king was infuriated by this violation of the treaty of Bayonne, hence the subsequent siege, but Burgundian intervention at home, together with Prince Ferdinand's reinforcements, enabled his father to save the situation. This was at a heavy price, however, as, in the peace treaty of July 1473, the French side demanded immediate payment, in recompense, of 300,000 *écus*, not the 200,000 stipulated in the 1462 treaty. In March 1475, Ferdinand, now titular king of Castile but not yet ruler of the Crown of Aragon, promised the Catalans that he would avenge them against the French, but two decades were to pass before he would be able to do so. In the meantime, he began to revive his father's anti-French coalition, persuading his wife to allow Castile to join it, despite her kingdom's longstanding alliance with the northern neighbour. The consequences of this change would take some time to unfold. In the meantime, in 1476, French troops continued to raid Catalonia, reaching Girona. John II made a truce with France in 1477 and, in the following year, as it were through gritted teeth, Ferdinand and Isabella felt constrained, by their troubles in Castile, to renew their own formal alliance with Louis XI.

Thus, when John II died, on 19 January 1479, there seemed to be no prospect of retrieving Rosselló and Cerdanya from French rule, while internal conflict continued to fester in Catalonia. For the first few years of Isabella's reign in Castile, Ferdinand was forced to devote himself to that kingdom's affairs and it was not until 1483, when the Granada war had already started, that he returned to the question of Rosselló and Cerdanya (see later). But, as has been noted (see Chapter 3), his wife insisted that he should give priority to the war with Islam and failure against France was guaranteed by the refusal of his Aragonese subjects to vote funds for a campaign. Yet Ferdinand had inherited other conflicts with France, as well as the question of the two eastern Pyrenean counties. One of these concerned the kingdom of Navarre, of which his father had been king. Straddling the western Pyrenees between Spain and France, this small state had for centuries been a bone of contention between its larger neighbours. Because of his military and political weakness in relation to Louis XI's France, John II of Aragon had been forced, by his second marriage to Blanche, the heiress to Navarre, to bequeath her kingdom not to his son Ferdinand, but to Leonor, his only surviving child by that alliance, who was the widow of a French Pyrenean nobleman, Gaston IV, count of Foix. She died shortly after her father, however, and the unstable kingdom, in which the Beaumont and Agramont factions warred and royal authority was weak, passed to her grandson, Francis Phoebus of Foix. As a result, Navarre floated in the French sphere of influence, since its new king's mother, Madeleine, was Louis XI's sister. Francis, in turn, died in 1483 and, after many unsuccessful marital manoeuvrings, involving France, Portugal and Castile, the kingdom went to his sister Catherine, who married Jean d'Albret. Ferdinand approved of this manoeuvre and, in 1494, Navarre became a Castilian protectorate, to be fully annexed in 1512.[6]

In contrast with this relative success, in 1480–1 a new threat appeared, when Louis XI inherited the claims of the Angevin line, both in southern France and to the kingdom of Naples, which had been held by an illegitimate branch of the Trastamaran dynasty since 1458. The result was to be a long-term realignment of both Spanish and general European politics. The first consequence was that Louis gained access to the ports of Provence, thus threatening the Catalan coast, but the development also focused attention once again on Rosselló and Cerdanya. Yet Ferdinand was in no position to launch a major campaign and it is possible that, on his deathbed in 1483, Louis even agreed to return the two counties, but things were to be very different in the reign of his son and heir, the boy king Charles VIII. The French regent, Anne, refused to hand over the territories, but Ferdinand was too weak and too distracted by Granada to exploit the instability that marred the regency in France. Ferdinand and his wife effectively let down their allies, England and the Empire (see Chapter 7) and allowed the French monarchy to recover its strength. The Granada war inevitably dominated the succeeding decade and it was only in 1493, when Ferdinand was at last free to return to historic Catalan politics, that he could plan to attack the French once more, with battle-hardened forces newly freed from the war with Islam. In the event, however, Rosselló and Cerdanya fell without a shot being fired. When he reached his majority, Charles VIII promptly married Anne, duchess of Brittany, thus thwarting one of the prime aims of the 'triple alliance' between Spain, England and the Empire, which had been to keep the duchy independent. But Charles had it firmly in his head that his destiny lay in Italy and, although his activity there would open up a terrible period of conflict in the future, in 1493 he needed to ensure that his neighbours would not attack him at home. Thus the 'triple alliance' had to be squared. Henry VII of England was paid off and Maximilian was given lands in the Burgundian inheritance in the Netherlands, while Ferdinand and Isabella were offered a treaty, which was signed in Barcelona on 19 January 1493. The document looked good from the French point of view, since the Castilian alliance was renewed and both Spanish monarchs undertook to give this alliance preference over any other, except that with the pope. Thus Ferdinand effectively abandoned his Trastamaran relatives in Naples, but he did receive Rosselló and Cerdanya in return. He and his wife were freed to organize another of their spectacular 'entries', to follow that of Granada on 2 January of the previous year. They solemnly entered Perpignan, amid general rejoicing, on 13 September 1493. Yet Charles's diplomats had not been wholly successful in their negotiations. They had not secured all the guarantees that should have accompanied the treaty of Barcelona, but the primary danger, from the French point of view, lay in the priority of the Spanish alliance with the pope. Charles's main target, the kingdom of Naples, had been a papal fief since the thirteenth century. This meant that the pope had to authorize the succession to the Neapolitan throne and this simple legal fact was greatly to complicate European politics for the next 20 years.

By the end of 1494 Charles was ready to act and during December entered the duchy of Milan, to which he also had a claim, with 22,000 men. Strictly speaking, the French move was not an invasion, as Charles was invited in by the Milanese ruler, Lodovico Sforza, 'Il Moro'. Although he was opposed by Trastamaran Naples and Pope Alexander VI, both Venice and Florence were likely to remain neutral in any conflict.

It remained to be seen how the king of Aragon would react. Up until this unexpected French move, Ferdinand had pursued historic Aragonese–Catalan claims against Provence and Genoa. He inherited from his father a temporary peace treaty with the mercantile republic of Genoa, which had such great economic influence in Spain, but Ferdinand, buoyed by John II's late success in suppressing a rebellion in Sardinia in 1478, decided to attack the Genoese, with the aim of wresting Corsica from their control. Catalan troops failed to achieve much on the island, however, and after a series of truces a new treaty was made in 1493. No doubt inspired by the need to cut off their trade with Nasrid Granada, Ferdinand devoted himself, during the 1480s, to achieving good relations with Venice and Genoa, while strong links with the Neapolitan Trastamarans were preserved. Under Ferrante I, Catalan merchants were prominent and some settled permanently, and ties became even closer when, in 1477, he took Ferdinand's sister Joanna as his second wife. In 1481 the Spanish rulers sent a Castilian fleet to help Ferrante against the Turks, who, to the horror and sensation of Europe, had occupied Otranto. No doubt Ferdinand was concerned also for his hereditary territory of Sicily. In 1482–3, the Spanish took the side of Naples in Italian diplomacy and conflict and in 1485 Ferdinand supported Ferrante against a rebellion by the pro-Angevin faction among the Neapolitan nobility. Ominously for politics after 1494, this revolt was backed by Naples' overlord, Pope Innocent VIII, but the pro-Angevin and papal candidate for the throne, René II of Lorraine, failed to appear, and the result was an increase in Ferdinand's influence in the kingdom. The French invasion would test its strength to the full.

Things began amazingly well for Charles. The Florentine ruler, Piero de' Medici, lost his nerve and surrendered his Tuscan territories. Pope Alexander VI, finding himself too weak to resist, had to endure a triumphal French entry to Rome on 31 December 1494, but he skilfully, and significantly, managed to avoid investing the French king with the crown of Naples, something only he could do. Unfortunately for the Trastamaran cause, not only had Ferrante died on 25 January 1494, but his son, Alfonso II, crumbled before the French threat and abdicated, on 21 January 1495. He fled to Sicily and was nominally succeeded by his grandson, Ferrante II, but the fight had evidently gone out of the Trastamaran cause and Charles was free to make a solemn entry to Naples on 22 February 1495. According to even to pro-French writers, such as the chronicler Philippe de Commynes, who was then French ambassador in Venice, the occupying power did not attempt to conceal its contempt for the native population. For once, an Italian league was effective, Charles had to fight his way back to France and, by 17 February 1496, Ferrante II was back in control of Naples. This outcome was not totally to the liking of Ferdinand of Aragon, even though he had played a large part in organizing the 'Holy League' against Charles VIII in 1495. He had, after all, stood aside while his Trastamaran cousins were driven out of Naples and seems still, at this stage, to have been anxious to preserve his newly minted alliance with France. Thus papal and Spanish interests, as on so many subsequent occasions, did not entirely coincide. It appears that Ferdinand had not in fact wanted Alexander VI to recognize Alfonso II and then Ferrante II as kings of Naples, for the simple reason that he claimed the throne for himself. It was on this basis that the Aragonese king intervened anew in Italy. He no doubt wanted to defend Sicily and Sardinia and was obviously sensitive to the Turkish threat, but his dynastic ambition did not stop there.

Ferdinand chose one of his Andalusian commanders from the Granada campaigns, Gonzalo Fernández de Córdoba, to intervene in southern Italy. The 'Great Captain' (Gran Capitán), as he was to become known, was first despatched to Sicily, with 300 light cavalry (jinetes) and 2000 infantry, under royal orders issued on 30 March 1495. Ferdinand told him that, if the French had gained complete control of Naples, he should remain in Sicily. If, contrariwise, Ferrante II still controlled some fortresses in his kingdom, Gonzalo should persuade him to hand them over, to be held by him on Ferdinand's behalf. This he duly did and on 30 April of that year Ferrante gave five Calabrian fortresses into Spanish custody, to be followed by others. Despite the Great Captain's epic reputation in Spain, his troops were not dominant in the Neapolitan campaign of 1495–6. While the major action was happening in the north of Italy, as Charles fought his way home, Gonzalo's light cavalry found the heavily armed and mounted French men-at-arms a tougher prospect than Boabdil and Al Zagal's Muslim horsemen. In the event, Naples fell mainly because of a rebellion by its citizens, as well as the French garrison's small numbers and lack of pay. Further blows for Ferdinand were to follow. On 7 October 1496 Ferrante II died, but once again the Aragonese king's claims were passed over and the late king's uncle, Federico, succeeded, being recognized at once by Venice and, on 11 June 1497, by Alexander VI. On 7 May 1497, Ferdinand had recalled Gonzalo de Córdoba to Spain, although asking him first to secure the Neapolitan fortresses, and it appears that the king's scheme for the partition of the kingdom of Naples was hatched at this point. As he and his wife pursued their plans for marriage alliances with the Habsburgs and England (see Chapter 7), first a truce was made with France, in February 1497, and renewed in November of the same year. Death intervened once again, however, with Ferdinand and Isabella's son John dying on 4 October 1497 and, equally unexpectedly, Charles VIII of France on 7 April 1498.

The accession of Louis XII, whom Alexander VI allowed to divorce his first wife and marry his predecessor's widow Anne of Brittany, caused a realignment of Italian politics. The new king was more interested in Milan than Naples and persuaded other European powers, including Spain, to allow him the freedom to attack and depose Lodovico il Moro, who had officially become duke of Milan after Charles VIII's invasion. Milan duly fell to Louis in September 1499. Meanwhile, Ferdinand's scheme for the partition of Naples with France was finally put into effect, under the terms of the treaty of Granada, signed there on 11 November 1500 and approved by Pope Alexander in the following year. Its basis was that both Spain and France had claims over Naples and it was asserted that Federico's alliance with the Turks, which had indeed been made in desperation, invalidated him as a Christian ruler. The cynicism of the partition seems to have shocked foreign rulers and also the Great Captain, who did not apparently wish to fight against a former ally. As for the protagonists, Ferdinand's interest in the manoeuvre is self-evident, but it is harder to see what Louis had to gain from it, given that his position in Italy was much stronger than the Spanish one. Nevertheless, his acquiescence in the partition scheme let Spain into Italy as a power that was to remain dominant, or at least influential, there for two centuries. Early in 1500, Gonzalo de Córdoba had been sent to Sicily with a significant fleet and a small army, consisting of 300 men-at-arms, 300 *jinetes* and 400 infantry. His initial enemies were the Turks and he duly drove them out of Corfu and, in December 1500, conquered Cephalonia. Finally, in the summer of 1501, he invaded Calabria and military conflict with the French became inevitable. Federico had in fact surrendered to French forces on 26 September 1500, but the Great Captain went on fighting, against the former king's heir, the duke of Calabria. An undeclared war then broke out between the supposed allies and, although Spanish troops captured Taranto, on 1 March 1502, the Great Captain was subsequently blockaded for eight months in Barletta, from September 1502 until April 1503, starved of money and supplies. His military brain was still at work, however, and it was during this time that he developed a new type of infantry formation, on the German model, which would become the much feared Spanish *tercio*, combining pikemen with the extensive use of firearms. Gonzalo de Córdoba's refusal, unlike his French opponent, to attack in the open, in the traditional 'chivalric' manner, contributed to his major victory at Carignola, on 28 April 1503. For the first time, Spain was recognized as a major military power in Europe.

After this victory, the fall of Naples was inevitable, taking place on 16 May 1503. Louis XII began at once to plot revenge, but his plan to secure good terms from Archduke Philip, the future Philip I of Spain, was thwarted by Ferdinand. A new French army was sent to Italy, but the Great Captain defeated it, on the Garigliano, on 28 December 1503 and in January 1504 Louis agreed a truce for three years, thus tacitly admitting that his Neapolitan ambitions were over. By the time of Isabella's death, in November of that year, Ferdinand was secure as king of Naples and Spain was established as a major player on the European scene. Wider expansion was also underway.[7]

Exploration and colonization

Canary Islands

Links with Africa were, for various reasons, among the inherited concerns of both Isabella and Ferdinand. Both under Roman and Muslim rule, Spain was, of course, part of imperial systems that covered lands on either side of the Straits of Gibraltar. In the late Middle Ages, both Aragon and Castile had firm African policies, which included economic, military and political aspects. In the Castilian case, the earlier fifteenth century had seen such activity, but it was only under Isabella's regime, and particularly after the fall of Granada in 1492, that the idea of extending the war of territorial conquest into Islamic North Africa began to be seriously entertained. Such a policy was given credence not only by past connections but more immediately by the active role of some North African troops in the Granadan war, especially in Málaga and the continuing plague of Mediterranean piracy, often supported by Muslim states on the southern shore. It was this longstanding interest in the Maghreb that led to southward explorations along the west coast of Africa, in which Castile and Portugal were rivals. As early as 8 July 1449 John II of Castile had granted to the duke of Medina Sidonia sovereignty over the Guinea coast, as far as Cape Bojador, but this was clearly an empty gesture. In the event, Portuguese activity in the area, sponsored by Prince Henry 'the Navigator' and supported by the papacy, developed to such an extent that Isabella, in the first few years of her reign, not only had to fight the Portuguese king on land but also faced a war at sea. The result was that the Canary Islands became the main focus of attention.[8]

Given the prevailing maritime conditions, it was perhaps inevitable that the interest of the Iberian kingdoms, and particularly Castile and Portugal, in West Africa should have led to contact with the Atlantic islands. Those that came to be called the Canaries had been known to Roman geographers of the Imperial period (first century AD onwards), but after the empire's collapse they were confined to imitative literary references, for example by Isidore of Seville (*c.*565–636), until the fourteenth century. The islands which became Portuguese colonies – the Madeira archipelago, the Azores and the Cape Verde islands – were uninhabited when first discovered by Europeans, but this was not the case when the Canaries, known to Isidore as the 'Fortunate Islands' (*Insulae Fortunatae*), were contacted in the mid-fourteenth century. In 1336, a Genoese merchant, Lanzarote Malocello, reached the islands with an expedition supported by Majorcans and Andalusians and, three years later, a navigator's coastal map was produced in Majorca by Angelino Dulcert. In 1345 Afonso IV of Portugal announced that he was interested in the islands and sent what appears to have been a reconnaissance expedition. Already, Europeans were interested in enslaving the native 'Fortunan' or Canarian population and there was rivalry in the attempt between Portugal and the Catalan slave traders of Majorca. In view of the exclusion of Aragonese and Catalans from the subsequent American enterprise, it is interesting to note that, at this early stage, there seems to have been much more level competition between the western and the eastern Iberian kingdoms. Significantly, both the Portuguese and the Majorcans, who sent two expeditions in 1342, announced their intention not just to trade but to *colonize.*

It was, however, a Castilian, Luis de la Cerda, who, in 1344, received a grant from Pope Clement VI of the 'kingdom of Fortuna', with the ineffective title of 'prince'. Around 1420 the Las Casas and Peraza families, from Seville, took complete control of El Hierro and captured La Gomera. Thus, until Isabella and Ferdinand intervened in 1477, the exploitation of the Canaries remained a matter for aristocrats and merchants, contested not only by the descendants of Béthencourt and the Peraza, but also by expeditions sent, on his own account, by Prince Henry 'the Navigator' of Portugal.[9] In rivalry with the Portuguese, the leading families of Seville, including the dukes of Medina Sidonia, increasingly regarded the Canaries as a useful staging post on the route between Iberia and the Guinea coast of Africa and as part of their own sphere of influence, this being the situation inherited by Isabella and her husband in 1474.

When the succession war broke out in Castile in 1475, the Portuguese attempted once more to secure control of the Canaries. In 1478, they fomented a rebellion in La Gomera, but it was a Portuguese attack on Gran Canaria which brought about the direct intervention of the Castilian Crown and an attempt to conquer the latter island, which had been regarded previously as too difficult a task. By this time the general war was coming to an end and in the 1479 treaties of Alcaçovas and Toledo, the Portuguese recognized Castilian sovereignty over the Canaries, along with a monopoly of maritime traffic with the Guinea 'gold coast'. Even before this, some Castilians had settled in various of the islands, beginning a process of colonization and acculturation that was to proceed rapidly between 1480 and 1515, with the active support of the king and queen. In this way, an increasingly aggressive and expansionist European civilization came into forceful contact with a technologically much less sophisticated one, which has been described as 'Stone Age', although it lacked neither social complexity nor military force. Direct royal interest in the Canaries began in 1476, when, after careful investigation of the relevant documents and titles, Isabella and Ferdinand formally recognized the title of the Peraza family to lordship over Lanzarote, Fuerteventura, La Gomera and El Hierro, but reserved to the Crown full jurisdiction over the main islands, Gran Canaria, La Palma and Tenerife. In their hard-pressed state at that time, the rulers had no intention of sending troops to the Canaries, but preferred to make *capitulaciones* with individual churchmen and military commanders to secure and settle the territory for them. The conquest of the island was a slow process, however, partly because of dissension among the Castilians themselves and partly because of the ferocious opposition of the indigenous population, which received active Portuguese support until the war ended in the Iberian Peninsula, in 1479. In Gran Canaria, Captain Juan Rejón adopted the techniques of war that were soon to be applied in Granada, these being *talas*, looting and imprisonment, but in August 1479, once free of the Portuguese threat, Ferdinand and Isabella sent a knight from Seville, Pedro Fernández de Algaba, to be their governor in Gran Canaria, with the tasks of ending conflict among the colonizers and completing the conquest.

In an episode that was to be much repeated in America, the captain in situ overcame the royal official who had been sent to discipline him. Not only did Rejón escape punishment in Spain, but he shortly returned to Gran Canaria with 400 new troops and Bishop Frías in tow. In addition, after a second visit of several months to Seville, the gallant captain returned once more to Gran Canaria in May 1480 to revenge himself on his enemies, dismissing Dean Bermúdez and having Algaba executed. His victory was short lived, however, as already, in February 1480, Isabella and Ferdinand had appointed a minor noble from Jerez de la Frontera, Pedro de Vera, as governor and captain-general of Gran Canaria, with full power to act on their behalf, under a new *capitulación*. As soon as Vera arrived in Las Palmas, on 18 August 1480, he deposed Rejón, who was killed soon after, while fighting in La Gomera. It was not until the following year that Pedro de Vera completed the conquest of Gran Canaria, with the help of native Gomerans under the command of Fernán Peraza. At about this time, Vera also succeeded in defeating a band of native Grancanarians, under the king of Telde, making them slaves, even though many of them had already converted to Christianity. This, too, would be an unfortunate precedent for America. In August, the main native leader on Gran Canaria, Doramas, died, and in November of that year the king of Telde was sent to Spain, being presented to Ferdinand and Isabella at Calatayud. Even before Boabdil's *volte face* after the battle of Lucena, the former ruler of Telde became an ally of Castile, also converting to Christianity. Although he used his influence to win over his compatriots, it was not until 29 April 1483 that a formal surrender agreement was reached.

Pedro de Vera's governorship was authoritarian and violent, having on occasion to be 'corrected' by the Crown, as when, in 1488, he enslaved the Gomerans, already Castilian vassals, who had risen against Fernán Peraza and assassinated him. There had already been a revolt in Gran Canaria, four years earlier, in protest against his manner of allocating lands to settlers, his disruption of native customs and his enslavement of indigenous Grancanarians. Yet those who survived at least appeared to assimilate, some of them visiting Spain and then returning to assist in the Castilian conquest of Tenerife. In the early 1490s, the most active colonizing leader was Alfonso Fernández de Lugo, whose technique was to ally with some native clans in order to subdue the more rebellious groups. In June 1492, Lugo agreed with Genoese and Spanish merchants a plan to conquer La Palma. On 29 September of that year, he landed on the island, but even with native allies, he was unable to achieve complete victory until May 1483. At once, he founded the settlement of Santa Cruz de la Palma and took advantage of the small amounts of lingering resistance to enslave the great bulk of the population, including many of his native allies. The same unfortunate traits were to be revealed in the conquest of Tenerife, which began in December 1493 and was finally completed, after much cruelty and bloodshed, in May 1496, when five local rulers (*menceyes*) surrendered. In the following month, several of them did homage to Isabella at Almazán. A pattern had been set for what would occur in America and, indeed, was already occurring in the

Caribbean. Apparently, arbitrary violence was being inflicted on native populations, who protested to the Crown and sometimes received at least a degree of redress.[10]

Christopher Columbus

While Pedro de Vera and his forces were going on their violent way in the Canaries, a seaman called Christopher Columbus (Cristóbal Colón in Spain) was planning an adventure that would transform the world: it would also directly involve Ferdinand and Isabella. The story has often been told, but the details still give rise to debate. To begin with Columbus's origins, there seems to be little doubt that he was Genoese, although claims have been made for his being Catalan, Portuguese, Galician, Majorcan or Ibizan. Claims that he was Jewish have also been made, but the documentary evidence seems to contradict this since, although he sometimes shows a generalized respect for Jews and Muslims, his anti-Jewish prejudices were conventional in the Europe of his day.[11] Columbus seems in fact to have been born in Genoa, to Christian parents (his father apparently a weaver), at some time between 25 August and 31 October 1451, thus being a virtual contemporary of his future patron, Isabella of Castile. For his first 25 years, he seems to have remained in Italy, in his home region of Liguria, acquiring the practical skills of seamanship, but apparently without any formal education. In 1476, he joined one of the regular Genoese expeditions to the western Mediterranean, the destination of its four carracks being England. The war of the Castilian succession was in progress, however, and the straits of Gibraltar and the bay of Cádiz were dangerous places, in which there was no such thing as a neutral ship. Columbus was captured by a Portuguese naval patrol and thus began his seven-year 'Portuguese period'. He married well, at some time between 1477 and 1480, and thus became directly connected with Atlantic colonization, his spouse being Felipa, the daughter of Bartolomeo Perestrello, who was governor of the island of Porto Santo. Increasingly, his interest turned from trade to voyaging and he visited English waters, as well as the Azores and the west coast of Africa. It seems to have been during these Portuguese years that Columbus first began to dream of sailing by a new route to 'Cipango' (Japan) and the lands of the 'Great Khan', which he had read about in the works of the thirteenth-century Venetian traveller, Marco Polo. The scheme was to sail westwards to East Asia and thus avoid the hostile Muslim states that formed a barrier to the east. This plan did not, however, fit in with Portuguese plans for exploration and expansion which, with papal approval, involved southward and eastward voyages to Africa and India. Thus Columbus was refused and the way was opened for his move to Castile, in 1485, although he was slow to abandon his links with Portugal.

His first years in Castile were difficult for him, as he struggled to find support for his Cipango scheme and suffered family problems, although he ultimately received the significant backing of the Franciscan friary at La Rábida (Huelva) and particularly of its guardian, Fray Antonio de Marchena, who was Castilian court astronomer and the sole expert supporter of the plan. Contemporary sources for this period in Columbus's life are largely lacking and it is not possible to know either when he arrived at court or when exactly the king and queen began to take an interest in his project. It appears, however, that later legends about instant recognition in Castile of Columbus's 'genius' cannot be substantiated. For example, the treasury accounts show no royal payments to him until 1493, after his first voyage, when the money is said to have been received by his Cordoban lover, Beatriz Enríquez de Harana.[12] There were, of course, many rival maritime projects that demanded royal attention and Isabella and her husband would naturally consult their advisers about them, these including churchmen such as Hernando de Talavera and Diego de Deza, as well as the University of Salamanca. A subsequent memorandum, prepared for the then newly installed King Charles I (1516), speaks frankly of Ferdinand and Isabella's motives for supporting Columbus's plans in 1492:

Your Majesty will also know that there was another very great doubt when the passage was attempted to discover the Indies, because there was no certainty apart from what Columbus said, and, in the end, with the little expenditure that was made for it, something was discovered in which the Faith was magnified in the whole world, and there were so many and such great benefits that they cannot be written or spoken of.[13]

In fact, the accounts of the Holy Brotherhood (*Santa Hermandad*), from 15 August 1490 to 15 August 1492, show a payment of 1,157,100 *maravedíes* to be handed over to the bishop of Ávila, Talavera, 'for the despatch of the Admiral [Columbus]'. Thus the Aragonese *converso* Luis de Santángel probably did not finance the expedition personally or, as is sometimes said, from Aragonese royal funds, but simply processed money from the Castilian exchequer, as treasurer to the *Santa Hermandad*. Discussions about the planned expedition took place in the town of Santa Fe, near Granada, in April 1492, the resulting *capitulaciones* being agreed on the 17th of that month. In this contract, Columbus undertook to find a new route to 'the Indies' (meaning the Asian landmass), along with any islands that might emerge on the way. Venturing his life itself rather than his reputation, he offered the cash-starved post-war Castilian treasury the succulent prospect of the treasures of the mysterious East. In return, the Crown agreed to provide the sum of money already mentioned, but not as a contractual obligation between equals but rather as a concession from monarch to subject. On the practical side, the Santa Fe agreement granted Columbus the splendid titles of 'admiral' (*almirante*), viceroy' (*virrey*) and governor' (*gobernador*). As far as economic rewards were concerned, Columbus was granted one-tenth of the value of all trade within his jurisdiction as admiral (*almirantazgo*), as well as the right to judge any disputes that arose in commercial matters. He was also to contribute one-eighth of the cost of any fleets sent to the newly discovered territories and receive one-eighth of any consequent benefits. Nothing was said in the Santa Fe agreement about religious matters.

Columbus reached the small south-western port of Palos de la Frontera on 22 May 1492 and his three ships left there on 3 August 1492, six days later putting into Las Palmas (Gran Canaria) for repairs and re-provisioning.[14] Famously, on 12 October, a lookout on the *Pinta* spotted 'a white headland of sand' and joyfully reported the news to the rest of the crew. The landfall appears to have been on what is now known as Watling Island, in the Bahamas, although the admiral named it San Salvador, after Jesus the Saviour. A landing was made and duly recorded notarially by Escobedo, before the expedition continued to Cuba and to present-day Haiti, which was named La Española (Hispaniola). The expedition wintered there, christening its settlement, on the north coast of Hispaniola, Navidad ('Nativity' or 'Christmas'). The *Santa María* had run aground, however, and both the ship and its crew were left behind when the two remaining vessels set sail for Spain on 16 January 1493. Columbus talks in his journal of a brief visit to Lisbon and even an interview between himself and King João II, but there is no corroboration for this. What is certain is that the ships arrived back in Palos on 14 March, and on the 30th of that month the king and queen summoned Columbus to court, which was then in Barcelona. This is unlikely to have been an elaborate, ceremonial visit, since it does not appear in the normally meticulous records of the city authorities, but there were nonetheless working sessions, in which the future juridical status of the admiral's discoveries was discussed. Out of these deliberations seems to have arisen the idea of securing a legal demarcation of newly discovered lands between Castile and Portugal, such as was achieved in 1494 in the treaty of Tordesillas. It was already accepted at Barcelona that only the pope could grant authority over the 'new' lands to Christian kingdoms.

Columbus seems to have left Barcelona in an optimistic frame of mind and, on 28 May 1493, Isabella and Ferdinand confirmed all his existing titles and grants and gave him further resources to plan a second voyage. The administrative responsibility for the new enterprise was entrusted to the highly experienced Juan Rodríguez de Fonseca, later to be a bishop. This second expedition was to be much larger than the first, consisting of 17 ships and 1500 crew and passengers, including, this time, Fray Bernardo Boil with the powers of an apostolic delegate. The fleet left Cádiz on 25 September 1493, called in the Canaries and set off, with much greater certainty than before and avoiding the Portuguese islands, in the direction of the north coast of Hispaniola. But instead of finding the crew of the *Santa María* at Navidad, they found the little fort in ruins and replaced it with the first town and trading station in the 'New World', which was named La Isabela, after the queen. Bernardo Boil took charge of religious matters there, while Pedro Margarit, another Catalan, was detailed to conquer and pacify the rest of the island. Columbus, meanwhile, sailed on, hoping to strike the mainland of the 'Indies'. He headed for Cuba, which was then believed to be the edge of Asia, sailed round the coast for three weeks, then returned to Hispaniola, before heading once again for Spain, in the *Niña*, in March 1496. His reception on this occasion was considerably less ecstatic than it had been three years earlier and for various reasons, including the cost of royal marriages and international affairs, there was some delay before the third voyage took place. In the spring of 1497 a new attempt was made, but the recruitment of crew proved to be difficult, mainly because reports had reached Spain of troubles in the Indies (see later). Eventually, some criminals were transferred from service on the royal galleys in order to make up the shortfall. The expedition was divided in two, the first part heading for Hispaniola, while the second, under Columbus's command, was to sail south-westward, in the vain hope, as it turned out, of finding the American mainland: Brazil was to be discovered soon afterwards by the Portuguese. Meanwhile, Columbus's fleet reached port in Trinidad, but the admiral was mainly concerned with seeking the 'earthly paradise', rather than exploring the Orinoco estuary. Eventually, however, in 1500, he headed back to Spain, this time not as a conquering hero but as a prisoner.

As a result of reports of rebellions in Hispaniola, against Columbus's brother, and deputy, Bartolomé Colón, the Crown had sent out an experienced servant, Francisco de Bobadilla, who blamed Columbus, started an investigation and trial against him and sent him back to Spain in chains. The admiral commented: 'If I stole the Indies [...] and gave them to the

Moors, they couldn't treat me as more of an enemy in Spain.'[15] Columbus had to work hard to achieve a measure of rehabilitation and it was not until just before Christmas 1500 that he achieved an interview with the king and queen, who had formerly been so open towards him. Finally, they agreed to fund a fourth expedition, but this took two years to prepare, during which time rival explorers, mostly Andalusian, continued making expeditions of their own, in opposition to the admiral and his claims. When it eventually set sail, in 1502, Columbus's last expedition consisted of only four ships and was aimed specifically at discovery, although in view of recent experience, the royal instructions warned him against abusing the native population. The little fleet called at the newly founded port of Santo Domingo, in Hispaniola, and in Veragua, Cuba and Jamaica. It was on the north coast of Jamaica, in June 1503, that the ships became stuck and virtually wrecked. It was not until 29 June 1504 that another boat arrived from Hispaniola and Columbus and his men were rescued. The admiral was shattered by the experience and never took part in any further activity in the Indies. By the time he reached Spain, Isabella was dying and, two years later, he himself died broken hearted, probably on 20 May 1506.[16]

This brief outline already indicates the prominent role played by the queen and her husband in setting in motion the great process of 'discovery' by Europeans in the Americas. Yet it would be wrong to assume from their initial interest that they had somehow acquired a strategic prescience that foresaw the significance of the blundering efforts of Columbus and his contemporaries. It would be a long time before anyone in Europe could see the 'New World' as redressing the balance of the Old. Instead, the monarchs and their advisers coped with problems as they arose, seeing them, in Azcona's phrase, 'on the level, [while] we [see them] from above'.[17] Right from Columbus's first landing in the Bahamas, his explicit intention was to occupy all newly discovered land for Castile, by an authority previously conceded by the papacy, which had similarly supported earlier Spanish and Portuguese efforts in the Atlantic and on the continent of Africa. This appears to have been enough for Isabella who, with her husband, had already gained increased powers from the pope in her own kingdom. During the fifteenth century it had been influentially argued, not least by Cardinal Juan de Torquemada, that popes should leave temporal matters to secular rulers and this seems to have been the basis of Alexander VI's legislation on the subject of the Indies. In addition, the treaty of Alcaçovas and Toledo (1479) had already legislated on the subject of dominion over newly discovered lands. This treaty, between two sovereign states, effectively removed the necessity for papal intervention. Thus Alexander's documents, often known as the 'Alexandrine' or 'Indian' bulls, served to give the Church's approval for actions that had already been taken by Castile. The first two, both beginning *Inter caetera* and issued in May and June 1493 respectively, granted to Ferdinand and Isabella all the 'new' lands that had been discovered or would be discovered in the future. The third, *Eximie devotionis*, issued in July 1493 but pre-dated 3 May, gave to the Castilians all the privileges in the area of conquest and colonization that had previously been granted by Nicholas V and Calixtus III to the Portuguese colonizers elsewhere. *Pies fidelium*, dated 25 June 1493, covered strictly ecclesiastical matters, referring to the monarchs' obligation to send missionaries to the newly conquered territories in the Indies, while *Dudum siquidem* (26 September 1493) confirmed and clarified the concessions made in the second *Inter caetera*. As a result of these bulls, which were effectively confirmed by the treaties of Tordesillas, made between Castile and Portugal in June 1494, the spheres of influence of the two kingdoms were to be divided by a north-south line 100 leagues (*leguas*), or about 550 km, west of the Portuguese Azores, but with all navigation south and west of the Canary Islands reserved to the Portuguese, who may already have been aware of the possibilities of Brazil.[18]

Apart from the conduct of negotiations such as these, it was inevitable that Ferdinand and Isabella, insofar as they realized the significance of what was being found by Columbus and his fellow explorers, would be forced to react to events that were largely determined by others. One notorious problem was that Columbus himself was no politician. When it came to controlling and developing the lands that he had discovered, he pursued his own personal ambitions, with his two brothers, Bartolomé, whom he named commander or scout (*adelantado*) and Diego. Archaeology is now revealing how the settlement of La Isabela, in Hispaniola, unsurprisingly showed no concession to native culture, but the often violent resistance of the Caribs made this virtually inevitable.[19] The Columbus brothers' desire for personal riches and the need to satisfy the financial demands of the Castilian Crown led them into highly oppressive behaviour towards the indigenous population. So, probably, did their lack of administrative experience. In any case, whatever theoretical debates about the degree of 'humanity' possessed by the natives may have taken place back in Europe, both in Isabella and Ferdinand's reigns and later, life in the colonized territories themselves was harsh and brutal for all concerned. As for the role of the king and queen in all this, it has to be borne in mind that they too were inexperienced, as were their advisers, in dealing with the problems posed by contact with native American populations. In addition, the explicit priority of both the Spanish rulers and Pope Alexander VI was to evangelize all those humans who were discovered in the 'Indies', as part of the longstanding strategy to encircle and eventually defeat and eliminate Islam.

As soon as Europeans began to settle on the Caribbean islands, economic factors – gold, and cheap or slave labour – came into conflict with missionary techniques and this contradiction was to haunt both the 'Catholic Monarchs' and their Habsburg successors. It is clear, however, that the influence of Crown officials in the new colonies would grow inexorably, although there would always be disputes between Peninsular officials and Spaniards who settled permanently in the Indies. After his imprisonment by Bobadilla, Columbus never regained administrative power, although he retained his title of admiral and dreamed of a return. In 1501, Bobadilla was succeeded as governor of Hispaniola by Nicolás de Ovando, who remained in post for seven years. In 1508, with Ferdinand once more 'governor' (*gobernador*) of Castile, a Columbus returned to the Caribbean, when Ovando was succeeded by the now deceased admiral's son, Diego Colón, who served, with the restored title of viceroy, until 1515. During this period, colonizers arrived in the Indies in ever increasing numbers. It is clear that the Crown was determined to keep a firm grip on what happened in its new American dominions and Diego never gained powers to match his father's, despite mounting an unsuccessful legal action that lasted until 1556. A significant development was the establishment in 1511, at Santo Domingo in Hispaniola, of a high court (*audiencia*).

By this time, not only had Vasco da Gama rounded the Cape of Good Hope and reached the real India, but Castilian rivals of the Columbus family had made further discoveries and settlements in the Americas, such expeditions having been authorized by the Crown from 1499 onwards. Progress was rapid so that, by 1500, when Christopher was sent back to Spain, the coast of the American continent had been visited, and to some extent explored, between the mouth of the Amazon and what was to become known as Venezuela. Those involved included Alonso de Ojeda, Juan de la Cosa, Pero Alonso Niño and Columbus's old companion, Vicente Yáñez Pinzón. Initially, some of these explorers were given governmental powers, but a more permanent system was quite rapidly developed, with the aim of integrating the American territories fully into the institutions of the Castilian state. For this purpose, the Casa de Contratación ('House of Trade') was set up, in Seville, in 1503 and regulated by further ordinances in 1510. In this building, close to the cathedral, all navigational, commercial, customs and colonization matters were regulated and, in 1509, Americo Vespucci, after whom the newly discovered continents were named, was appointed as its chief pilot (*piloto mayor de la Casa*). The Casa also acted as a legal tribunal for matters arising out of the new settlements. Juan Rodríguez Fonseca was in charge in Seville from 1504, while Lope de Conchillos joined the institution later, to supervise the administration and, above all, to see that the Crown duly received its fifth share (*quinto real*) of precious metals from the colonies. Hispaniola was the main centre of settlement and an effort was made to build up a new economic system, to compensate for the unwillingness of the native Caribs to labour systematically and their catastrophic losses through diseases (mainly smallpox) imported by the Europeans.

Most of the Spanish settlers in this period came from Andalusia or Extremadura, although some originated from León and both Old and New Castile. They were generally from the middle or lower classes and sought both riches and 'honour', which would raise their social status in the eyes of their compatriots at home. They had infinite confidence in the superiority of their own religious and cultural values and no scruple about imposing these on native Caribbeans and Americans. In these respects they fully shared the attitudes and perceptions of their monarchs. Among the latter were, on the one hand, a messianic belief in Spain's destiny, accompanied by a desperate need and desire for wealth that did not seem contradictory to them or their subjects and, on the other, an evidently sincere desire to rule their new territories in accordance with the tenets of religious and secular law. A prime example of this nexus of values, although it appeared after Isabella's death, was the legal code that emerged from deliberations of the special committee (*junta*) that met in Burgos in 1512 and is, hence, commonly known as the 'Laws of Burgos'. The code was in part a reaction to denunciations by missionaries, notably the Dominican Fray Antonio Montesino, of the abuse of 'Indians' by Spanish colonists. It reaffirmed the legal view that the natives were free subjects of the king, even though they were required by law to perform certain work for the colonists in the estates (*encomiendas*) that had been granted to them by the Crown. In deference to the missionaries, and notably the Dominicans, colonists with such estates (*encomenderos*) were also required to ensure that Indians had facilities to enable them to receive instruction in, and subsequently to practise, the Christian faith. The religious basis for Spanish colonization in America was, in parallel, affirmed in the legal 'requirement' (*requerimiento*), devised by a lawyer on the Royal Council, Juan López de Palacios Rubios, which was to be read publicly to native authorities, in order to demand their allegiance to the Castilian sovereign. The debates surrounding these measures, carried out in the reigns of Isabella and Ferdinand, were to rage on for many decades, both in America and in Europe.[20]

Notes

1 For an overview of the conquests of western Andalusia and Valencia, see O'Callaghan, J. F. (2003) *Reconquest and Crusade in Medieval Spain*, University of Pennsylvania Press, pp. 78–123.

2 Ladero Quesada, M. A. (2002) *Las guerras de Granada en el siglo XV*, Ariel, p. 171.

3 Ibid. pp. 171–83; Harvey, L. P. (1990) *Islamic Spain, 1250–1500*, University of Chicago Press, pp. 334–9.

4 Edwards, J. (1982) *Christian Córdoba. The city and its region in the late Middle Ages*, Cambridge University Press, p. 135.

5 Ladero, M. A. (1988) 'La repoblación del reino de Granada anterior al año 1500' and 'Mercedes reales en Granada anteriores al año 1500' in Ladero, M. A. (1988) *Granada después de la conquista. Repobladores y mudéjares*, Diputación Provincial de Granada, pp. 3–88, 89–185; Ladero, M. A. (2002) pp. 183–4.

6 Suárez Fernández, L. (1985) *Fernando el Católico y Navarra. El proceso de incorporación del reino a la Corona de España*, Rialp, pp. 57–207.

7 Cf Hillgarth, J. N. (1978) *The Spanish Kingdoms, 1250–1516*, vol. 2, *1410–1516. Castilian hegemony*, pp. 540–59; Ladero, M. A. (1999) *La España de los Reyes Católicos*, Alianza Editorial, pp. 431–58; Belenguer, E. (1999) *Fernando el Católico*, Ediciones Península, pp. 214–82.

8 Azcona, T. de (1993) *Isabel la Católica. Estudio crítico de su vida y su reinado*, Biblioteca de Autores Cristianos, pp. 813–15.

9 Fernández-Armesto, F. (1987) *Before Columbus: exploration and colonisation from the Mediterranean Atlantic, 1229–1492*, Macmillan, pp. 171–85; Russell, P. (2000) *Prince Henry 'the Navigator. A life*, Yale University Press, pp. 264–90; Ladero, M. A. (1985) 'Conquista y colonización' in 'La conquista de Canarias', *Cuadernos Historia 16*, no. 79, pp. 13–18.

10 Ibid. pp. 18–22; Azcona, T. de (1993) pp. 817–24; Ladero, M. A. (1999) *La España de los Reyes Católicos*, Alianza Editorial, pp. 401–15.

11 Fernández-Armesto, F. (1991) *Columbus*, Oxford University Press, pp. viii–ix; Leivovich, S. (1986) *Christophe Colomb Juif: défense et illustrations*, Maisonneuve & Larose.

12 Cabrera Sáchez, M. (1999) 'Los amigos cordobeses de Cristóbal Colón' in *Las ordenanzas de limpieza de Córdoba (1498) y su proyección*, Universidad de Córdoba, p. 97.

13 Archivo General de Simancas Patronato Real 28–31, cited in Azcona, T. de (1993) *Isabel la Católica. Estudio crítico de su vida y reinado*, Biblioteca de Autores Cristianos, p. 831.

14 Columbus, C. (1990) *Journal of the First Voyage* (Ife, B. W. ed. and trans.), Aris and Phillips.
15 Cited in Azcona, T. de (1993) p. 843.
16 For accounts of Columbus's career, see Fernández-Armesto, F. (1991) pp. 1–175; Azcona, T. de (1993) pp. 837–44; Phillips, W. D. and Phillips, C. R. [1990] (2002) *The Worlds of Christopher Columbus*, Cambridge University Press, pp. 136–240.
17 Azcona, T. de (1993) p. 846.
18 Ibid. pp. 847–52; Phillips, W. D. and Phillips, C. R. (2002) pp. 187–8.
19 Deagan, K. and Cruxent, J. M. (2002) *Columbus's Outpost among the Taínos. Spain and America at La Isabela, 1493–1498*, Yale University Press.
20 Azcona, T. de (1993) pp. 854–71; Ladero, M. A. (1999) pp. 421–5.

Chapter 6

Court and Culture

The courts

In recent years, the study of royal courts and their activities has become a preoccupation of many historians who concern themselves with late medieval and early modern states. In most cases, and notably those of France, England and Burgundy, it is a question of a single focus of royal power, but in Spain this was not so, because of the very nature of the alliance between Isabella and Ferdinand and their respective kingdoms. Both spouses inherited established court systems, which continued, legally as well as politically, to govern the couple's respective territorial inheritances. Despite the growing 'unification' of Castilian and Aragonese policy, which took place between 1474 and 1504, the two courts continued to possess their own identities, as well as treasuring their separate histories. Until Isabella's accession in 1474, the most significant development in the organization of the Castilian court had been the growth in the importance of the chamber (*cámara*), which gradually became an administrative department, and which gave the chamberlain (*camarero*) an ever more prominent role. Under the terms established by the Cortes of Toro, in 1371, during the first consolidation of the Trastamaran regime, there was a clear distinction between court offices that were 'outside the royal household' and those 'of the household', the latter including the chief chancellor (*canciller mayor*), the chief notary (*notario mayor*), the chief constable (*alguacil mayor*) and the household and court magistrate (*alcalde de casa y corte*). The fifteenth century had seen a growing sense of independence in the various sections of the court and particularly in the increasingly sedentary chancellery (*chancillería*), or High Court, which was commonly known as the *audiencia*, and in the Royal Council (*consejo real*), the treasury (*hacienda*) and the army (*ejército*). Parallel developments took place in this period in the Crown of Aragon. Isabella and Ferdinand, preoccupied by the financial weakness of both Crowns, and particularly Castile, carried out a detailed investigation into the accounts of the Royal Household and the Court, including the households of their children, especially that of Prince John. This unprecedented attention to financial detail was accompanied by a further fragmentation of the traditional court into specialized departments, including the office of the head steward (*mayordomo mayor*), the kitchens, the King's and Queen's Chambers and their respective Royal Chapels.[1]

Ferdinand and Isabella's strong and practical devotion to Christianity is evident in many contexts and it is therefore natural that there should have been a vigorous religious life in their own household and court. As far as the monarchs themselves were concerned, here was the inner core of lives that expressed themselves, elsewhere, in work to reform the Church, in warfare against Islam and in the battle against Judaism, both within and outside the Church. The Royal Chapel, which, as in the case of the Church in general, meant both worshippers and places of worship, was inevitably the main visible focus of Christian devotion and activity and it has already been noted that the Catholic Monarchs made it into an instrument of royal ecclesiastical patronage (*patronato real*), not only offering religious services to courtiers, but also providing leadership for the wider Church. The chapel traditionally consisted of a hierarchy of clergy, with jurisdictional as well as sacramental powers, a group of singers and instrumentalists, who not only provided liturgical music but also sang and played in secular royal ceremonies. In Isabella and Ferdinand's reign, there were still two royal chapels, one Castilian and the other Aragonese. In addition, the queen endowed a dedicated 'chapel' for her ladies-in-waiting and one each for her children, although death and foreign marriages gradually caused these to disappear. In addition to their court chapels, the monarchs later founded a Royal Chapel adjoining Granada cathedral, on the model of the earlier chapel of the 'New Kings' (*reyes nuevos*), in Toledo cathedral. In 1474 Isabella inherited a chapel that had last been reorganized by her father, in 1436. The dual role of a royal chapel, in Spain as elsewhere, was to accompany the monarch both in life and in death. It was to celebrate the royal liturgy and portray, in word, sacrament and music, the divine aspect of the monarch as priest-king (*rex sacerdos*) and whatever problems may have been perceived by some in the arrival of a female ruler, these do not appear to have affected the work of the Castilian royal chapel in Isabella's time. During her reign, the Castilian Royal Chapel grew into the largest 'department' of the household. The main expansion took place in the 1490s, when the number of personnel in the chapel rose from 62 to 140, including senior and junior chaplains, preachers, singers, sacristans, schoolmasters and an almoner (*limosnero*), who distributed royal charity within and outside the court. Ferdinand worked to emulate this organization in his separate Aragonese chapel.[2]

Great importance was attached, in both chapels, to the correct daily performance of Catholic worship. About one-third of the chapel staff were 'boys' (*mozos*) or 'upholsterers' (*reposteros*), the first category being responsible for bringing the liturgical objects of the cult to the priest sacristans and the latter bringing curtains, carpets and other fittings to enable the queen to hear Mass in comfort as well as state. This special team of *reposteros*, in addition to that in the Royal Chamber, was needed to accommodate the queen not only during the daily Mass, but also for the singing of the Divine Office. One thing which emerges from contemporary sources is that, despite the queen's ostentatious Christian devotion, even greater kudos seems to have been attached to those servants of the chapel who immediately surrounded her than to those who handled the sacred vessels of the sanctuary and altar. Given the nature of the liturgical offices of the chapel, it was inevitable that music played a prominent part in its daily life. The large team of chapel choristers and instrumentalists not only sang the Mass and the Hours, but also provided musical accompaniment for court ceremonies, the Castilian musicians being mostly recruited locally, while, in 1477, Ferdinand appointed Juan de Urreda as director of his Aragonese chapel. Like other contemporary rulers, he regarded his own chapel as an important manifestation of royal power and leading magnates adopted a similar attitude. Thus both the king and the duke of Medina Sidonia took their chapels with them into the field, during the Granada war, including, in the duke's case, boy choristers, adult singers and instrumentalists playing trumpets, pipes (*cheremías*) and sackbuts. The permanent Royal Chapels also included organists to play sacred music and minstrels, trumpeters and drummers for secular ceremonies. Tess Knighton notes the increasing influence in Castile of the Franco-Burgundian musical school. This was particularly obvious in liturgical music, including settings of the common of the Mass, such as the *Kyries, Sanctus, Benedictus* and *Agnus Dei*, although native forms remained prevalent in secular music.[3] Referring to the work of the composer Francisco de Peñalosa in Ferdinand's Aragonese chapel, Knighton states that 'in his Masses it can clearly be seen that he knew very well how to adapt the techniques of his Netherlandish colleagues, but the style of his motets reveals another emphasis, that of giving expression to, and projecting the words of the text'.[4] This is a significant religious and cultural point, which will be further discussed later. Among the most notable composers in the Castilian royal chapel were Juan de

Anchieta, Lope de Baena, Alonso Pérez de Alba, Juan del Encina, Francisco de Millán and Alonso de Mondéjar.

The 1503 inventory of the royal library in the Alcázar in Segovia contains several liturgical texts, including missals, the liturgy of the Passion, the festivals of the Virgin, the office of St James the Great and Talavera's office for the conquest of Granada, which combined plainsong with organ music. There were also seven books of 'organ song' (canto de órgano) and clearly secular works for voices and organ.[5] In the Aragonese chapel, which in Ferdinand's time, like its Castilian equivalent, was increasingly dominated by native musicians, the most prominent composers were Francisco de Peñalosa and Francisco de la Torre.[6]

Fernández de Córdova argues that the singers in Isabella's Castilian chapel had more weight and influence than their equivalents in other European courts. There were four times as many chaplains as singers and although the latter constituted only 15 per cent of the total chapel staff, the fact that they received 50 per cent more salary than chaplains appears to indicate the extent to which their services were valued. A singing teacher was responsible for training the adult cantores and it is likely that the choirboys received their musical education in the same manner. Surviving scores from the period were evidently written for all parts and Ferdinand and Isabella's chapel Constitutions distinguish between 'vulgar' polyphony, based on plainsong and sung alternately with the chant as faux-bourdons, which was the everyday staple of chapel music, and the more elaborate contrapuntal polyphony that was reserved for major festivals. Crucial to the musical activities of the Castilian chapel were the organists, who sometimes doubled as chaplains. In 1494 the salaries of three organists ranged between 20,000 and 56,000 maravedíes a year, while a 'master of organs' (maestro de hórganos) was employed to keep the various instruments in good repair. Ferdinand appears to have paid less attention to the role of organs in the liturgy, however, as he seems to have employed only one in his Aragonese chapel. The instruments talked of here were small, compared with those of later centuries, and were often portable. In 1480 Isabella had in her chamber, and presumably not only for chapel use, organs that were stored in leather and iron cases, while in 1500, her chamberlain, Sancho de Paredes, refers to three such instruments, as well as two 'clavicembalos' and other early types of keyboard instrument. The queen lavished organs and clavicembalos on her son, John, and also presented him with a 'clavi-organ' (possibly an early clavichord with pedals), designed by a Muslim from Zaragoza called Mofferriz. This was the first instrument of the kind to appear in Spain and it was much admired both within and beyond the court. The organists and choristers in Isabella's chapel were supplemented by numerous instrumentalists, who received payments (*raciones* and *quitaciones*), as well as clothing. Although they were on the chapel staff, they were mainly employed in performing secular music in the royal chamber and at more public court ceremonies, but they also took part in the most important liturgical celebrations in chapel. Nearly all these musicians were native Castilians and the fact that there was a considerable turnover in the musical staff, from year to year, suggests a fairly vibrant musical life in the kingdom as a whole in this period. Also notable is the existence of 'dynasties' of singers in Isabella's service. Senior minstrels received 30,000 *maravedíes* per year, while the drummer (*atabalero*) Juan de Dueñas received 50,000. The queen also employed six 'chamber players' (*tañedores de cámara*), who performed secular music on *vihuelas* (generally meaning the predecessor of the guitar, although the early violin was also referred to by this term) and the *vihuela de arco*, an early viol, which was not plucked but played with a bow. (This last instrument appears not to have reached the Aragonese Royal Chapel at this time.) These musicians performed at dances and other ceremonies and the permanent staff could be expanded by four or five times, by extra hirings, for special occasions. The 1503 inventory of royal possessions in Segovia castle also includes harps, flutes and lutes, in addition to the pipes, sackbuts and trumpets noted by contemporary chroniclers.[7]

Isabella's chapel naturally followed the Catholic liturgical year, giving priority to the major festivals associated with Jesus himself – Christmas, Holy Week, Easter, Whitsun, Ascension and the Octave of Corpus Christi. Great reverence was also given to the feasts of the Virgin Mary, from her Nativity to her Assumption, and including the Annunciation of Jesus and her Purification (Candlemas). Among the apostles, particular attention was paid to St James (Santiago), the patron of Spain, and to St John the Evangelist, the personal patron of the queen and her husband. Other saints who received particular commemoration were Pope St Gregory the Great, St Augustine of Hippo, St Martin of Tours, St Francis of Assisi and St Dominic Guzmán. It is notable that the calendar of Isabella's chapel also included eight commemorations of female saints – her name saint Elizabeth, mother of John the Baptist, whom Mary visited before the birth of Jesus, Anne the mother of Mary, the Empress Helena, mother of the Emperor Constantine, and the virgin martyrs Cecilia, Catherine of Alexandria, Barbara, Lucy and Agatha. In addition, Isabella's chapel had the duty of liturgically commemorating the major military victories of her and Ferdinand's reign, notably the battle of Toro, during the war against Portugal, and the conquest of Granada, in 1491–2. The liturgical propers for the latter were composed by Archbishop Fray Hernando de Talavera, a year after that victory. Not surprisingly, the queen nagged her former confessor to show her the text as soon as possible and in any case before publication. The propers, or texts specific to this office, are full of Easter joy and celebrate the conquest of the Muslim state as a triumph of God's work and the Spanish Christian monarchy, working in harmony, presenting it as the culmination of the history of Spain. Interestingly, in view of the then recent edict for the conversion or expulsion of Spain's Jews, Old Testament figures provide role models for the king and queen. Thus Ferdinand is compared to Joshua, who led the children of Israel into the Promised Land of Canaan, while Isabella is compared to Deborah and Judith. The queen is said to be endowed with the seven gifts of the Holy Spirit – wisdom, understanding, counsel, fortitude, knowledge, piety and fear of the Lord. This and other liturgical offices of the period, which were designed to praise royalty as well as God, typically contained forms for vespers, matins and Mass.[8] Despite this stress on the divinely sanctioned glories of the 'Hispanic' monarchy, the greatest liturgical concentration of the year, at the Royal Court as elsewhere, was on Holy Week and Easter, and particularly the 'Triduum' of Holy (Maundy) Thursday, Holy (Good) Friday and Holy Saturday (Easter Eve).[9]

Royal baptisms, marriages and funerals were inevitably given prominence. On the happier occasions, the liturgical celebration was normally followed by more secular entertainments, such as jousts with lances or canes (see later), bullfights, banquets and dances. A case in point is the baptism of Prince John, in Seville in July 1478, as recounted by the chronicler Andrés Bernáldez. A procession of nobles accompanied the infant prince to the Cathedral and the ceremony bore a marked resemblance to the New Testament account (Luke 2:22–39) of the Presentation of Christ in the Temple, although Isabella, as it were in the role of Mary, did not attend, or follow Jewish Law (a sensitive matter in Seville at that time) by offering two turtledoves or young pigeons, but instead gave two gold *castellanos*, worth 50 *excelentes* (c.375 *maravedíes*) each.[10] Accordinging to the seventeenth-century Sevillian annalist, Diego Ortiz de Zúñiga, the city's population joined in these celebrations with services in their own local churches and masques and light shows (*almenaras*), which continued for a week and were repeated when the queen arose from her *accouchement*.[11] The marriages of Ferdinand and Isabella's children were celebrated with comparable splendour, as were royal funeral ceremonies, although the terms of Isabella's will somewhat restricted the elaboration of her own exequies.[12]

Although historians have naturally tended to concentrate on the more spectacular aspects of the activity of the royal chapels, in Spain as elsewhere, it is important to remember that a daily round of Masses and Hours was celebrated throughout the year, on ferial days and lesser feasts. Isabella's interest in the minutiae of the liturgy seems to have developed at an early age. In 1466, when she was just 15, the princess obtained a concession from Pope Paul II that she might have a portable altar of her own and permission to hear Mass, with the company of no more than 12 people, during times of interdict. This privilege, which was renewed by subsequent popes, enabled her to be close to the Sacrament of the Altar, and its celebration, at all times. In accordance with the best liturgical practice, Mass was celebrated daily in the royal chapels. The queen normally heard the first Mass of the day, in the early morning, from a mobile platform which was brought in for her personal use, complete with chair, cushions, carpet and curtains. Ferdinand, too, occupied what was effectively a sacred space of his own, separated physically as well as spiritually from his subjects. One of the English ambassadors who negotiated the marriage contract for Catherine's marriage to Prince Arthur of Wales in 1489 (see Chapter 7), Roger Machado, offers a vivid description of her parents worshipping in the chapel of La Mota castle, at Medina del Campo:

And entering the chapel they found both the Kings [*Rois*] seated inside the curtain, which was of very rich cloth of gold, and everything was fitting to their estate, and the whole chapel draped with beautiful and rich tapestry, and the altar very richly adorned and ready.[13]

The 'hiding' of dignitaries, such as kings and dukes, who revealed themselves by the drawing back of a curtain at a certain moment in the liturgy, seems to parallel the Byzantine and Orthodox *stasis*, which separates the people from the clergy who offer the Eucharist.

The so-called 'Isabella Breviary', now in the British Library, which seems to have been presented to her in 1497, at the time of the marriages of Prince John and Princess Joanna, is a splendid example of the best liturgical books that were used in the royal chapels.[14] The queen also had many vestments and liturgical objects made for use in the celebration of Mass in her chapel. During the service itself, she made offerings on a fixed scale, in gold ducats and florins or silver *reales*, which were handed to her for the purpose, and accounted for afterwards, by the chapel receiver (*receptor*). The largest of all (301 florins, or 80,491 *maravedíes*, in 1484) was made on Maundy Thursday ('*el Jueves de la Çena*'). During the Lenten Hours, as well as offering 8000 *maravedíes*, the queen would buy a Crusading bull (*bula de la cruzada*) and sometimes others for favoured members of religious orders, monasteries and members of her own household. Since the thirteenth century, the Castilian Royal House had possessed a special pax (*portapaz*), which would normally be exchanged with the peace during Mass, but in this case would be kissed only by the celebrant and royalty. Isabella's chapel had several *portapaces*, which were used further to emphasize the special role of monarchs before God. As was customary elsewhere, celebrations of major festivals in the Royal Chapel began with a 'vigil' of vespers on the previous day and the general preoccupation with good order in the liturgy received strong impetus from the queen, who set great store by praying the Hours. Clergy, servers and singers must have felt that the all-seeing eye of God had its counterpart in the monarch's seat in chapel.[15]

Since Ferdinand and Isabella's courts consisted of personnel, including a full range from secretaries to huntsmen, rather than fixed places, it was necessary for them to have residences situated throughout their respective territories. In many cases these castles, palaces and hunting lodges were directly under royal jurisdiction, while in others the monarchs and their entourages would lodge in the palaces of nobles, or else in monasteries, while on their almost ceaseless journeys in both Aragon and Castile. In the absence of the rulers, many of these establishments operated as centres of local government, for example as the headquarters of *corregidores*, and in some cases, as in the Castillo de San Jorge in Seville and the Alcázar in Córdoba, as bases for the Inquisition. Thus the monarchs aimed to make themselves visible and accessible to their subjects.[16]

Culture

The 'royalist' nature of much liturgical activity in the court chapels has already been noted, as has the fact that chapel musicians were also required, often with additional musical support, to play and sing in secular ceremonies. There were numerous pretexts for these and Isabella and Ferdinand, whether in their Castilian or their Aragonese territories, seem consciously to have used such performances, for that is what they were, to bolster their own prestige and that of their monarchies. Thus ceremony surrounded the banquets, plays and dances that took place in the great hall of whatever may have been the monarchs' residence at the time. Music was also performed in the more intimate circumstances of the King's or Queen's Chamber, where every incident in the rulers' lives, from rising in the morning to going to sleep at night, was accompanied by servants, noble courtiers and ceremonial, so that privacy did not exist for them. Formal acts and ceremonies also took place outside the court itself. These included formal entrances by the monarchs into cities, similar to the 'Glorious Entries' of their French and Netherlandish neighbours and allies, and public processions, whether linked to political or religious purposes. Also involving both ceremony and cultural outpourings were the normal public acts of government, such as the reception of foreign ambassadors or of native dignitaries, the personal administration of justice by the rulers and the opening of meetings of the Castilian or Aragonese Cortes.[17] All these acts served to put into practice the high ideology of monarchy that Ferdinand and Isabella cultivated throughout their reigns.

Also prominent in court life under Ferdinand and Isabella were chivalric activities. Both rulers enthusiastically revived the knightly culture of John II of Castile, which had been somewhat diluted under Henry IV, and their main motives for doing so seem to have been to raise their own prestige and, more particularly, to stimulate enthusiasm for the Granada war. Thus their court(s) enjoyed a diet of jousts and tournaments, often with the full panoply of 'knights errant' and elaborate heraldic games and motto writing, which successfully combined the interests of military men, kings of arms and poets.[18] Other noble pastimes, commonly associated with court ceremonial, were bull fighting, then done by knights and nobles on horseback, as in the case of present-day *rejoneros*, and the so-called 'cane games' (*juegos de cañas*) in which horsemen kept in trim by fighting each other with sticks, rather than the lances used in more formal jousts and tournaments.[19]

The chivalric character of Ferdinand and Isabella's court was pronounced and often took an Arthurian form. The earliest known Spanish reference to the Arthurian romances dates from the end of the twelfth century and later writings were generally rescensions of the thirteenth-century French cycle known as the *Roman du Graal* ('Romance of the Grail'). The 1503 Segovia Alcázar inventory includes three works in this 'Arthurian' tradition, all 'in romance'. One was the *Historia de Lanzarote* ('History of Lancelot'), containing the story of the love of the hero and Guinevere, which had not been stressed in earlier Iberian versions. The queen's copy seems to have been printed and published in about 1496 and the same edition existed in a Catalan translation. The second, the *Balandro de Merlín* ('Ballad of Merlin'), also derived from the French 'Post-Vulgate' Arthurian tradition, the inventory stating that 'it speaks of Joseph [of] Arimathea', in other words, the earlier history of the Grail.

The third book in the royal library was *La demanda del Santo Grial* ('The quest for the Holy Grail'), including the death of Arthur.[20] Long before Miguel de Cervantes (1547–1616) ridiculed them in *Don Quijote*, such romances of chivalry were controversial. Even Gonzalo Fernández de Oviedo, whom the king and queen had chosen for their son's chamber, later condemned them as:

[V]ain and fabulous treatises, full of lies, and based on loves and vices and absurdities . . . which move these [foolish men] . . . and weak-minded women, to fall into licentious errors and accumulate sins, which they would not have committed if they had not heard these readings.[21]

Isabella's nineteenth-century eulogist, Diego Clemencín, saw a contradiction between the possession of these books and her evidently deep Christian faith: 'And is this the princess who wishes to be painted as being of an awe-inspiring religiosity?'[22] In this tradition, which appears to be supported by Sánchez Cantón, Daniel Eisenberg states, in relation to such chivalric literature, that:

The Reyes Católicos, though not completely immune to its charms, took their responsibilities too seriously, and were too interested in concluding the reconquest, to have much time for idle reading.[23]

Against this, Ian Michael plausibly argues that:

In the second half of the fifteenth century: references to the *matière de Bretagne* [the Arthurian 'matter of Brittany'] abounded in all kinds of verse (including ballads) and prose, when the surviving number of manuscript fragments of Spanish versions of the Arthurian prose romances suggests that they were much read and adored, and when we find among the first fictional works printed between 1494 and 1509 no fewer than nine chivalric works translated from the French, two of them appearing in more than one edition.[24]

In any case, it is clear that the *Balandro de Merlín* and the *Demanda del Santo Grial* were deliberately deployed and exploited in order to motivate Christian forces during the Granada war.[25]

The only major Castilian contribution to this genre was Pedro del Corral's *Historia sarracina* ('Saracen history'), published *c.*1450, but more new titles were published in Portuguese and Catalan. Works such as *Tirant lo Blanch*, in Valencian, *Curial e Güelfa*, in Catalan, and *Palmerim de Inglaterra*, in Portuguese, were translated into Castilian and circulated widely in that form. Most famous of all, however, was the Castilian romance *Amadís de Gaula*, which was descended from a mid-thirteenth-century French prose *Lancelot*. The Spanish critic, Martí de Riquer, emphasizes the importance of French writing, such as that of Chrétien de Troyes, in the development of chivalric romances and novels in the Iberian peninsula.[26] Also highly influential on the literature of Isabella and Ferdinand's day was an early fourteenth-century Castilian romance entitled *El libro del caballero Zifar*. This was based on the *matière de Bretagne*, contained much chivalric lore and was to influence subsequent Castilian literature in this genre. Isabella seems to have owned a fine manuscript copy of *Zifar*, which was probably made either for John II or for Henry IV.[27] In addition, much of the philosophical and political advice contained in part three of *Zifar* derived from the *Flores de la filosofía* ('Flowers of philosophy'), a manuscript of which was in the royal library at Segovia in 1503.[28] The whole of *Zifar* was in print by 1512, four years after *Amadís*.[29] Deyermond observes that the latter, an original, immensely popular and influential work, is 'in its essentials the Arthurian story transposed into a new setting'.[30] Although the direct influence of the 'Lancelot' tradition in Iberia was somewhat limited, in *Amadís* it received new life, not least in behaviour approved and encouraged at Isabella's court – this despite the adulterous character of the eponymous hero. Intriguingly, it seems that Isabella exploited the fashion for chivalric literature, and to some extent behaviour, to strengthen her hold over the aristocracy, thus following the example of her grandmother, Philippa of Lancaster, queen of Portugal.[31] Over all, as Fernández de Córdova has observed (and the same applies in Ferdinand's Aragonese and Catalan territories), chivalric literature, while looking back to a supposed earlier 'golden age' of knighthood, was consciously used 'to galvanize the forces of the anxious Castilian aristocracy towards the military projects, and those of religious reform, which were pushed forward by the Catholic Monarchs'.[32]

Parallel to the Arthurian tradition in late medieval Europe, including Spain, was a literary and historical preoccupation with the Trojans and their defeat by the Greeks. The main focus of attention was the siege and destruction of Troy, which appealed to two of the main enthusiasms of Europeans in the period, these being courtly love and the downfall of greatness. Love interest was naturally attached to the relationship of Hector with Helen of Troy, but also to that between Troilus and Cressida (in Spain, Troilo and Breseyda), whose prominence was much greater in medieval literature than in the original Greek and Roman epics.[33] The numerous Spanish romances concerned with Trojan matters will undoubtedly have been familiar to the Catholic Monarchs and their courtiers and, in addition, these and other chivalric themes and romances were illustrated in the extensive royal collections of tapestries.[34] The

Trojan story was, however, only part of the complex myths of racial and dynastic origin, which ideologically sustained the major monarchies of late medieval Europe.

In the case of Spain, the main creative effort in this direction was made in fifteenth-century Castile, and closely involved Jewish 'New Christians'. In the course of the development of historical and political writing in this period, Jewish and pagan types and myths came to form a heady mix of monarchical ideology and propaganda, which was to influence not only Spain itself but also its incipient empire. The notions of Castilian patriotism inherited by Isabella have been described as 'neo-Gothic', not in the sense of late medieval artistic and architectural styles, but rather in that of a supposed organic link with the Christian Visigothic monarchy, which had preceded the Muslim invasion of Spain in 711.[35] In the mid-thirteenth century, at a time when major conquests of territory from the Muslims had been achieved by the Castilians in western Andalusia, and by the Aragonese and Catalans in Valencia, Rodrigo Jiménez de Rada, archbishop of Toledo and historian, expressed the view that the Castilian Royal House was descended from the Visigoths and that the rulers of all the Spanish kingdoms descended from those of Castile. Much was to be made of these notions in the fifteenth century, with the resulting debate proving to be formative in the development of anti-*converso* measures under Ferdinand and Isabella. This process began in earnest with the conversion to Christianity, in 1390, of a rabbi in Burgos, Shlomo ha-Levi, together with his family. Under his baptismal name of Pablo de Santa María, he became bishop of Burgos, but at the time of his conversion he already had a family and, by the time that he died, in 1435, he had created a powerful ecclesiastical, political and cultural dynasty.[36] From the point of view of the Spanish monarchy, its origins and its nature, the most influential member of the family was his son, Alonso García de Santa María, commonly known as Alonso de Cartagena (1384–1456). His work on this subject was paralleled by that of his younger contemporaries, the *converso*, Diego de Valera (1412–88) (see Chapter 3), and of the non-Jewish *hidalgo*, Rodrigo Sánchez de Arévalo (1404–70). In the mid-fifteenth century, the 'Gothic' myth, as developed some 200 years earlier by Jiménez de Rada and his contemporary Lucas of Tuy, received new impetus from Alonso de Cartagena and Sánchez de Arévalo. Indeed Cartagena's *Anacephaleosis* ('Recapitulation') was explicitly based on Jiménez de Rada's work.[37] Nevertheless, in Brian Tate's view, these fifteenth-century writers produced new emphases, reflecting the conditions of their own time, in which the nature of Jewishness assumed ever greater importance.[38] Also still important were feudal concepts, such as lordship and vassalage, which were used to link the Visigoths with the reigns of the Trastamaran rulers. Although such terms were rarely explicitly mentioned in the fifteenth-century treatises, it is clear, from the works of Sánchez de Arévalo and others, that monarchy was not to be unlimited, whatever the apparently absolutist characteristics of the Jewish, Greek, Roman and Visigothic models that they adopted. The ambiguous impact of the Jewish experience of monarchy, as recorded in the Bible, plays an important part in several of these treatises, including those by Sánchez de Arévalo and Valera. Yet all the relevant Jewish texts were seen in the light of Christian revelation and quoted alongside references from the New Testament, frequently juxtaposed with Classical references.[39] Alonso de Cartagena's *Anacephaleosis*, written in 1455–6, illustrates these points.

After Henry IV's death, the new Castilian queen soon found herself the object of adulation from prose writers and poets, both Old Christian and *converso*. Both groups had high hopes of Isabella and these were well represented by the Franciscan poet, Fray Iñigo de Mendoza, whose mother was of Jewish origin. He wrote two works to celebrate what he imagined would be the arrival of a new era of religious toleration and understanding. In one of these works, he refers to the queen as the one who 'undoes our wrong' and whose works are our salvation (*salud*).[40] In one of his verses (*coplas*) for Isabella, probably also written in the 1470s, Mendoza, like Martín de Córdoba before him (see Chapter 1), appears to speak of the queen as though she were the Virgin Mary. He attributes to her the power to 'remedy our ills', since she had:

Come [to the throne] through the grace of God,
As when our life was lost,
Through the fault of a woman.

The poet adheres to the then conventional Christian view, that just as New Testament Scripture described Jesus as 'the second Adam', who restored to humankind what had been lost by Adam's sin in the Garden of Eden, so his earthly mother, Mary, wiped out the sin of Eve, who had urged her husband to eat the forbidden fruit. The allusion would not have been missed by any Christian reader or listener. Another case in point is that of Diego de San Pedro, author of the 'The treatise on the loves of Arnold and Lucinda' (*Tractado de amores de Arnalte y Lucenda*). This 'sentimental novel' includes an apparently extraneous episode, in which the lovelorn hero, Arnold, tries to forget his suffering by asking the 'Author' (*Auctor*), who intervenes in the plot, to tell him about Queen Isabella. The author replies in verse form, stating that:

The highest marvel of any that can be thought of,
After the one without stain [the Virgin Mary],
Is the queen of Castile.[41]

This does not imply that San Pedro regarded Isabella as in any way divine, but he starkly contrasts her regime with that of Henry. After saying that the latter's reign was full of injustice and discord, he continues:

[She] is a queen who never errs,
She is a brake upon the unequal,
She is glory for the earth,
She is peace for our war,
She is good for our evil . . .
She is a yoke for the strong,
She is life for our deaths,
She is light for our darkness.[42]

Perhaps, however, the most spectacular poetic praise of Isabella is to be found in the 'Song in praise of the queen, Lady Isabella of Castile' (*Canción en loor de la Reyna doña Ysabel de Castilla*), which was written by the Cordoban *converso* poet Antón de Montoro, between 1474 and his death in 1477. In this poem, Montoro goes so far as to imagine how things would have been if Isabella, rather than Mary, had given birth to the Son of God. Just as the Virgin had been 'perfect, except for divinity' (*perfecta, la divinidad ecepta*), so, in the case of the queen:

Since by you [Isabella] is gained our life and glory,
If St Anne [Mary's mother] had not given birth before you were born,
From you the Son of God would have received human flesh.[43]

It would hardly be possible to identify the Castilian queen more closely with the Queen of Heaven without risking accusations of heresy and it may be argued that Montoro did indeed cross that line in these verses. Thus, in a poignant mix that was not untypical of Jewish *conversos* in this period, he managed to produce dubious Christian theology as well as being accused of Judaizing, but all was done in the cause of intense royalism.

An additional example of poetic praise of Isabella in Christian language is to be found in the 'Verses of Juan Álvarez Gato to the Queen our Lady' (*Coplas de Juan Álvarez Gato a la Reyna Nuestra Señora*). Gato, who was probably a *converso*, seems to have written this poem in the late 1470s, when he was associated with Ferdinand and Isabella's court. As well as expressing *converso* hopes that the new reign would usher in greater stability, this poet, too, linked the queen with divine attributes.

Despite some critical theories to the contrary, it seems likely that Gato's verses were part of the *converso* writing that accompanied the early years of Isabella's reign:

Worthy of mighty praises, the sacred right hand
Made you a much closer neighbour of His Divine Majesty
Than of that common [human] form of ours.
So even if I were to remain silent about it,
Your action is a good witness to the grace [God] gave you,
And how hard he worked to make you equal to him.[44]

Thus, in the late 1470s, there appears to have been a fairly coherent effort by poets, many of them Jewish *conversos*, to build up the image of the queen, in the process seeming to accept enthusiastically the rule of a woman. Literary critics have generally identified these poems in praise of the Castilian queen with 'feminist' (in the medieval sense of 'non-misogynist') literature in fifteenth-century Spain. Yet there seems to be a distinction between verse which praises women in general terms, for example, for their beauty, chastity or other virtues, and the works noted here, which appear to be more specific and to go much further. When Isabella carried out her coup and seized the Castilian throne, she achieved something that was effectively unique in her lifetime. As Margaret King has rightly observed: 'Most women in the ruling classes [of the period] did not rule, but only shared some of the prerogatives of sovereignty. In the vibrant artistic and intellectual climate of the Renaissance ... this meant that they [mainly] exercised the power of patronage.'[45] Of course, Isabella was such a patron, but she was far more than that, being an active and determined ruler, who, in the process of state building, with her husband, cruelly frustrated the yearnings of her *converso* subjects (see Chapter 4).

This discussion has inevitably been focused mainly on Castile, but it should not be supposed, despite what Jocelyn Hillgarth has described as the 'Castilian hegemony' of the fifteenth and subsequent centuries, that both local patriotic myths of origin and royalist writing did not exist in parallel in Aragon and the Catalan lands. In his *Crónica de Aragón*, published in 1499, Fabricio de Vagad, a Cistercian monk, attacked his Catalan neighbours for failing to note Aragonese developments and achievements in their chronicles. He was inordinately proud of his Aragonese origins, and was as anti-Castilian as he was anti-Catalan, reflecting the jealous pride of his compatriots, concerning their independence and freedoms. The Catalan subjects whom Ferdinand inherited in 1479 had a strong 'national' sense, which had been reflected in chronicles and other literature for several centuries. Particularly after the Compromise of Caspe, in 1412, it was evident that Aragon and the Catalan territories intended to stay together, but the arrival of the Trastamaran dynasty threatened an ever growing domination by Castile. Royalism in the Crown of Aragon still involved, however, the passionate defence of the traditional *fueros*.[46]

After 1480 the attention of all Spaniards was increasingly concentrated on the war in Granada. Thus it was perhaps inevitable that Castilian should be the language of that genre of poetry known as the 'frontier ballad' (*romance fronterizo*), which arose out of life along the border between Castile and the emirate of Granada (see Chapter 3). Poems of this kind had become especially popular during the reign of John II (1406–54) and reflected both actual events, with varying degrees of accuracy, and the chivalric mentality that naturally developed as a result of the long period of confrontation and co-existence, between Christian and Muslim, which had developed in Andalusia since the mid-thirteenth century. Real incidents are referred to, although often in an idealized form and, although some of the poems seem to have been composed originally at a time close to the events described, they followed the normal path of literary development and became 'set in stone'. Events commemorated in this manner include the unsuccessful attack on Baeza (then in Muslim hands) in 1407, the death in battle, in Setenil in 1410, of the governor (*alcaide*) of Cañete, as well as the Christian capture of Antequera in the same year and the bravery of its governor, Rodrigo de Narváez, in the battle of 'the Killing' (*La Matanza*) on 1 May 1424. In 1431 Isabella's father, John II, raided the vega (plain) of Granada, and this too was commemorated in laudatory verse, while another ballad mourned the death, three years later (May 1434), of the then commander or 'scout' (*adelantado*) of Andalusia, Diego Gómez de Ribera, in an assault on Álora. The mounted raids (*cabalgadas*) by Christian troops on Granadan territory, which took place with some regularity in the years immediately preceding Isabella and Ferdinand's birth, were also commemorated in verse and the genre continued into the campaigns of 1482–92. It would be dangerous to regard these ballads as 'simple' or 'literal' accounts of what happened on the frontier during these years but, as well as providing diversion at Court, they do appear to have given moral support to Christian Andalusians, who faced their Muslim neighbours day by day. Their formulaic nature lent itself to ease of memory and recitation and also revealed a grudging admiration for the bravery and sophistication of a 'good' enemy.[47] The 'frontier' poems were a fine of example of the blend of courtly and popular culture over which Isabella and Ferdinand presided and in which they participated.

Notes

1 Fernández de Córdova, A. (2002) *La Corte de Isabel I. Ritos y ceremonias de una reina (1474–1504)*, Editorial Dykinson, pp. 25–6, 38–40, 127–44.

2 Ibid. p. 41; Knighton, T. (2001) *Música y músicos en la Corte de Fernando el Católico, 1474–1516*, Diputación Provincial de Zaragoza, p. 62.

3 Knighton, T. (1987) 'Northern influence on cultural developments in the Iberian peninsula during the fifteenth century', *Renaissance Studies*, vol. 1, pp. 220–37; Knighton, T. (2001) pp. 59–61.

4 Knighton, T. (1992) 'Fernándo el Católico y el mecenazgo musical', p. 45.

5 Sánchez Cantón, F. J. (1950) *Libros, tapices y cuadros que coleccionó Isabel la Católica*, CSIC 1950, pp. 35, 83–4.

6 Domínguez Casas, R. (1993) *Arte y etiqueta de los Reyes Católicos: artistas, residencias, jardines y bosques*, Editorial Alpuerto, pp. 160–7.

7 Fernández de Córdova, A. (2002) pp. 183–9; Knighton, T. (2001) pp. 65–107.

8 Azcona, T. de (1992) 'El oficio litúrgico de Fray Fernando de Talavera para celebrar la conquista de Granada', *Anuario de Historia de la Iglesia*, vol. 1, pp. 71–92.

9 On the Feast of the Annunciation (25 March), the ceremony was repeated for nine women.

10 Bernáldez, A. (1962) pp. 590–2.

11 Ortiz de Zúñiga, D. (1988) *Anales eclesiásticas y seculare de la ciudad de Sevilla*, vol. 3, p. 96.

12 Fernández de Córdova, A. (2002) pp. 282–5.

13 Bello León, J. M. and Hernández Pérez, B. (2003) 'Una embajada inglesa a la corte de los Reyes Católicos y su descripción en el "Diario" de Roger Machado. Año 1489', *En la España Medieval*, vol. 26, pp. 167–202.

14 Backhouse, J. (1993) *The Isabella Breviary*, British Library.

15 Fernández de Córdova, A. (2002) pp. 285–91.

16 Domínguez Casas, R. (1993) pp. 283–526, 536–40.

17 Fernández de Córdova, A. (2002) pp. 244–79, 291–374; Knighton, T. (2001) pp. 143–61.

18 Riquer, M. de (1967) *Caballeros andantes españoles*, Espasa Calpe: Macpherson, I. (1998) 'Secret language' and 'Five *invenciones* and the Ponferrada affair' in Macpherson, I. and MacKay, A. (eds) *Love, Religion and Politics in Fifteenth-century Spain*, Brill, pp. 82–98, 223–35.

19 Fernández de Córdova, A. (2002) pp. 343–65.

20 Sánchez Cantón, F. J. (1950) pp. 23, 51; Deyermond, A. D. (1971) *A Literary History of Spain. The Middle Ages*, Ernest Benn, pp. 156–7.

21 Fernández de Oviedo, G. (1880) *Las quincuagenas de la Nobleza de España*, Real Academia de la Historia, p. 233.

22 Clemencín, D. (1821) *Elogio de la Reina Católica Doña Isabel*, Real Academia de la Historia, p. 44.

23 Eisenberg, D. (1982) *Romances of Chivalry in the Spanish Golden Age*, Juan de la Cuesta, pp. 35–6.

24 Michael, I. (1989) 'From her shall read the perfect ways of honour: Isabel of Castile and chivalric romance' in Deyermond, A. and Macpherson, I., *The Age of the Catholic Monarchs, 1474–1516. Literary studies in memory of Keith Whinnom*, Liverpool University Press, p. 104.

25 Fernández de Córdova, A. (2002) p. 85.

26 Introduction to Eisenberg, D. (1982) pp. viii–ix.

27 Michael, I. (1989) p. 105; Walker, R. (1974) *Tradition and Technique in* 'El libro del cavallero Zifar Tamesis', pp. 19–20, 51, 70.

28 Sánchez Cantón, F. J. (1950) p. 47 (no. 66-C).

29 Michael, I. (1989) p. 105.

30 Deyermond, A. D. (1971) p. 159.

31 Goodman, J. R. (1993) 'The lady with the sword: Philippa of Lancaster and the chivalry of the Infante Dom Enrique (Prince Henry the Navigator)' in Vann, T. M. *Queens, Regents and Potentates*, University of Texas, pp. 149–65.

32 Fernández de Córdova, A. (2002) pp. 83–9.

33 Deyermond, A. D. (1971) pp. 159–60.

34 Sánchez Cantón, F. J. (1950) pp. 89–150.

35 For the development of this theory up to the fourteenth century, see Linehan, P. (1993) *History and the Historians of medieval Spain*, Clarendon Press.

36 Hillgarth, J. N. (1978) *The Spanish Kingdoms, 1250–1516*, vol. 2, *1410–1516. Castilian hegemony*, Clarendon Press, pp. 198–9.

37 Linehan, P. (1993) pp. 313–412.

38 Tate, R. B. (1959) 'The *Anacephaleosis* of Alonso de Cartagena' in *Hispanic studies in honour of J. González Llubera*, Dolphin, pp. 387–401.

39 Edwards, J. (1996) 'Conversos, Judaism and the language of monarchy in fifteenth-century Castile' in Edwards, J. *Religion and Society in Spain, c.1492*, Variorum, no. XVII.

40 Rodríguez Puértolas, J. (ed.) (1968) *Fray Iñigo de Mendoza: Cancionero*, Espasa Calpe, p. 331.

41 San Pedro, D. de (1973) *Obras completas*, vol. 1, *Tractado de amores de Arnalte y Lucenda*, Whinnom, K. (ed.), Castalia, p. 93.

42 Ibid. p. 94.

43 Ciceri, M. (ed.) (1991) *Antón de Montoro. Cancionero*, Universidad de Salamanca, pp. 219–20.

44 Artiles Rodríguez, J. (ed.) (1928) *Obras completas de Juan Álvarez Gato*, Blass, p. 126.

45 King, M. L. (1991) *Women of the Renaissance*, University of Chicago Press, p. 160.

46 Hillgarth, J. N. (1978) vol. 2, pp. 200–1.

47 MacKay, A. (1976) 'The ballad and the frontier in late medieval Spain', *Bulletin of Hispanic Studies*, vol. 53, pp. 15–33, reprinted in MacKay, A. (1987) *Society, Economy and Religion in Late Medieval Castile*, Variorum, no. VIII; Ladero Quesada, M. A. (2002) *Las guerras de Granada en el siglo XV*, Ariel, pp. 75–81.

Chapter 7

Dynasty and Legacy

Royal marriages

Like other European monarchs of the period, Ferdinand and Isabella sought to strengthen their political position by placing their children in alliances with the rulers of other kingdoms. Within two years of their victory in the Castilian civil war and war against Portugal between 1475 and 1479, the Spanish monarchs were attempting to arrange the marriage of their second daughter, Joanna, then only two years old, to the heir to the Navarrese throne, Francis Phoebus, who was of the same tender age. The boy died in 1483, but Isabella and Ferdinand did not abandon the notion of a Navarrese alliance, trying to persuade the queen mother to countenance a marriage between Princess Catherine and their four-year-old son, John. These unsuccessful schemes were to be the first of many that occupied Queen Isabella, at least, for the rest of her life and that were to suffer many more of fortune's slings and arrows thereafter.

A part of the peace settlement with Portugal, and embodiment of the well-recognized need to keep that peace, despite the continuing presence of Joanna the 'Beltraneja', was a projected marriage between Isabella, and Ferdinand's eldest daughter, also called Isabella, and Afonso, son of John II of Portugal. Before the agreement was made, John had to swear that he would never allow Joanna to leave Portugal or even the convent in which she was by this time residing (see Chapter 1). The marriage finally took place in 1490, but the young Afonso died just a year later, as did his father, who left no direct heir to the Portuguese throne. The succession went to the last surviving scion of the ducal house of Braganza, Manoel, who in 1497 had married Afonso's widow and had an infant son named Michael, who died young. But the cycle of death continued, with the demise of the younger Isabella herself, in 1498, after which the Portuguese king married Ferdinand and Isabella's fourth daughter, Mary. It was in the context of these repeated attempts at a dynastic alliance that

Castile and Portugal were able to settle many of their colonial differences in the treaty of Tordesillas in 1494 (see Chapter 5) and finally, in 1509, agreed separate spheres of influence in North and West Africa.[1]

Ferdinand and Isabella's only son, John, conceived seven years after his elder sister Isabella, was born in the Alcázar of Seville, probably in the middle of the day on 30 June 1478, although some contemporary sources offer a slightly earlier date. The Cortes of Toledo swore allegiance to him in April 1480 and in the following year, Aragon, Catalonia and Valencia followed suit. Marriage plans for the male Trastamaran heir were clearly a high priority and the first proposal was that he should be betrothed to Catherine of Navarre, who in the event was allied instead with John d'Albret, although the couple offered their own daughter, Anne, as a substitute. Further unsuccessful proposals followed, including, in 1486, a marriage between John and the heiress of Naples. In the meantime, Prince John's eventual future wife, Margaret of Austria, had been betrothed, in 1481, to Dauphin Charles of France, by agreement between Maximilian and Louis XI. In 1488, however, when John had attained the age of ten, serious moves began to be made to assure his place in his parents' dynastic plans. By the following year, it had been provisionally arranged that the prince should marry Margaret of Austria, daughter of the future Emperor, Maximilian, who succeeded his father Frederick III in 1493, while his sister Joanna should wed Margaret's brother, Philip.

John's marriage took place in Burgos on 2 April 1496, after a betrothal on 19 March, and it should be noted that the Habsburgs were by then effective exponents of the technique of dynastic advancement by means of marriage alliances, which Isabella and Ferdinand attempted to emulate. This had not been the first arrangement apparently on offer. Attempts to create a triple dynastic alliance, involving Burgundy, Spain and England, had begun as early as the 1460s. A marriage had been proposed, in 1461, between Duke Charles the Bold of Burgundy's daughter, Mary, and Ferdinand of Aragon and there had been efforts on the Castilian side too. As early as 12 September 1471, Dr Juan de Lucena, as the representative of Princess Isabella, had signed a treaty of alliance against France. All these arrangements had collapsed, however, after Charles the Bold's death in battle near Nancy, in January 1477. Nevertheless, in the mid-1480s, serious negotiations had begun for the marriage of Philip to Joanna. According to a letter from Philip to the royal secretary, Miguel Pérez de Almazán, in November 1486, the main agent on the Spanish side was Ferdinand and Isabella's ambassador to the Roman See, Comendador Francisco de Rojas. By July 1490 it appears that the king and queen were thinking in terms of a marriage between their son, John, and Anne of Brittany and although this scheme was quickly frustrated, it clearly indicates their anxiety to seek blood links with other European powers, generally at the expense of France. At this stage, Maximilian, too, was a candidate for the hand of Duchess Anne. The most ambitious scheme produced at this time by Isabella and Ferdinand would have led to a very different political landscape in Western Europe. It involved a double marriage of Prince John with Margaret, but of Joanna with Charles of France. The scheme collapsed, however, and the alternative double marriage was arranged instead. Negotiations to achieve it may have begun in 1490, but it was not until five years later, with the signing of the 'Holy League' against France, that the two parties were able to come to an agreement. In the existence of conflict in Italy between Spain and France and with the growing threat of disruption by the French of Hispano-Netherlandish trade, the attraction of the Habsburg marriages came to seem overwhelming. Thus in Worms, on 25 August 1495, Maximilian and Ferdinand and Isabella's ambassador, Francisco de Rojas, negotiated formal terms.[2] On 20 January 1495, the formal agreement for the two marriages was signed in Antwerp, on the Spanish side by Francisco de Rojas and on the Burgundian side, in person, by Maximilian, Philip and Margaret.

According to a minute that appears to date from either December 1495 or January 1496, the Antwerp agreement was ratified by the prince of Asturias in Madrid, five days after it had been made, on 25 January 1496, while the current document ratified the legal marriage in Malines, on 5 November.[3] After this ceremony, Rojas had returned to Spain, accompanied by Flemish ambassadors bearing the necessary documents from Maximilian, and also in January 1496, John made public his marriage to Margaret of Austria. Soon afterwards, Isabella felt able to send her new brother-in-law a message of friendship and congratulation on the marriages of their respective offspring, expressing the view, so sadly to be disproved, that 'these sons and daughters being as they are, they cannot be anything other than very well matched, because of which their parents should live happy and content'. Probably on the same day, the Castilian queen wrote to her new son-in-law, Archduke Philip, sharing with him her delight at his marriage to her daughter.[4] At that time, Philip and Margaret were in the eastern Spanish port of Tortosa, to be received in the Catalan Corts, having previously attended the Cortes of Valencia. The court stayed in Tortosa until after Easter 1496, moving then to the Sorian town of Almazán, where Prince John was to be formally installed as *señor* of the lands, towns and castles that had been included in his principate of Asturias. There, also, John received his new bride, and his sister Joanna was prepared for her departure to Flanders. While the Spanish court was spending the early part of the summer in Almazán, French ambassadors arrived, offering dubious 'guarantees' of stability on the Franco-Catalan border. Not deceived, Ferdinand decided nevertheless to head for Girona, arriving there on 11 August via Calatayud, Zaragoza and Barcelona, while Isabella left for Cantabria, on the north coast of Castile, with Princesses Mary and Catherine.

By then, and poignantly, in view of the subsequent fate of the latter princess, complications with ecclesiastical law had already surfaced in relation to the Trastamaran–Habsburg marriages. On 20 March 1496, Pope Alexander VI issued two bulls, which were sent to Almazán, no doubt at the request of Ferdinand and Isabella, who evidently wished all to be in canonical order before the religious solemnization of John and Margaret's wedding took place in Spain, and Philip and Joanna's in the Netherlands. In the first of the bulls, Alexander authorized the celebration of the two weddings during Lent and other forbidden liturgical seasons. In the second bull, the pope granted to Margaret the same ecclesiastical indulgences that were enjoyed by her future parents-in-law. Isabella, indeed, seems to have awaited her first sight of the Habsburg princess with eagerness and some trepidation. On 10 December 1496 the court humanist Piero Martire d'Anghiera wrote that one of her numerous preoccupations at that time was 'the desire that she has to see, speak to, and embrace Margaret, her future daughter-in-law'.[5] Eventually, Ferdinand was able to despatch the *corregidor* of Burgos, García de Cortés, to Santander, to meet the fleet bearing Princess Margaret to Spain, having heard that she had landed there on 6 March. The king and his son, the latter having recently arrived from Almazán, set out from Burgos to meet her, coming on her escort at Villasevil, near Reinosa, where the couple were introduced to each other by Diego Hurtado de Mendoza, titular Catholic Patriarch of Alexandria. It seems that the young people's delight with each other pushed protocol to the limit, their frustration having been increased by the delays enforced, as on so many occasions, by the weather in the Channel and the Bay of Biscay. The Admiral of Castile, Don Fadrique Enríquez, reported, on the way to Burgos, that he had wanted to set sail from Flushing back in November 1496, but the weather had prevented his doing so until 22 January 1497. Once again, however, there were storms and the fleet had to take refuge in Southampton until 21 February. The original plan had been to land at Laredo, but the weather and currents had directed the ships to Santander and even then, a typical Cantabrian storm (*galerna*) had nearly made an end of the whole fleet, princess and all. Margaret was allowed four days to recover in Santander and the couple and their entourage finally made their formal entry to Burgos on 19 March. It was later noted that the new princess of Asturias' fleet had brought the plague to the Cantabrians and northern Castile, killing 6000 people in Santander alone.

In Burgos, the royal party stayed at the palace of the count of Haro, duke of Frías and Constable of Castile, Don Bernardino Fernández de Velasco and it was in its chapel that Cisneros, as archbishop of Toledo, blessed the marriage on 4 April 1497. The religious completion of the wedding was accompanied by bullfights, jousts, fireworks and other entertainments, as well as a distribution of bread to the poor. The court left Burgos for Valladolid at the end of May and arrived in Medina del Campo. Thus 1497 became the 'year of royal marriages' in Spain, with not only John and Margaret's wedding but also agreement for Princess Isabella's marriage to Manoel of Portugal (see earlier) and the marriage of Catherine to Arthur of Wales. There seems little doubt that John and his new wife quickly became devoted to each other and, before long, Piero Martire was writing, both to Cardinal Carvajal in Rome (13 June) and to Archbishop Talavera in Granada (15 July), to say that some advisers were suggesting, unsuccessfully, to the queen that the handsome young couple should not be allowed to spend so much time together.[6] It is largely out of Piero Martire's writings that the popular tale of 'the prince who died of love' arose, but it appears unlikely that her husband's early death resulted from the excessive and precocious sexual appetites of Princess Margaret, since, although she had been married twice before, she was still only an inexperienced girl. In any case, by September, signs of Prince John's ill health begin to be discernible in court records. The plan had been that, in September 1497, Isabella, Ferdinand, John and Margaret would all accompany the younger Isabella to the Portuguese border, preparatory to her marriage to King Manoel, but the trip had already been postponed for two months and, in the event, the prince went instead to Salamanca. During that month, John suffered a second attack of smallpox, and a special tabard (*gabán*) was made to protect his now delicate form.

The purpose of sending him and his wife to Salamanca, with a small escort, was that his tutor, Diego de Deza, now bishop there, should preside over nursing him back to health. John and Margaret seem still to have been in Medina del Campo on 20 September, while the main royal contingent had already left for the Portuguese border. The best account of John's last days is to be found in a letter from Piero Martire to Cardinal Carvajal, since the Milanese humanist was an eyewitness of events. The prince and princess, and their entourage, made a ceremonial entry to Salamanca on 23 September 1497, amid many entertainments that must have tested John's constitution. Three days later, his health was conspicuously worse and by the end of the month Bishop Deza had sent two anxious letters on the subject to the king and queen. On receipt of Deza's second letter, dated 29 September, Ferdinand set off at once, to go to his son's bedside. On 4 October John made his will, conventional in its religious and secular provisions, although in contemporary and later sources there is a surprisingly large number of versions of the date of his death, varying between 3 and 7 October. It seems most probable that the prince died, with his father at his side, on 4 October, the Feast of St Francis of Assisi, and was buried at Salamanca, temporarily as it turned out, in the early hours of the following morning. Thus one vital piece of Isabella and Ferdinand's dynastic jigsaw was lost for good.[7]

Ferdinand and Isabella's second daughter, Joanna, was born in Toledo, on 6 November 1479. She was nine years younger than her sister Isabella and just over a year younger than her brother John. Isabella allocated servants to take particular charge of her as the court travelled around Spain, and it was not until 1496 that she could be said to have had a household of her own. Joanna began her formal studies at the age of seven, with Dr Andrés de Miranda, a Dominican from the order's Burgos house of Santo Domingo. In 1490–1, when her younger sister Mary reached the age of six, the two girls began to study together. Joanna received less instruction in the performance of public ritual than did her older sister and brother, although she received considerable training in horsemanship, and showed bravery when, in 1494, her mule threw her, while they were crossing the Tagus near Aranjuez. Like her brother, Joanna was granted her own separate household, as preparation for her Habsburg marriage. Unlike Prince John, however, Joanna was educated not to govern but to shine in a foreign court, as a cultured and submissive wife. It has already been noted that, in 1488, Isabella and Ferdinand had offered Joanna as a wife for Archduke Philip of Austria, alongside an alliance between John and Margaret of Austria. It is notable that Joanna was the only one of the Catholic monarchs' progeny to marry someone who was, at least at that stage, beneath the rank of a reigning prince. Literary propagandists felt it necessary to try to upgrade Philip, so as not to suggest that Joanna had stooped to conquer. One anonymous poet took the initiative of unilaterally conferring on him, as Maximilian's heir, the title of 'King of the Romans'.[8] In August 1496 Joanna set out for Flanders, with 15,000 men and more than 130 ships. As so often in those climes, the weather was distinctly unhelpful and on 31 August the fleet was forced to take refuge off Portland, continuing its voyage on 2 September. (Her eventual return to Spain will be discussed later.)

Isabella and Ferdinand's youngest daughter, Catherine, was born in the archbishop of Toledo's palace at Alcalá de Henares, north-east of Madrid, on 16 December 1485. The poet and historian Juan Barba celebrated the birth as the culmination of a 'good year of much glory', in the Granada war, taking place in the month of Christ's birth. Knights and nobles, who were relaxing between campaigns, held jousts in honour of the new princess, named after her Lancastrian grandmother, who was expected to inspire further military endeavour.[9] In the event, Catherine was almost immediately brought into her parents' dynastic plans and it soon became plain that England was to be her destination. The idea of a marriage between Catherine and Prince Arthur of Wales (born 19 September 1486), seems to have originated in the mind of the Tudor king, Henry VII, when the Spanish princess was just two years old. Still fairly insecure on his throne, Henry needed continental allies, while Ferdinand and Isabella were keen to include their new daughter in their dynastic scheme to encircle France. Spanish ambassadors were sent to England late in 1487, not just to discuss political and economic relations between the two countries, but also to negotiate a marriage between Catherine and Arthur. One poignant aspect of these and subsequent proceedings is that Henry's Yorkist predecessor, Edward IV, had inherited a claim to the Castilian throne. This originated with his great-grandmother Isabella, daughter of Peter ('Pedro the Cruel'), the last pre-Trastamaran king, who had married Edmund Langley, earl of Cambridge and subsequently duke of York. Edward's father, Richard, duke of York, certainly took the claim seriously and, since Edward IV included the arms of Castile and León in his own, Ferdinand and Isabella can hardly have been unaware of it. Presumably, their thought was that a new era had begun with the accession of Henry Tudor.[10]

Nevertheless, despite their apparent shift towards an English alliance, the Spanish monarchs seem still to have hankered after the traditional pro-French policy of the Castilian branch of the Trastamarans and it was only after the failure of a final effort to marry their eldest daughter, Isabella, to Charles VIII of France that they undertook negotiations in earnest with England. Henry VII responded with alacrity to the new Spanish enthusiasm and, on 10 March 1488, he appointed ambassadors to agree terms for the marriage, as well as to negotiate on trade and political relations. In the conventional manner of the time, Isabella and Ferdinand thought that the marriage would be the best method of securing a strong political relationship and, on 30 April 1488, they gave full negotiating powers in the matter to their *converso* ambassador in London, Ruy González de Puebla, and also to Diego de Guevara. In the first part of 1489, Henry VII's ambassadors spent a month at Ferdinand and Isabella's court, then in Medina del Campo, and the result of these negotiations was the treaty of that name, dated 27 March 1489, which effectively ended the century-old alliance between Castile and France. Most of this document concerned politics and trade, setting up a mutual defence pact, as well as free trade between Castile, Aragon and England, but it was also agreed therein that Catherine and Arthur's marriage should be deferred until they came of age.[11] In the meantime, Henry VII would have further time to secure his throne, while Ferdinand and Isabella pursued victory in the Granada war.

From the Spanish point of view, the English alliance had always been seen as just one piece in a diplomatic jigsaw that encompassed all of Western Europe. Thus, in the cases of Prince John and Princess Joanna, the Habsburg dynasty, as well as France, had come to play a major part in their calculations, but the agreement for Catherine's marriage to Arthur was never formally repudiated. Charles's invasion of Italy, in 1494, produced a further shuffling of the diplomatic cards. Thus Ferdinand and Isabella, slighted by the French king's violent ambition, in a region where they too had dynastic and territorial interests (see Chapter 5), felt free to renew their ties, not only with the Habsburgs' possessions in the Low Countries but also with England. By this time, however, a new complication had arisen in the relations between England, Spain, France and the Empire, with the appearance of two successive pretenders to the English throne, whose presence soured Anglo-Burgundian relations.

The threat of the young man known to history as Lambert Simnel, who was claimed to be the earl of Warwick, son of Edward IV's brother, the duke of Clarence, had been eliminated by military action, in the battle of Stoke, on 16 June 1487. Far more threatening, however, was the arrival on the international stage, in 1491, of another young man, who claimed to be Richard, duke of York, the younger son of King Edward IV, whom most believed to have been murdered in the Tower of London, probably at some time in 1483. All Western European rulers were faced with making a decision as to whether or not they were prepared to believe the story or at least to act as though they did. What inexorably drew Ferdinand and Isabella into the midst of the affair, however, was the strong support quickly given to 'Richard IV' by his supposed aunt, Margaret of York, widow of Charles the Bold, and dowager duchess of Burgundy. As Edward IV's sister, Margaret was determined to make every effort to overthrow the Tudor dynasty and the emergence of the supposed Yorkist heir (no one ever seems seriously to have supposed that his elder brother, Edward V, had survived his imprisonment in the Tower of London) appeared to present an ideal opportunity to achieve this. 'Perkin Warbeck', as he is known to history, was almost continually exploited by Henry VII's enemies, between November 1491, when he landed in Cork and attempted to raise a rebellion in Ireland, and October 1497, when he was at last captured by the Tudor authorities. The pretender received support from some Anglo-Irish nobles, from James IV of Scotland and from Charles VIII of France. Most significantly of all, however, not least from the Spanish point of view, was the fact that 'King Richard' soon gained recognition from the Emperor Maximilian and from his son, Archduke Philip, no doubt as a result of vigorous lobbying by Margaret of Burgundy, who seems genuinely to have believed that the young man was her lost nephew.

During this period, from 1491 to 1497, Ferdinand and Isabella were in a difficulty, since they wished to form dynastic links with two powers that, despite their longstanding and close trading relations across the Channel and North Sea, were now on a political collision course. If the Habsburg and English marriages were to be successfully established, forming a triple alliance against France, it was evidently in the Spanish rulers' interest, as well as that of Henry VII, that 'Perkin Warbeck' should disappear from the political scene as soon as possible. Indeed, it was as a result of their anxiety to oblige the English king that Catherine's parents became involved in Scottish politics, sending Pedro de Ayala, in late 1495, as their ambassador to the Scottish court. Ayala soon discovered, apparently to his surprise, that James IV was interested in a Spanish bride. Isabella and Ferdinand were not keen to send Mary, their only remaining uncommitted daughter, to Scotland, but instead offered James one of Ferdinand's illegitimate daughters, in exchange for an effort to obtain a cardinal's hat for the bishop of Glasgow, which they duly undertook in November 1495.[12] To complicate matters further, it was at about this time that Maximilian came out openly in support of Warbeck as king of England, demanding that the agreement for the alliance, between the empire, England and Spain, should contain a clause stating that the Spanish would give no support to Henry VII, if he took action against the pretender. The king of the Romans stated, however, not that Warbeck was the son of Edward IV, but that he resulted from an alliance between the dowager Duchess Margaret of Burgundy and an unnamed bishop of Cambrai, who may have been either John of Burgundy, who did indeed father more than 30 illegitimate children, or his successor, and chancellor of the Order of the Golden Fleece, Henri de Berghes. Thus was confusion heaped on confusion and a further crisis produced in Isabella and Ferdinand's attempt to marry Catherine to Arthur. Even by the standards of the time, the diplomatic manoeuvres that followed, in 1496 and 1497, were of dizzying complexity, the Spanish rulers and their youngest daughter being at the centre of them. First, north of the Border, on or about the feast of the Epiphany (6 January) 1496, James IV had Warbeck married off to Lady Katherine Gordon, daughter of Scotland's leading magnate, the earl of Huntly. Uncertainty concerning the true identity of 'Richard IV' remained, however, and Isabella and Ferdinand, apparently still committed to an alliance with Henry Tudor and to a marriage between Catherine and Arthur, obtained some new evidence concerning the pretender, which they proceeded to make available to the English government. The story illustrates the close and complex ties which existed between the Iberian kingdoms and their trading partners in England and the Netherlands. On 25 April 1496 Ferdinand and Isabella's ambassador in Portugal, Don Alonso de Silva, went to the town of Setubal, south of Lisbon, to initiate a judicial investigation, which was to be carried out before the Apostolic protonotary, Fernão Peres Mexía. Witnesses were to be interrogated concerning the identity and biography of the self-proclaimed 'duke of York'. The ambassador had three simple and direct questions to ask them: whether they had known the duke of York in England; whether, and to what extent, the pretender resembled the real duke whom they had known as a boy; and whether they thought that pretender, who was then at the Portuguese court, was in fact the duke of York.[13]

De Silva went back to Spain with the information that 'Perkin' was a boatman's son from Tournai and Ferdinand and Isabella immediately employed the news to revive negotiations with Henry VII. A new agreement was reached in London, on 1 October 1496. It settled the issues which had arisen out of the 1489 Treaty of Medina del Campo, stating that that the marriage would not take place until the prince of Wales reached the age of 14, although it might happen two years earlier if either party requested it. All these negotiations, and their apparently happy outcome, evidently arose not only from the Setubal evidence but also from wider political developments, involving the Empire, the papacy, Venice and Milan, as well as England and Spain. As far as Catherine and Arthur's marriage was concerned, a papal dispensation would be necessary because of their young age, although not, apparently, because of consanguinity, and both parties agreed to request the relevant document. As in 1489, the dowry was set at 200,000 gold écus, and the value of Catherine's trousseau was to be 15,000 écus, together with gold and silver plate to a similar value, and precious stones worth 20,000 écus. Catherine was to receive her share of the revenues from Arthur's lands as soon as the marriage was solemnized. This treaty duly received its second ratification, from Ferdinand and Isabella, on 1 January 1497, but Catherine's parents still kept their options open by intimating, through their ambassador Ayala, that she might marry James IV of Scotland instead. With true duplicity, on this very same day, the Spanish ambassador in London, de Puebla, was empowered to act as Catherine's proxy in her marriage to Arthur, which was probably still her parents' real goal. On 19 May 1499, Catherine and Arthur were married by proxy at Tickhill Manor, near Bewdley, and the princess and her entourage eventually landed at Plymouth on 2 October 1501. They were ceremonially welcomed to England and the couple were married in St Paul's Cathedral on 14 November of that year and, after some debate at court, set out together to Ludlow, on 21 December. But Arthur was sickly and, although he survived the winter, he died on 2 April 1502, probably of pneumonia, without anyone being precisely aware of whether he had consummated his marriage with Catherine, who was herself too ill to attend his funeral, in Worcester Cathedral.

Even if her future troubles could not have been imagined at this stage, it was clear that Ferdinand and Isabella's dynastic plans had suffered a further serious blow. As soon as the news of Arthur's death reached them, they suggested that Catherine should marry the new heir to the throne, Henry. The English appeared to entertain this possibility and the usual hard bargaining began again, although it is important to note that no mention was made, in the subsequent negotiations, of any doubts about either the legality, or the feasibility, of a marriage, within 'the first degree of affinity', between the brother- and sister-in-law. Although there were Spanish complaints about King Henry's shabby treatment of Catherine, a new marriage treaty had been drafted by September 1502. According to its terms, a betrothal was to take place within two months and the marriage was to be solemnized once the required papal dispensation had been received, the second instalment of the dowry agreed for the first marriage had been paid and Prince Henry had attained of the age of 15 (one year older than Arthur), which would happen on 28 June 1506. The betrothal immediately followed the conclusion of the Anglo-Spanish treaty, on 25 June 1503. The whole treaty was based on the notion that Catherine and Arthur had indeed consummated their marriage and negotiations took place on this basis, as a result of the statement made to that effect by de Puebla, on the authority of Catherine's tutor and confessor, Alessandro Geraldini. By way of contrast, Catherine's chief lady-in-waiting, Doña Elvira Manuel, was firmly of the opinion that there had been *no* intercourse between the couple and wrote a letter to that effect to Ferdinand and Isabella, as a result of which Geraldini was hurriedly recalled to Spain.[14] Ferdinand accepted the English view, however, which was that the relevant papal dispensation should cover all eventualities.[15] The relevant bull, fictitiously dated 26 December 1503, but received in Spain in November 1504, did not arrive in England until March 1505. The reason for the papal delay is not known, although it may have been due to concern about the canon law issues involved or else to a desire to frustrate Ferdinand's ambitions in Naples. The views stated in the two documents were not identical, the brief stating firmly that Arthur did indeed consummate the marriage, while the bull was more circumspect, granting dispensation for Catherine's marriage to Henry 'even if' (*forsan*) the previous one had indeed been consummated.

The marriage negotiations were inevitably affected by the political turmoil that arose in Castile after Isabella's death (see later). Since Joanna and Philip were designated as her heirs, Henry began to see Ferdinand's importance to him as diminished, and even lent £108,000 to Philip, 'for his next voyage [from the Netherlands] to Spain'.[16] On 27 June 1505 Henry VII gave himself further room for manoeuvre by having his son formally repudiate his betrothal to Catherine, alleging that he had not consented to the arrangement. In fact, the English seem only to having been reserving their position until the outcome of events in Castile became clearer, hoping to increase Prince Henry's value as a diplomatic counter. The question of the Castilian succession divided Catherine's own household. Doña Elvira tried to involve her mistress in a plot to secure an alliance between Henry VII and Philip, her brother Juan Manuel being the latter's active supporter, but in August 1505 de Puebla persuaded the princess to write to the English king, saying that she no longer wished to see her sister Joanna, if she came to England. Finally, in November of that year, Elvira was expelled from Catherine's household, but in January 1506, as the result of a storm, Philip and Joanna were indeed forced to land in England, while on their way to claim their rights in Castile. Thus Catherine did in fact meet her sister and Henry and Philip made a close alliance. After Philip's death, on 25 September 1506, and Ferdinand's return to influence in Castile, Henry continued to keep his options open. On the basis that Ferdinand was still refusing to pay the second instalment of Catherine's dowry for her first marriage, Prince Henry continued to be offered on the international marriage market and the English king even proposed himself to marry the widowed Joanna, who appears to have charmed him. Indeed, in 1506–7, an alliance between England and the Habsburgs seemed much more likely than one with the Aragonese and Catherine continued to suffer. Not unnaturally, she complained bitterly to her father about her treatment, so that he actually gave her the credentials of an ambassador, to act alongside de Puebla.[17] This she duly did, although she struggled with diplomatic correspondence, finding it hard both to read and to write in cipher. It seems that she had to work without the help of a private secretary.[18]

In February 1508, now secure in the governorship of Castile, Ferdinand decided to cement the alliance with England and sent Gutierre Gómez de Fuensalida to join de Puebla as ambassador, with the wherewithal to pay the remainder of Catherine's dowry and to negotiate her marriage to Henry, duke of York. Things did not go well at first, as Henry was still more interested in an alliance with the Habsburgs, which was to be ratified by the marriage of his daughter to the future emperor Charles V. Thus the English Council was instructed to quibble over the details of the payment of the dowry and especially over the question of Catherine's plate and jewels. By the end of 1508 both Fuensalida and the princess's household were convinced that the marriage to Henry would never take place, although Catherine and her confessor, Diego Fernández, remained sure that it would. Despite this, by March 1509, even the dogged and faithful Catherine had despaired, asking her father to let her return to Spain and become a nun.[19] The denouement was unexpected to all, as, after Henry VII died, on 21 April 1509, the new king wasted little time in summoning Fuensalida to tell him that the marriage was to take place as soon as possible, without any further quibbles. Not only was the Spanish ambassador astonished, but so, apparently, were Henry VIII's own counsellors, who suddenly swept away all the objections that had seemed insuperable only days before.[20] Young Henry claimed, in a letter to Margaret of Savoy, that he was simply obeying his father's dying wish, but it is equally possible that the idea was his own.[21]

Isabella's will

Back in 1504, on 12 October, the twelfth anniversary of Columbus's first landfall in the Americas, Isabella of Castile made her will, before the Court notary Gaspar de Gricio and numerous counsellors. Wills are, of course, notoriously problematic sources of evidence, in that notaries and clergy commonly dictated the format and often the terms of the resulting document. In Isabella's case, however, it seems unlikely that any adviser, even on the threshold of death, could have significantly affected the content of the queen's wishes. As in the case of her son John's will in 1497, a protestation of Catholic orthodoxy introduces the text and is followed by supplications for God's mercy. Then follow details of arrangements that the queen wished to have made for her funeral. Her burial was to be in the Franciscan house in the Alhambra at Granada, either among the friars or among the adjoining community of nuns. She was to be buried in a Franciscan habit. Yet despite the obvious symbolism of being laid to rest at the scene of her greatest triumph, if Ferdinand wanted to be buried elsewhere, Isabella should be laid alongside him. After making provision for the settlement of her financial debts and the saying of twenty thousand masses for her soul, followed by various charitable benefactions and instructions to carry out the terms of her father's will, the queen turned to political matters. The resulting provisions give a clear indication of the extent to which, as she approached the moment of death, Isabella thought that her policies had failed or fallen short.

First, she broached the question of excessive Crown offices (*oficios acrecentados*), admitting that her policy of reducing them, as announced at the Cortes of Toledo in 1480 (see Chapter 2), had not been successful. Any surplus posts that had not already been extinguished were to be wound up, when their holders resigned or died. She then turned to grants (*mercedes*) of royal resources, which she and her husband had made to individuals. Criticism of the excessive liberality of her father and her half-brother in this connection had been a notable feature of the early years of her reign in Castile, but now she admitted that necessity had forced the royal couple to relax their policy on grants and give away royal towns, villages, castles, vassals and lands. She ordered that all grants and confirmations contained in a separate list, appended to the will, should be revoked and invalidated. As an important example of the ramifications of this problem, she turned to the case of her loyal friends and servants, Andrés de Cabrera, marquis of Moya, and his wife, Doña Beatriz de Bobadilla. As rewards for their crucial role in her seizure of power in 1474–5, Isabella and her husband had not only granted them the lordship of Moya, as a marquisate, but also some villages and vassals in the territory (*tierra*) of the royal city of Segovia. The queen evidently had these grants on her conscience, even though they had been made to some of her most dedicated supporters. Now, however, the conservation of the royal patrimony was to be given priority. If it turned out, on closer scrutiny, that the grants of Moya and Segovian possessions had not been licitly made, they should be revoked, and the marquis and marchioness should receive, in compensation, equivalent possessions in the kingdom of Granada. The next case to be considered was that of possessions of the city of Ávila, which had been granted by Henry IV to Garci Álvarez de Toledo, duke of Alba. These villages and vassals had been inherited by

Garci's son, Pedro de Toledo, who had recently died. There was thus an opportunity, which Isabella's executors were to take, to return the lands and population in question to Ávila city council. The heirs of Duke Pedro were to receive equivalent Granadan possessions in compensation. Another reference to the tormented early years of Isabella's reign concerned the former marquisate of Villena. The queen had evidently been traumatized by her battle with Juan Pacheco and thus, more than 20 years on, she instructed Joanna and Philip never again to release the town, castle and lands of Villena from the royal patrimony. Also still, apparently, on Isabella's conscience was her half-brother's alienation of Gibraltar to Enrique de Guzmán, duke of Medina Sidonia. 'Queen of Gibraltar' was one of her official titles, repeated on every royal document, but Isabella had revoked the grant after the duke's death and she now instructed Joanna and Philip never to alienate this part of the patrimony either.

Another of Isabella and Ferdinand's main policies, from the mid-1470s, had been to increase the Crown's revenues by preventing the diversion of taxes into private hands. Now, Isabella admitted that she and her husband had 'tacitly tolerated' (tollerado taçitamente) the collection and retention of the alcabalas, and other taxes, by nobles, knights and others. She ordered that all such grants and concessions should be revoked, although money already paid to the individuals concerned should not be reclaimed. This was a major admission of failure and it was followed by the confession that royal justice was not, despite the monarchs' best efforts, reaching their subjects in large areas of the country. The problem was a characteristically 'feudal' one, in which nobles and others were preventing their vassals, and others under their control, from gaining access to the royal High Courts (chancillerías). Isabella now ended all such practices 'by my own will and certain knowledge and absolute royal power' (de mi propio motu e çerta sçiençia e poderio real absoluto). The expense of the Granada war was cited as the reason for the monarchs' failure to carry out their policy of reducing, or eliminating, the assignment of royal revenues to individuals, in the form of juros, either for one life or in perpetuity. Isabella instructed her heirs not to make any new grants (mercedes) of this type and to ensure that, when holders of life juros died, the revenues in question were resumed to the Crown.

After dealing with these financial questions, the queen turned to political matters, urging Joanna and Philip to use their best efforts to ensure compliance with the terms of the agreements for the marriage of Princess Mary to King Manoel of Portugal and that of Princess Catherine to the Prince of Wales. These provisions were followed by a formal designation of Joanna as Isabella's heiress, to be obeyed by all the authorities of the Crown of Castile. The queen then turned to the vexed question of foreigners who held public offices, secular or ecclesiastical, in her realm. In what would prove to be a vain request, both under Philip I and in the reign of his son Charles, she urged her successors not to make such appointments. After reaffirming Castilian rights over the Canaries and the Indies, the will then moved on to the question of the succession to Isabella's throne. Doubts over her daughter Joanna's capacity to govern had been live for several years and the queen now ordered that, if necessary, Ferdinand should be *gobernador* of Castile on their daughter's behalf. She then went on to instruct her heirs to give their full support to the Inquisition and to pursue the war against Islam in Africa. She instructed Joanna and Philip to obey Ferdinand in all things and to live in concord with one another, giving good government to the kingdom. After this, the will briefly turned to the matter of rewarding royal servants, ordering a monetary benefaction to Joanna and Philip's son, the future Emperor Ferdinand of Austria and then making detailed provisions for the succession in Castile. Isabella left her jewels to Philip and Joanna and bequeathed her collection of religious relics to Granada cathedral, except for a piece of Jesus' robe, which was given to the Franciscan convent of San Antonio in Segovia. Having named her executors and granted them legal power to act, she instructed them to give to various monasteries and churches the wherewithal for the proper celebration of the Eucharist and ceremonies connected with it. While ordering that Joanna should be provided with all that was required to rule in state, she also provided for grants to any needy people among her servants who might be identified by her executors. After further legal provisions, Isabella returned to the matter of family burials. Wishing herself to be buried in the monastery of Santa Isabel de la Alhambra in Granada, she requested that, if this happened, her daughter, the former Queen Isabella of Portugal, should be brought to lie there too. An alabaster tomb should be erected in the monastery of Santo Tomás, Granada, in which Prince John should be placed. The document ends with legal formulae, her signature and those of the seven witnesses.[22]

This was not the end of the story. Still in the castle of La Mota, in Medina del Campo, while her health continued to deteriorate, and indeed, only three days before her death, which would occur on 26 November 1504, the queen added a short codicil to her will. In it, as was common in the period, the imminent approach of mortality led her to respond to further requests from some of her subjects. She asked her heirs and executors to sort out jurisdictional disputes between the archbishop of Santiago and the secular authorities in Galicia, and between the bishop of Palencia and the local authorities there, control having effectively been taken from him by the Crown in the early years of her reign, during the war with Portugal. She also ordered the fortress of Rabe to be returned to the bishop of Burgos and the removal of royal governors (*alcaides*) from other episcopal fortresses, and instructed that the small town of Fuenteovejuna, which had been seized by Córdoba city council in 1476, and over which there was a lengthy dispute still pending in both secular and ecclesiastical courts, should be returned to the military order of Calatrava.[23] A dispute with Navarre, over the border towns of Arcos and La Guardia, should be settled in a similar manner. The queen then turned to matters concerning royal revenues, asking her heirs, with the proper advice, to settle certain unresolved disputes. They were to ensure that all the revenues granted by the pope for wars against Islam were assigned to that purpose, and to complete a pending investigation of the collection of the *alcabala*, in the kingdom in general and particularly in Granada, as well as the *servicio* and *montazgo* (see Chapter 2). Her successors were also to pursue Church reform with continuing vigour, both in Spain and in the Indies. Finally, in addition to those which were to be said for her soul, under the terms of her will, a further 20,000 requiem masses were to be said, in 'Observant' churches and monasteries (see Chapter 4), 'for the souls of all those who have died in my service'.[24] Thus the queen prepared to meet her Maker and it would soon be seen how far her wishes, so firmly expressed, would be fulfilled.

Underlying both her will and its codicil was Isabella's strong desire that her beloved husband should continue to have authority in her hereditary territories as well as his own. Yet the queen's influence over the government of Castile had been declining for several years before her death. She had been devastated by her only son's death, in 1497, and her capacity to rule was obviously diminishing by the early 1500s. Inevitably, and willingly, Ferdinand had filled the vacuum, but no one knew whether he would have the same power and influence without the immense moral support and influence of his wife. In any case, the king of Aragon would no longer be king of Castile and thus the somewhat creaky edifice of Peninsular 'unity', which in reality resided only in the persons of the royal couple and in the Inquisition, threatened to collapse as rapidly as it had been constructed. After his wife died, Ferdinand was forced to balance the need to attend to his affairs in Italy, especially after the pliable Alexander VI was replaced as pope by the pro-Neapolitan, and therefore anti-Spanish, Julius II, in 1503, with the demands of a largely unfriendly Castile. During Isabella's last years, of illness and depression, Ferdinand's supporters, including the *converso* Aragonese secretaries,

Miguel Pérez de Almazán and Lope de Conchillos, had strengthened their influence at the expense of Castilian colleagues and institutions. Complaints were beginning to be made publicly about the quality of some who received Crown appointments, and the royal secretaries were being blamed. At the local level, two phenomena were becoming increasingly noticeable. First, the system of *residencias*, under which legally qualified inspectors (*pesquisidores*) assessed the conduct in government of urban *corregidores*, was beginning to break down. Second, and perhaps even more ominously, the Castilian upper nobility, which had largely been expelled from urban government in the late 1470s, was beginning to reappear and flex its muscles. In Córdoba, for instance, the marquis of Priego entered the council chamber on 18 November 1504, just eight days before the queen's death, and presided as *alcalde mayor*, as his father had done, with dire consequences for law and order, before his suspension by the Crown in 1478.[25] At the time, Andalusia and part of the central Meseta were suffering from harvest failure, hunger and epidemics, with a consequent revival of the traditional conflict between cultivators and stockbreeders, the latter mainly in the form of the ancient transhumant graziers' association known as the Mesta, which had received extra support from the Crown as recently as 1501.

It is worth noting at this point that the monarchs and their advisers had but a limited grasp of the economic pressures to which their lands were being subjected and, in the manner of most medieval rulers, resorted to vain regulation. Thus they succumbed to the pressure for higher wool production, which was demanded by the textile manufacturers in the Netherlands, but failed to protect the native cloth industry. In 1502–3, in response to growing social instability, they attempted to impose price controls (the *tasa*) on grain, but were forced soon afterwards to abandon the policy. None of this augured well for the post-Isabelline era. Neither did the fact that, in the year in which Isabella died, while Castile was a source of massive revenues for the Crown, about a quarter of them were already being deployed in 'Aragonese' projects, on the Catalan border with France and in Italy. The inevitable succession to the Castilian throne of Joanna, with her husband Philip as consort, was not destined to stabilize this situation. It is probably fair to say that Spanish historians have traditionally tended to see Philip's brief reign as a tiresome irrelevance, since the Habsburg archduke had little understanding of his new subjects, caused unnecessary irritation to them and provided an unfortunate precedent for the first few years of his son Charles of Ghent's sojourn on the thrones of Castile and Aragon. Recently, however, biographers of Philip and Joanna have shown a much greater appreciation of the

European, and in particular the Netherlandish, dimension of Philip's formation and politics.[26] The cultural and economic links between Spain and the Netherlands were already longstanding and intense, but the arrival of Philip in Spain was to bring unresolved issues into clearer focus.

Isabella's provision, in her will, that her husband should resume the governance of Castile if Joanna became incapable of ruling, was based on the events that followed the couple's visit to Spain, six years after their marriage in Flanders, to be sworn in as heirs to the Castilian throne. Philip, anxious to achieve a reconciliation between his Burgundian hereditary territories and France, had returned as soon as possible to the Netherlands, while a distraught Joanna, madly in love with him but rightly convinced of his infidelity, defied her parents in an attempt to rejoin him, this aim being finally achieved early in 1504. By the time of his wife's death, Ferdinand was as doubtful of Philip's capacity to rule as they both were of their daughter's. He immediately summoned the Cortes to Toro, scene of his earliest success in Castile (see Chapter 1), in order to recognize him as *gobernador* of the kingdom, in the name of Joanna, the proprietary queen. As 1505 began both Castilians and foreigners seem to have been uncertain whether Philip or his father would prevail in the struggle for dominance. It was evident that both had prominent supporters among the administration and the wider nobility, and the ambitions of both were generally known. Early in that year, a steady trickle of Spanish notables began to head for Philip's court in Flanders and, with the encouragement of Juan Manuel de Lando (see earlier), a minor Andalusian noble and former ambassador from Isabella and Ferdinand to Philip and his father Maximilian, the trickle had become a flow, both in person and by correspondence. Desperate to hold on to Castile, Ferdinand even offered Philip the kingdom of Naples if he would only abandon his claim, but his rival insisted that Joanna was perfectly sane, so that he, and not her father, should be regent of Castile.

Legacy

In September 1504 a treaty had been made between Maximilian, Philip and Louis XII, which was ratified in April of the following year and was accompanied by a secret agreement for the invasion of both Naples and Castile, if Ferdinand did not give Philip what he regarded as his rights. Since many of the nobles on the frontier were hostile to Ferdinand, such a scheme appeared to have a good chance of success. By 12 September Philip felt sufficiently assured to issue a letter ordering Castilians to refuse to obey Ferdinand as *gobernador*. In the meantime, however, the Aragonese king had turned the tables on his Habsburg enemies by himself negotiating an alliance with France, which was ratified in the Treaty of Blois on 12 October 1505. Now unable to invade Castile by land, Philip was forced to accept a compromise agreement, made at Salamanca on 24 November, whereby the kingdom would be ruled jointly by Joanna, Philip and Ferdinand. Philip still wanted complete control over Castile, however, and arranged a winter voyage with Joanna, during which storms in the Channel forced an unscheduled stop at the court of Henry VII of England. Joanna and Catherine saw each other for the last time in the course of this stopover. Eventually, on 26 April 1506, the new king and queen arrived at A Coruña, with an army of 3000 Flemish and German troops. As Ferdinand waited in Burgos, it appeared that events might resemble those surrounding Afonso of Portugal's invasion in 1475, as Philip used a delay in Galicia, supposedly meant to allow his wife to recover from the voyage, to make contact with likely supporters among the Castilian nobility and administration.

Such efforts amounted to more than wishful thinking. Ferdinand's marriage to Louis XII's niece, Germaine of Foix, who had no legal interest in Castile and was by many compared unfavourably with Isabella, was unpopular. Another factor behind Philip's unwillingness to meet his father-in-law, apart from a mutual suspicion fomented by the gossip of interested parties on both sides, was the new king consort's apparent fear for his wife's mental health, which he had previously maintained to be good. Meanwhile, rumours began to spread, with the active support of Spaniards who had previously been in Flanders, that Philip intended to suspend, or even abolish, Isabella and Ferdinand's beloved Inquisition. In the midst of the political and social turmoil of the years since 1500, its tribunals had come under increasing attack and, at the time of Philip's arrival in Spain, the longstanding resentment of Jewish *conversos*, since 1502 added to by that of forced *morisco* converts from Islam in Castile, was mainly focused on a notorious case in Córdoba. Diego Rodríguez Lucero, or as the Italian court humanist Peter Martyr nicknamed him 'Tenebrero' (shedding darkness rather than light), had been inquisitor in that city since 1499 and had burned hundreds of *conversos*, apparently in the sincere belief that secret synagogues were being operated there by Jewish Christians.[27] Given Ferdinand's known attachment to the Inquisition, this was undoubtedly an opportunity for the new king to gain further credit and support. During May 1506 it seems that even Ferdinand's most loyal supporters, such as Archbishop Cisneros, were abandoning him and, on 9 June, the Aragonese king announced that he was now willing to meet Philip at any time and place of his choosing. The result of two uneasy interviews was the so-called Treaty of Villafáfila, dated 27 June, in which Ferdinand admitted defeat. He ceded complete power in Castile to Philip and Joanna, or to Philip in the event of Joanna's death, and promised in the future not to intervene in any way in the kingdom's affairs. He retained only some bequests from Isabella and the undeniably lucrative masterships of the military orders of Santiago, Calatrava and Alcántara. The great political operator, so much praised in Niccolò Machiavelli's *Prince*, had been brought to this pass by a collapse in his political support in Castile, manifested by the closing of many city gates against him on the orders of the newly resurgent nobility. Retiring to Aragon, with his tail between his legs, Ferdinand plotted revenge and it was not long before his conflict with Philip erupted onto the international stage.

Ferdinand's first move was to encourage Louis XII to attack Philip's Netherlandish territories, while the new Castilian king retaliated by urging his father, Maximilian, to attack Spanish Naples. Now Philip was in pursuit of sole sovereignty in Castile and Ferdinand began to see a role for himself as Joanna's defender against accusations of insanity, but Philip's sudden death, apparently of natural causes, on 25 September gave the wheel of political fortune another turn. Ferdinand was informed of his adversary's death while sailing to defend Naples and stopped at Portofino to send a general letter to Castile, ordering the people to obey Joanna. The queen's extreme reaction to her husband's death, which has inspired much literary as well as historical comment and speculation, made it ever more unlikely that she would reign effectively, although she did activate measures, in the latter part of 1506, aimed at eliminating Philip's supporters from government and especially from the Royal Council. Although she urged all to await her father's return, he delayed for nearly a year in Naples, finally arriving in August 1507. As in changes of regime in the previous century, leading nobles rushed forward in the hope of gaining control of the Crown's resources, which, although once more somewhat depleted, were still large. Soon after Philip I's death, some tried to seize his infant son Ferdinand, but were thwarted by the citizens of Valladolid. At this time, Cisneros tried to have Joanna declared insane, but Ferdinand now objected to this, as he needed her authority in order to rule Castile. Yet the queen's night-time travels with her husband's open coffin, which she intended to take to Granada, convinced many that she was indeed mad and that the instability of Henry IV's reign had returned. In Andalusia, the duke of Medina Sidonia besieged and captured Gibraltar, which had been taken from him by the

Crown in 1502 and the count of Lemos similarly reoccupied Ponferrada, in Galicia. These events took place against a background of continuing social and economic disturbance, a plague epidemic and controversy over the Inquisition. Ferdinand would arrive not a moment too soon.

To begin with, earlier events seemed to be repeating themselves. As in 1475 Ferdinand found Burgos castle closed to him and, before he left Naples, the chronicler Gonzalo de Ayora wrote to one of the king's secretaries, warning that the government was so unpopular, mainly because of corruption and high tax demands, that more or less any foreign prince who was interested – and there were several – might easily seize the kingdom. Ayora, a non-resident *veinticuatro* of Córdoba, was a major campaigner against Lucero's activities in his native city. In the event, Ferdinand was able, with the small army that he had brought from Naples, to recapture Burgos castle, while the count of Lemos took the hint and withdrew from Ponferrada. During 1507–8, the new 'governor' pursued the magnates of Andalusia, occupying the lands of the new duke of Medina Sidonia and sacking his base at Niebla, as well as crushing a rebellion by the marquis of Priego in Córdoba. Despite pleas from the latter's uncle, the 'Great Captain', Gonzalo Fernández de Córdoba, the marquis's castle at Montilla was demolished on royal orders, its blocks of stonework still to this day lying embedded in the castle mound.[28] In many cases, however, Ferdinand's attitude was more conciliatory, because he desperately needed Castilian resources if he were to pursue his ambitions in Navarre, elsewhere in Europe, and in North Africa, where Cisneros had briefly occupied Oran in 1508–9. Thus he obtained a cardinal's hat for the archbishop, also appointing him Inquisitor General and even allowed the bishop of Zamora to retain the see, having previously captured it by force and driven off royal officials.[29]

Joanna's decline, with an increasing refusal, from 1507, to wash, dress or feed herself, followed by her seclusion in rooms adjoining a convent at Tordesillas, which would last from 1509 until her death in 1555, only made it easier for Ferdinand to control Castile.[30] His marriage to Germaine of Foix had inevitably opened up the prospect of Castile and Aragon going their separate ways and any discussion of the vexed question of the supposed 'unity' of Spain under Ferdinand and Isabella has to take place in this light. The monarchs' dynastic plans, thwarted as they were in so many respects, had been developed in the context of constant European plots and negotiations with matrimony, and consequent political alliances, in mind. It is important to remember that rulers, like their aristocratic subjects and aspiring members of lower orders, were constantly pulled between conflicting desires: both to hand their often painstakingly assembled heritage intact to a chosen heir and at the same time to be fair to all their children. In the last years of Ferdinand's life these desires were undimmed, as is shown by his ferocious effort to regain and retain his hold over Castile, this being supported by the annexation of Navarre to that Crown, in and after 1512. Yet, after the tragic early loss of his son John who, with his sister Joanna's marriage to a Habsburg archduke and possible future Holy Roman Emperor, would have secured both the Trastamaran succession and a Habsburg alliance, everything had to be done by means of marriages between the daughters and foreign rulers.

Also, by 1510 Spanish settlement in the Americas was becoming established and royal authority was being strengthened. Thus Diego Columbus was never permitted to inherit his father Christopher's powers as 'Admiral of the Ocean Sea' and in 1511 a further crucial step was taken, in the establishment of a Royal High Court (*audiencia*) for the 'Indies' at Santo Domingo, on the island of Hispaniola. Already, in 1503, a central 'trading office' (*casa de contratación*) had been established in Seville, to secure royal control over all trade between Europe and the newly discovered American territories. While Spanish settlers there, many of whom came from the southern and western provinces of Andalusia and Extremadura, seem effortlessly to have combined a sense of 'messianic' destiny with an insatiable appetite for slaves and gold, some at least, in the religious orders and among Crown administrators, were developing a conscience about the growing mistreatment of native Caribbeans and Americans. Debates about the moral basis of the Spanish conquests were to rage on for several decades.[31]

In his last years, Ferdinand seems to have developed a strong desire for further children, which Germaine proved unable to provide after the early death of a son, in order to exclude Charles of Ghent from the Spanish succession. In this he was, of course, conspicuously unsuccessful, however the more favoured Prince Ferdinand did, indeed, eventually become Holy Roman Emperor. As he grew up, Charles seems to have come to suspect that his grandfather intended to leave his Castilian possessions to young Ferdinand. In 1515 the brothers made an agreement to share their various future possessions, but it was overtaken by events, as, on 23 January 1516, while on his way to Seville, with the future Pope Adrian VI, in order to assemble a military expedition that might be deployed either in North Africa or against France or Italy, Ferdinand died, in the Extremaduran village of Madrigalejo. The assessment of his and his wife's achievements began at once and still continues.

Notes

1 Hillgarth, J. N. (1978) *The Spanish Kingdoms, 1250–1516*, vol. 2, *1410–1516. Castilian hegemony*, Clarendon Press, pp. 539–40.

2 AGS Patronato Real, leg. 57, fol. 106.

3 RAH Est. 1 gr. 1.A.9.

4 AGS Estado, Castilla leg. 1–2, fol. 182.

5 Anglería, P. M. de (1953) *Epistolario*, López de Toro, J. (ed.), Imprenta Góngora, p. 325.

6 Ibid. pp. 334–5, 338–40.

7 Alcalá, A. and Sanz, J. (1999) *Vida y muerte del príncipe don Juan. Historia y literatura*, Junta de Castilla y León, pp. 145–93.

8 Anon (1496) *Coplas fechas sobre el casamiento de la hija del rey de España*, Frederch Biel [Burgos], cited in Aram, B. (2001) *La reina Juana. Gobierno, piedad y dinastía*, Marcial Pons, p. 61.

9 Cátedra, P. M. (1989) *La historiografía en verso en la época de los Reyes Católicos. Juan Barba y su consolatoria de Castilla*, Universidad de Salamanca, pp. 276–8.

10 Hughes, J. (2002) *Arthurian Myths and Alchemy. The kingship of Edward IV*, Sutton Publishing, pp. 35, 118.

11 Starkie, W. (1952) 'Reflejos en Inglaterra de la personalidad del Rey Católico' in *V Congreso de la Corona de Aragón*, CSIC, pp. 209–14.

12 Torre, A. de la (ed.) (1949–1956) *Documentos sobre las relaciones internacionales de los Reyes Católicos*, CSIC, 5, 137 (letter from Ferdinand and Isabella to Pope Alexander VI, 12 November 1495).

13 Suárez, L. (ed.) (1971) pp. 526–9, translated in Wroe, A. (2003) pp. 471–3.

14 *Span. Cal. 1485–1509*, pp. 322, 325, 327.

15 Ibid. p. 370.

16 Chrimes, S. B. [1972] (1999) *Henry VII*, Yale University Press, p. 289.

17 Ibid. pp. 520, 526.

18 Ibid. pp. 514, 520, 526, 541; *First Supplement*, pp. 13, 16, 21.

19 *Span. Cal. 1485–1509*, p. 603.

20 *Span. Cal. 1509–25*, p. 16.

21 *Letters and Papers of Henry VIII*, 1, 1, 84.

22 Isabel la Católica 1958, *Testamento y codicilo*, Ministerio de Asuntos Exteriores, pp. 13–58.

23 Cabrera, E. and Moros, A. (1991) *Fuenteovejuna. La violencia antiseñorial en el siglo XV*, Editorial Crítica.

24 Ibid. pp. 61–71.

25 Edwards, J. (1982) *Christian Córdoba. The city and its region in the late Middle Ages*, Cambridge University Press, p. 156.

26 Aram, B. (2001) *La reina Juana. Gobierno, piedad y dinastía*, Marcial Pons; Calderón, J. M. (2001) *Felipe el Hermoso*, Espasa Calpe.

27 Edwards, J. [1986] (1996) 'Trial of an inquisitor: the dismissal of Diego Rodríguez Lucero, Inquisitor of Córdoba, in 1508' in *Religion and Society in Spain, c.1492*, Variorum, no. IX.

28 Edwards, J. (1982) pp. 159–60.

29 García Oro, J. (2002) *Cisneros. El cardenal de España*, Editorial Ariel, pp. 198–209.

30 Fernández Álvarez, M. (2000) *Juana la Loca, la cautiva de Tordesillas*, Espasa Calpe, pp. 153–64.

31 Azcona, T. de (1993) pp. 854–71; Ladero, M. A. (1999) pp. 421–3.

Epilogue

Despite their close blood relationship, gender meant that Isabella and her husband came to monarchy in the midst of very different assumptions and prejudices. As a woman, Isabella, although certainly not short of advice, had to shape her life as a ruler in a 'man's world'. Ferdinand could simply adopt a well-recognized and generally esteemed role. The circumstances of their respective successions also differed. From birth, Ferdinand knew that he would eventually be king of Aragon, even though his father lived to so great an age. Isabella could have no such confidence and her conduct, at Segovia in the winter of 1474–5 and from then until her death towards Joanna 'La Beltraneja', may well betoken a fundamental sense of insecurity. In such circumstances, it is all too easy for a strong sense of duty and responsibility to turn into cruelty. Another temptation was the constant stream of flattery and adulation, whether sincere or not, that emerged from servants, counsellors, poets and musicians. Even the most devout might succumb to constant comparison with the divine or, in the case of Isabella, the Virgin Mary, especially when, from 1476 onwards (particularly in and after 1492), political and military victories began to arrive. There was no need for either spouse to question the divinely sanctioned privileges and powers of monarchy and there is no evidence that either of them did. The fact that their status was implicitly believed by others to be sanctioned by religion not only strengthened their hold over their subjects, especially in Castile, but also indicated some of their main policy lines, in the conquest of Granada, with its extension across the Mediterranean, in the attempt to remove Judaism from their kingdoms and in the mission to the Atlantic islands and the Indies. As far as their personal faith was concerned, and especially Isabella's, the elaborate outward forms of Catholic worship contained an individualistic piety that owed something to Netherlandish devotion, but more to Spanish experience. Such individualism did not necessarily help either ruler to a socially compassionate understanding of Christianity in relation to their subjects. Indeed, Ferdinand was much admired by Machiavelli for his cynical use of 'religion' to cloak less worthy motives and it was only in 1972 that a process began in the Vatican for Isabella's 'beatification', the step before sainthood.

Understandings of religion may, in some cases, have changed since the Catholic monarchs' lifetime, but the snares and restrictions of power in essence have not.

Chronology

1451	(22 April) Birth of Isabella at Madrigal de las Altas Torres (Ávila)
1452	(10 March) Birth of Ferdinand at Sos (Zaragoza)
1461	(23 September) Death of Carlos de Viana, Ferdinand's half-brother, at Barcelona
1462–72	Civil war in Catalonia
1468	(5 July) Death of Prince Alfonso of Castile at Cardeñosa (Ávila)
1469	(18 October) Marriage of Isabella and Ferdinand at Valladolid
1470	(2 October) Birth of Princess Isabella
1474	(11–12 December) Death of Henry IV of Castile in Madrid
1474	(13 December) Accession of Isabella, in Segovia, as queen of Castile
1475	(2 January) Ferdinand recognized as king of Castile and León (28 March) Isabella grants Ferdinand powers to govern in the Crown of Castile
1475–9	War of succession in Castile
1475	(19 September) Afonso V of Portugal is defeated by Ferdinand in the battle of Toro
1478	(30 June) Birth of Prince John (July) 'Congregation' or synod of the Castilian and Leonese Church at Seville (1 November) Bull issued by Pope Sixtus IV for the foundation of a new 'Spanish' Inquisition in Castile
1479	(19 January) Accession of Ferdinand in Aragon, on the death of his father, John II (4 September) Peace treaty (Alcaçovas-Toledo) ends the war with Portugal (6 November) Birth of Princess Joanna
1480	(February–May) Castilian Cortes held at Toledo (6 February) Prince John is proclaimed as heir to the Crown of Castile, during the Cortes of Toledo
1481	(19 May) Prince John is proclaimed as heir to the Crown of Aragon, during the Cortes of Calatayud

1482	(February) Granada war begins
	(28 June) Birth of Princess Mary
1484	(May) Castilian Inquisition spreads to Aragon and Catalonia
1485	(16 December) Birth of Princess Catherine
1486	(22 May) Ferdinand's 'Sentence of Guadalupe' ends the *Remensa* wars in Catalonia
1487	(May–August) Christian siege and capture of Málaga
1489	(December) Christians besiege and capture Baza, Guadix and Almería
1490	(18 April) Contract is signed for the marriage of Princess Isabella to Afonso V of Portugal
	(11 November) Princess Isabella leaves for Portugal
1491	(June) Final siege of Granada begins
1492	(2 January) Fall of Granada and incorporation of Nasrid Emirate into the Crown of Castile
	(6 January) Isabella and Ferdinand solemnly enter Granada
	(31 March) Parallel edicts issued for the Jews of Castile and Aragon either to be baptised or to leave
	(12 October) Christopher Columbus's flotilla lands in the Bahamas (Watling Island)
	(7 December) Attempted assassination of Ferdinand in Barcelona
1493	(19 January) By Treaty of Barcelona, France returns Rosselló and Cerdanya to Ferdinand
	(3–4 May) Pope Alexander VI grants to Ferdinand and Isabella full sovereignty over lands discovered in the 'New World'
1495	(21 February) Charles VIII of France enters Naples and war between France and Spain begins
	(31 March) 'Holy League' signed in Venice, between Spain, Austria, the Papal States, Milan and Venice, to oppose France
	(5 November) Betrothal agreement made in Malines between Princess Joanna and Philip 'the Handsome', later Philip I of Castile
1496	Prince John is betrothed to Archduchess Margaret of Austria
	(22 August) Princess Joanna leaves for Flanders, to marry Philip 'the Handsome'
	(19 December) Pope Alexander VI grants Ferdinand and Isabella the title of 'Catholic monarchs'
1497	(19 March) Marriage, in Burgos, of Prince John and Archduchess Margaret

(30 September) After the death of Afonso V, Queen Isabella of Portugal marries the new king, Manoel

(4 October) Death of Prince John

1498   (29 April) Isabella and Manoel are sworn as heirs to the Crown of Castile

(5 August) Peace treaty between Spain and France is signed in Zaragoza

(23 August) Birth of Prince Michael, heir to Portugal, Castile and Aragon

1499   (18 December) A Muslim revolt begins in Granada (Albaicín) and spreads to the Alpujarras

1500   (25 February) Birth in Ghent of the future Charles I of Spain (Emperor Charles V)

(20 July) Death of Prince Michael

(24 August) Princess Mary marries Manoel of Portugal by proxy, leaving for Portugal a month later

(11 November) Treaty of Granada, between Ferdinand and Isabella and Louis XII of France, partitioning the kingdom of Naples

1501   (21 May) Princess Catherine leaves for England, to marry Prince Arthur of Wales

1502   (12 January) Order issued for the conversion or expulsion of Muslims in Granada and Castile

(2 April) Prince Arthur of Wales dies at Ludlow

(22 May) Philip and Joanna are sworn in at Toledo as heirs to the Crown of Castile

(27 October) Princess Joanna is sworn in at Zaragoza as heiress to the Crown of Aragon, subject to Ferdinand having no male heir

1503   (10 March) Birth of Ferdinand, second son of Philip and Joanna, and future Holy Roman Emperor

(28 April) Spanish forces, under the 'Great Captain', defeat the French in the battle of Cerignola

(16 May) Spanish troops enter Naples

1504   (30 April) Spain makes a truce with Louis XII of France, which results in Spain securing possession of the kingdom of Naples

(26 November) Isabella dies. Joanna is sworn in as her heir and Ferdinand as governor of Castile

1505   (12 October) The Treaty of Blois is concluded between Ferdinand and Louis XII. It includes the stipulation that Ferdinand should marry Germaine of Foix

1506 (7 January) Philip and Joanna set sail for Flanders, arriving in A Coruña on 26 April, after an unplanned stay in England

(22 March) Marriage of Ferdinand and Germaine of Foix

(27 June) Agreement of Villafáfila, under which Philip and Joanna were to govern Castile, Ferdinand being obliged to return to Aragon

(4 September) Ferdinand sets sail for Naples

(25 September) Death of Philip I

(1 November) Ferdinand makes a triumphal entry to Naples

1507 (29 June) Meeting in Savoy between Ferdinand and Louis XII

(25 July) Ferdinand and Germaine make a solemn entry to Valencia

(29 August) Ferdinand meets Joanna in Tórtoles and is recognized once more as governor of Castile, remaining with his daughter in Burgos until 15 July 1508

1508 (June) A 'Catholic Congregation' in Burgos, summoned by Ferdinand, investigates, and dismisses, Diego Rodríguez Lucero, inquisitor of Córdoba

(10 December) League of Cambrai is concluded against Venice, between Ferdinand, Louis XII and Maximilian

1509 (13 February) Ferdinand goes to Arcos, to fetch Joanna to the monastery of Santa Clara in Tordesillas, where she arrived on 5 March

(3 May) Prince John born to Germaine of Foix, dying soon afterwards

(17 May) Castilian troops, commanded by Cardinal Cisneros, capture Oran

(11 June) Princess Catherine marries Henry VIII of England

1510 (5 January) The count of Olivero captures Bougie for Aragon and, on 25 July, captures Tripoli

(23 July) Pope Julius II formally invests Ferdinand as king of Naples

1511 (10 October) A 'Holy League' is formed by Ferdinand, Pope Julius II, Henry VIII and the Venetian Republic, against Louis XII and Maximilian

1512 (11 April) French troops defeat a Spanish army in the bloody battle of Ravenna

(21 July) Troops under the command of the duke of Alba invade Navarre

(25 July) Pamplona surrenders and the kingdom of Navarre is formally annexed to Castile

(19 November) Maximilian joins the Holy League, thus isolating Louis XII

1513   (5 April) League of Malines/Mechlen is formed by Ferdinand, Pope Leo X, Maximilian and Henry VIII, against Louis XII and Venice

1514   (4 May) Ferdinand, Leo X and Maximilian sign the formal requirements of the Holy League against Louis XII

1516   (23 January) Ferdinand dies at Madrigalejo (Cáceres)

Monetary Values

The monetary unit of account in late medieval Castile was the *maravedí* (from the Arabic *morabitun*). This had once been a gold coin but, by 1474, had become no more than a money of account. The coins noted here, some Castilian and some Aragonese, were calculated in its terms, as were taxes, prices and wages.

Values of gold and silver coins, *circa* 1500:

Castile

Castellano de oro (gold)	475 maravedíes (mrs)
Ducado (gold)	375 mrs
Dobla (gold)	365 mrs
Florin (gold)	265 mrs
Real (silver)	34 mrs

Aragon (silver)

Solidos of Valencia or Jaca	52 mrs
Solidos of Barcelona	46.5 mrs

Various base metal coins also circulated within Castile and Aragon, some of them, such as *blancas*, being minted in Spain, while others were foreign.[1]

Note

1 Edwards, J. (1982) *Christian Córdoba. The city and its region in the late Middle Ages*, Cambridge University Press, pp. 202–3.

Glossary

adelantado   literally, 'scout', a senior military and administrative official in a frontier region of Castile

alcalde   magistrate

alcázar   castle

capitulacion[es]   pact or agreement, or a set of such agreements, made between Iberian monarchs and their subjects

concejo   municipal council

Consejo Real   Royal Council, in both Castile and Aragon

condestable   constable

corregidor   literally, 'corrector' or 'co-ruler', the senior administrative official, on behalf of the Crown, in a major Castilian town

Cortes (in Catalonia, **corts**)   assembly of estates or parliament

cruzada   crusade or ecclesiastically sanctioned war against non-Christians or heretics

encomienda   group of estates allocated to a knight of a military order. Later, the term was used for estates held in the Indies. Such holders were known as *encomenderos*

escribano   Castilian and Aragonese word for a scribe or notary

jinete   lightly armed cavalry soldier, riding in the Muslim manner, like a racing jockey

letrado   literally, 'learned person', but commonly used in Castile to refer to a university graduate in civil law

parias   payments in money or goods made by the Nasrid emirs to Castilian rulers, in return for peace

pechos   Castilian term for direct taxes

privado   Castilian term for a royal favourite

requerimiento   demand, in written and spoken legal form, made by a public authority or an individual, against another legal party

señorío   lordship, in the sense of a group of estates granted by the Crown to a nobleman or else held by military orders, churchmen or a Church institution

tala   large-scale Christian raid across the Castilian–Granadan front into Muslim territory

vecino   citizen and inhabitant of a Castilian or Aragonese town

Further Reading

Perceptions of the basic outline and shape of the history of Spain between 1474 and 1516 have not changed markedly since William H. Prescott published his *History of the Reign of Ferdinand and Isabella the Catholic*, in 1838, Richard Bentley and many subsequent editions. This is because no serious scholar can ignore such events as the Granada war, the expulsion of the Jews from Spain and the 'discovery' of America. Neither can they discount the difficulty experienced by both sovereigns in establishing their regimes in Castile and Aragon or the fact that, after Ferdinand's death in 1516, Spain was increasingly known as a successful continental and soon a world power. Short surveys of the Catholic Monarchs' reigns thus tend to preface surveys of the so-called 'Golden Age' of Spain's imperial greatness. Still a reliable introduction, despite more recent research advances, is J. H. Elliott (1963) *Imperial Spain, 1469–1716*, Edward Arnold, updated in H. Kamen (1991), *Spain, 1469–1714*, Longman, and, with an American perspective, in H. Kamen (2002) *Spain's Road to Empire. The making of a world power, 1492–1763*, Penguin. From the medieval direction, T. N. Bisson (1991) *The Medieval Crown of Aragon. A short history*, Clarendon Press, and D. Abulafia (1997) *The Western Mediterranean Kingdoms, 1200–1500. The struggle for dominion*, Longman, offer an Aragonese and Mediterranean perspective. The appropriate sections of J. N. Hillgarth (1978) *The Spanish kingdoms, 1250–1516*, vol. 2, *1410–1516. Castilian hegemony*, Clarendon Press, are invaluable, especially concerning Aragon and religion. The translated articles in R. Highfield (1972) *Spain in the Fifteenth Century, 1369–1516*, Macmillan, are still useful, and the most recent surveys of the relevant period are J. Edwards (2000) *The Spain of the Catholic Monarchs, 1474–1520*, Blackwell (with bibliographical essay), and M. A. Ladero Quesada (1999) *La España de los Reyes Católicos*, Alianza Editorial. An excellent set of studies, representing recent research, is in J. Valdeón Baruque (ed.) (2001) *Isabela la Católica y la política*, Ámbito, while A. MacKay (1987) *Society, Economy and Religion in Late Medieval Castile*, Variorum, and J. Edwards (1996) *Religion and Society in Spain, c.1492*, Variorum, survey various religious social aspects of the period.

In English, only Isabella has received biographies, these being W. T. Walsh (1931) *Isabella of Spain*, Sheed and Ward, reflecting a strong Catholic commitment, and P. K. Liss (1992) *Isabel, the Queen*, Oxford University Press, which eschews archival sources but supplies an accurate and lively narrative. In Spanish, T. de Azcona (1993) *Isabel la Católica. Estudio crítico de su vida y su reinado*, Biblioteca de Autores Cristianos, is an essential study, particularly strong in religious matters, while T. de Azcona (2002) *Isabel la Católica. Vida y reinado*, La Esfera de los Libros, covers the same ground with less scholarly apparatus, and L. Suárez (2000) *Isabel I, reina*, Editorial Ariel, distils this great scholar's years of research in a compact and 'popular' form. There are no biographies of Ferdinand in English, the best in Spanish being the magisterial work of J. Vicens Vives (1962) *Historia crítica de la vida y reinado de Fernando II de Aragón*, CSIC, and more recently E. Belenguer (1999) *Fernando el Católico*, Ediciones Península. J. M. Calderón (2001) *Felipe el Hermoso*, Espasa Calpe, is a lively biography of Philip I of Castile, while M. Fernández Álvarez (2000) *Juana la Loca. La cautiva de Tordesillas*, Espasa Calpe, gives equally vivid treatment to Joanna 'the Mad'. Wider issues concerning her life and reign are effectively analyzed in B. Aram (2001) *La reina Juana. Gobierno, piedad y dinastía*, Marcial Pons.

The years before Isabella's accession in Castile are best analyzed in M. I. del Val Valdivieso (1974) *Isabel la Católica, princesa*, Universidad de Valladolid, while the best current treatment of her rival Joanna 'La Beltraneja' is T. de Azcona (1998) *Juana de Castilla, mal llamada 'La Beltraneja', 1462–1530*, Fundación Universitaria Española. In addition to the surveys of the reign noted here, the fullest study of an individual Castilian city in the period is J. Edwards (1982) *Christian Córdoba. The city and its region in the late Middle Ages*, Cambridge University Press. English accounts of the Granada war are provided in J. Edwards (2000), above, and L. P. Harvey (1990) *Islamic Spain, 1250–1500*, University of Chicago Press. In Spanish, the fundamental recent works on the war and Granadan society are M. A. Ladero (1987) *Castilla y la conquista del reino de Granada*, Diputación Provincial de Granada, and M. A. Ladero (1988) *Granada después de la conquista. Repobladores y mudéjares*, Diputación Provincial de Granada. There is a vivid account of the war itself and its background in M. A. Ladero (2001) *La guerras de Granada en el siglo XV*, Ariel. There are useful essays on various aspects of the Granadan frontier by M. González Jiménez, E. López de Coca and A. MacKay (1989) in R. Bartlett and A. MacKay (eds) *Medieval Frontier Societies*, Clarendon Press, and in E. López de Coca (ed.) (1987) *Estudios sobre Málaga y el reino de Granada en el V centenario de la conquista*, Diputación Provincial de Málaga.

There is now an immense bibliography in English on Judaism and the Inquisition, and the following are particularly useful. Spanish Jews in this period are usually considered in the context of the Inquisition and the two subjects are duly treated in T. de Azcona (1993) and M. A. Ladero (1999), above. General surveys of the Inquisition are J. Edwards (1999) *The Spanish Inquisition*, Tempus, and in greater detail, H. Kamen (1997) *The Spanish Inquisition. An historical revision*, Weidenfeld & Nicolson. The Inquisition's work in northern and eastern Spain and Sicily is efficiently treated in W. Monter (1990) *Frontiers of Heresy. The Spanish Inquisition from the Basque lands to Sicily*, Cambridge University Press. Not to be ignored is B. Netanyahu (2001) *The Origins of the Inquisition in Fifteenth-century Spain*, New York Review of Books, which mainly discusses the background to the post-1474 period. In Spanish, A. Alcala (ed.) (1995) *Judíos, sefarditas, conversos. La expulsión de 1492 y sus consecuencias*, Ámbito, is a valuable collection of specialist papers, while R. García Cárcel and D. Moreno Martínez (2000) *Inquisicion. Historia crítica*, Temas de Hoy, contains a stimulating discussion of the Catholic Monarchs' Inquisition. An impressive study of the Seville tribunal is J. Gil (2000) *Los conversos y la Inquisición sevillana* (five vols), Universidad de Sevilla. The Spanish Church and Christianity in Spain are less well served, although J. N. Hillgarth (1978) and J. Edwards (2000) are fairly comprehensive guides. In Spanish, T. de Azcona (1993), above, is invaluable, as are Chapters 1–5 of R. García-Villoslada (ed.) (1980) *Historia de la Iglesia en España*, vol. 3, pt. 1, *La Iglesia en la España de los siglos XV y XVI*, Biblioteca de Autores Cristianos. Among Spanish churchmen of the period, only Cisneros has recent biographies: E. Rummel (1999) *Jiménez de Cisneros: on the threshold of Spain's Golden Age*, Arizona Center for Medieval and Renaissance Studies, and J. García Oro (2002) *Cisneros*, Ariel. Spanish Islam in this period is even less well served, although some information is provided in the works on the Granada cited and in W. Monter (1990), above. A. G. Chejne (1983) *Islam and the West: the Moriscos. A cultural and social history*, State University of New York Press, is a useful general survey, while there are valuable and up-to-date essays on all three religions in M. D. Meyerson and E. D. English (eds) (2000) *Christians, Muslims and Jews in medieval and early modern Spain*, University of Notre Dame Press.

The economic aspects of Isabella and Ferdinand's court are discussed in M. A. Ladero (1999), above and in M. A. Ladero (1998) 'La Casa Real en la Baja Edad Media', *Historia Instituciones Documentos*, vol. 25, pp. 327–50. Isabella's cultural collection is discussed in F. J. Sánchez Cantón (1950) *Libros, tapices y cuadros que coleccionó Isabela la Católica*,

CSIC, while R. Domínguez Casas (1993) *Arte y etiqueta de los Reyes Católicos. Artistas, residencias, jardines y bosques*, Editorial Alpuerto, and Fernández de Córdova Miralles (2002) *La Cortes de Isabel I. Ritos y ceremonias de una reina (1474–1504)*, Dykinson, are wide-ranging studies of the organization and culture of Ferdinand and Isabella's courts. Court music is comprehensively covered in T. Knighton (2001) *Música y músicos en la Corte de Fernando el Católico, 1474–1516*, Diputación Provincial de Zaragoza.

Index